# TV ADVERTISING

# TV

# ADVERTISING

## A HANDBOOK OF MODERN PRACTICE

**ARTHUR BELLAIRE**

*Vice President in Charge of Television and Radio Copy*
*Batten, Barton, Durstine & Osborn, Inc.*

**FOREWORD BY HENRY M. SCHACHTE**

HARPER & BROTHERS, PUBLISHERS. NEW YORK

*To RUTH*
*Douglas*
*Gary*
*Barbara*

# CONTENTS

Preface     **xiii**

Foreword     **xv**

## CHAPTER 1

**The Picture of Television**     **1**

The Family—The Advertiser—How National Advertisers Regard Television—How Local Advertisers Regard Television—Approaches to the Medium

## CHAPTER 2

**The Network Program**     **6**

Part I, Networks: Rates—Contiguity—Discounts—Audience Composition—Time Periods—Time Buying—Cost per Thousand—Part II, Programs: Program Formulation—The Pilot Film—Scripts and Outlines—Program Trends—Types of Programs—Methods of Sponsorship—The "Special" —Daytime Programing—Program Openings—Program Research—Legal Considerations—Publicizing the Program

## CHAPTER 3

**Evaluating Program Ratings**     **29**

What Is a Rating?—A. C. Nielsen Co.—ARB—

Trendex—Pulse—Instantaneous Rating Systems
—Criticisms of Ratings—Improvements in Ratings—Basic Information Standards—Procedure
Standards — Accuracy Standards — New Proposals—The "Rating Trap"

## CHAPTER 4

### Spot Television                                    41

Status of Spot TV—Spot Buys—The Spot An-
nouncement: Forms—Costs—Rates—Copy—
Production—The Local Live Program—The
Syndicated Film Program: Advantages—Exam-
ples—Growth—Time Clearance—The "Film
Network"—Role of the Station "Rep"—Role of
the Time Buyer—Merchandising Services—Late-
Night Viewing

## CHAPTER 5

### Local Stations                                     53

Local TV Advertising—Station Managers Survey: Hours per Day of Station Operation—Hours
of Network Programs Carried per Week—Number of Live Cameras—Film Projection—Remote
Equipment—Rear Screen Projection—Studios—
Size of Station Staff—Merchandising Help—Stations Producing Film Commercials for Local Advertisers—Stations Creating Commercial Copy
for Local Advertisers—Spots Sold by Local Stations in Class "A" Time—New Development on
I. D. Specifications—Local Rate vs. National
Rate—Average Number of Spot Announcements
per Week—Types of Local Business Concerns
Advertising on Television—Reasons for Not
Using TV—Per Cent of Revenue from Local
Advertisers—Personalities Selling On-Camera

## CHAPTER 6

**How to Create Television Advertising**     **66**

The Television Copywriter—Four Steps to TV
Selling: 1. The Basic Theme—2. The Copy Plan
— 3. The Campaign — 4. The Commercials —
Creating the Commercial — The Script — The
Copywriting Secret — Keep It Simple — Script
Forms—Storyboards—How to Present the Idea
—Creativity

## CHAPTER 7

**Creating and Producing the Film Commercial**     **84**

Advantages of Film—The Copywriter's Task—
Basic Techniques—Supplementary Techniques
—Opticals—Special Effects—Which Technique
to Choose—Role of the TV Art Director—Pro-
duction Costs—Costs of Color—Competitive
Bids—Delivery Time—Commercial Cost vs. Pro-
gram Cost—Short Cuts in Production Costs—
Film Sizes—Stages of Film Production—Servant
Not Master

## CHAPTER 8

**Creating and Producing the Live Commercial**     **106**

Mechanics of "Live"—Advantages of "Live"—
The Copywriter's Task—Basic Approaches—
Special Visual Effects—Opticals—Which Tools
to Use—Steps in Production—Costs—The
"Risks"

## CHAPTER 9

**Videotape**     **120**

Advantages—Development—Splicing—Effect
on Film—Effect on Live—Program Uses—Local
Station Uses

## CHAPTER 10

### How to Demonstrate on Television                 129

When to Demonstrate—Where to Begin—
Types of Demonstrations—Safeguards

## CHAPTER 11

### Making the Words Work                              148

Kill the Cliché—Don't Take the Ad Too Liter-
ally—Don't Overwrite—Relate Audio to Video
—Write As People Talk—Suspect the Obvious—
Find the Right Word—Our Complex Language
—Words Complete the Picture

## CHAPTER 12

### Jingles                                            160

Public Acceptance—When to Use a Jingle—
What a Jingle Offers—Where Jingles Originate
—Qualities of a Good Jingle—Where to Begin
—The Melody—The "Tag" Jingle—Jingle Re-
cording—Singers—Emotional Appeal—Future
of Jingles

## CHAPTER 13

### Humor in Television Advertising                    173

Humor in Early Advertising—Enter Television
—Humor As an Art—Sell-"Soft" or "Hard"—
When to Use Humor—Implanting the Image—
When Not to Use Humor—Touches of Humor
—Humor in Perspective

## CHAPTER 14

### Talent in Television Commercials                   186

The Commercial Announcer—Actors and Actresses—Celebrities—"Star of the Show"—Singers—Models—Children—Role of the Advertising Agency—Talent Unions

## CHAPTER 15

**Selling the Corporate Concept**      **204**

Why Television?—Uses of Television—Corporate Objectives—The "Bigness" Factor—Typical Subjects—Measuring Effectiveness—Corporate-Product Relationship—Creating the Corporate Message—Financing the Corporate Effort

## CHAPTER 16

**How to Use Television Commercial Research**      **219**

Status of TV Research—Development of Research—Methods of Measurement—Reliability of the Recall Method—The Truisms of Television Research—The Likability Factor—The Believability Factor—The Psychological Factor—The Wearability Factor—Pre-Testing of TV Commercials — Copy Testing — New Areas for Television Research—Climate Testing—Costs of Television Research—An Appraisal of Television Research

## CHAPTER 17

**Growth and Effect of Television**      **237**

Rise of Television—The "Progress" of Color Television—Television's Effect on Other Media—Television As a Social Force—Television in Education—Television and Politics

## APPENDIX

I Television Code of the National Association of Broadcasters      **249**

xii   **Contents**

II Local Television                                          **257**

III Further Script Examples of Corporate Television
      Advertising                                            **262**

IV Top 150 U. S. Television Markets                          **275**

Glossary                                                     **279**

# PREFACE

This book is written for the advertiser, agency man, station man, network man, producer, director, copywriter, announcer, actor—anybody concerned with television advertising as it actually functions in daily practice; and for the student who seeks general understanding on the subject.

It would be presumptuous, of course, to claim for any book the power to teach complete mastery of a medium as complex and changing as television. However, I have tried here to present the facts of television advertising, including the newest developments, in such a way as to answer the questions most asked by advertisers and others concerned with day-to-day contact with the medium. In this sense, then, "how-to-do-it" is an apt way to describe the spirit in which this book was written and how it may most profitably be read.

As a full-time agency man specializing in television advertising since the birth of this exciting medium, I hold far less patience for theory than for practice. Consequently I purposely postponed any attempt at the "how-to-do-it" approach until the medium had matured to the point where basic principles could be set down as both timely and timeless fact. The time has now come when practical, everyday experience in this medium can, for the most part, be labeled as standard practice.

Television has given growth to the greatest roster of specialists advertising has ever seen. The result, in too many cases, is a lack of general understanding of the over-all industry. For this reason, regardless of the reader's connection with the medium, he will derive the most from this book by casting himself, temporarily at least, in the role of either an advertising manager of a company utilizing the medium or of an agency television account executive. The duties of both require an understanding of all aspects of television advertising and a knowledge of how to apply the facts thus gathered. An ounce of information is worth a pound of finesse in these duties, and "how-to-do-it" is ever in the minds of men filling such jobs.

The book is organized to cover in detail the facts which apply to actual practice. The early chapters treat the vital areas of networks, programs, local stations, ratings and spot announcements. These are followed by detailed basics on the creation of effective television advertising.

For their valued advice and assistance during the preparation of this book, I am especially grateful to the following:

Mrs. "Teddy" Anderson, H. C. Barksdale, Fred Barrett, Lawrence Berger, George Beyer, Wynn Bussmann, Charles S. Cady, A. E. Cantwell, John Caples, William J. Colihan, Jr., George Dalen, William K. Eastham, Miss Aina Ebbesen, John Elliott, Jr., Karl Fischer, Edward Fleri, Robert L. Foreman, Miss Bessie Jean Garnant, Stewart Garner, Miss Katherine Gens, Jack Goldsmith, Robert Grebe, Jack L. Gross, Bernard Haber, Everett Hart, Otto Kleppner, Dr. D. B. Lucas, Bert Mangel, Miss Nan Marquand, Edwin Marshall, W. Barry McCarthy, C. R. McKeever, George Mihaly, August Nelson, L. C. Nickerson, Alphonse Normandia, J. A. Patterson, E. J. Pechin, George Polk, Spencer Rowe, Joe Ryan, Miss Marianne Ryan, Henry Schachte, James Schule, Karl W. Schullinger, Douglas L. Smith, Charles B. Tranum, and Herminio Traviesas:

A.B.

New York City
February 1, 1959

# FOREWORD

BY HENRY M. SCHACHTE, EXECUTIVE VICE PRESIDENT
LEVER BROTHERS COMPANY
CHAIRMAN, ASSOCIATION OF NATIONAL ADVERTISERS

It is high time that somebody wrote the book herein authored by Arthur Bellaire.

Lots of people want and need to know about television advertising; and there *have* been some printed sources of information. But most of them have been in fractionated bits. For the reader, it has been like trying to understand the United States by studying Schenectady, New York.

To learn television advertising, one needs, first, a view of the totality of television itself—of the whole frame within which TV *advertising* fits.

This is what Mr. Bellaire's book provides—first, a broad scanning of television's growth, leading to its current status and practices; then, in related detail, a close look at the central subject of television advertising itself.

Viewed in this way, TV advertising is revealed for what it truly is, a new and exciting professional craft, based in creative imagination, but thoroughly disciplined by the codes and practices of the broadcasters, the technical limitations of TV equipment, the facts about the products advertised, and the learning speeds and skills of the viewers.

Surrounded and badgered by such restrictions, little wonder that the TV commercial writer is seldom overwhelmed with critical acclaim for his efforts.

The complicated situation of the TV writer, however much it might evoke our understanding, cannot explain away two major criticisms of today's television commercials.

First, why are there so many?

Secondly, why are so many of them so bad?

The answers to both questions are simple and only partially satisfactory.

There is a great deal of TV advertising (so much that we hear frequently about the "over-commercialization of television") because television *sells goods efficiently.* For this reason, more and more companies are buying more and more of it to help sell more products. Thus, television is becoming increasingly important to our companies' and our country's economic health.

Since the total amount of television available for sponsorship is limited by the hours of the day and night, the increasing number of TV messages have to be accommodated within the same twenty-four hours. Magazines or newspapers can handle increased advertising by printing more pages. Television can't stretch the clock.

While we should not promise *fewer* TV commercials, perhaps it is comforting to know that there probably won't be *more.* Most stations and networks are today carrying about all that their codes of practice allow.

On the "quality" front, though, the picture is more promising. Commercial television grew so quickly that there was never time to do two basic things that control quality:

1. Build up a "lore" of good and effective practices. Writers were so busy just getting out the work that there was little time to be a student of it.

2. Train the professional commercial writers which television needed. Its requirements were so new, so foreign to any previous kind of advertising practice that there was no simple transition from print or radio. Here, again, the lack of both time and study made training difficult.

But the very appearance of this studious handbook suggests that the days of hectic scrambling "just to get on the air" may be ending.

No one would be happier than the TV commercial writer himself to see the day of the studied, thoughtful, tasteful preparation of television commercials. No one, that is, except the public.

# TV ADVERTISING

# The Picture of Television

NO medium of communication has ever taken hold of the lives and habits of its audience so quickly as the colossus that is television.

Mark its commercial beginning as 1947, when there were sufficient stations available to make it worth the while of some advertisers, or 1950, when national television became a fact—no matter. The result was a force that became a part of our daily lives four times faster than radio, ten times faster than the telephone.

There is hardly a family in the United States outside the range of television's coverage. Almost 85 per cent of U. S. homes own television sets. More than 80 per cent of these homes can receive at least four stations. In Boston more people reportedly own television sets than telephones; in Baltimore, more own television sets than bathtubs!

As a form of entertainment, and as a powerful selling tool in the hands of business, television has thus altered drastically the habits and patterns of two basic groups: (1) the American family; (2) the American advertiser. Although these pages are concerned directly with the latter group and how it can take best advantage of the opportunities in this relatively new billion-dollar industry, it is first necessary to examine the former, the audience on whose reception of the medium the success of television advertising depends.

## The Family

In the comfort of the living room—or bedroom or family room ("the room that TV built")—the family can witness, and sometimes participate in, events happening thousands of miles away. In the space of a few hours people of all ages and incomes can watch the news as it is

1

made, sob at a daytime serial, snicker at a cartoon, cheer at a sporting event, thrill to an Indian chase, ponder over a panel discussion, laugh at a comedy skit, sweat out a melodrama, worry at the weather report. And any so inclined can top it all off by relaxing with a late movie.

Do families really spend many hours by their sets? In January, the peak viewing month, the television set is in operation more than six hours a day, seven days a week. The TV family, in fact, spends more time before the set than in any other human activity apart form working and sleeping.

Six hours a day actually represents total set usage, not individual viewing. It takes in the cumulative viewing of the housewife during the day, the children during the late afternoon and early evening, and the family during the evening. It also includes miscellaneous week-end viewing of various special programs. With television a dawn-to-bedtime attraction, advertisers enjoy the ultimate opportunity to reach new customers.

The greatest numbers of viewers are available, of course, during the evening hours. Most sets are in use from 7 to 11 P.M., with the peak from 8 to 10. Audience size drops during the summer months, notably during the early evening hours, but not so sharply as to make television impractical as a medium of selling. January and February are generally the heaviest viewing months. July and August are the lightest.

For nearly everybody television is a friend, a companion, an entertainer, a teacher, a servant, even a baby-sitter while mother is getting dinner. Television has been hailed as a widener of horizons. It has been cursed as an opiate of the masses. Whatever else it may be, television has moved in to stay.

### The Advertiser

How important is television to the advertiser? One has only to watch carefully the many programs over a cycle of two or three weeks to count the big-name companies as well as local business firms investing in the medium.

In an average of the total budgets of the nation's top twenty national advertisers, almost as much money is allocated to network television alone as to magazines, newspapers, radio, outdoor, and all other media combined. This comparison does not include the additional millions spent by the same advertisers in television spot announcements and programs on local stations.

Of course, some national advertisers use no television at all. The reasons may include limited budgets, products of specialized appeal, or products not allowed on television such as liquor and intimately personal items. There are also some advertisers who have tried television and failed to find it sufficiently effective.

Adding all expenditures of all advertisers, national and local, television accounts for less than 15 per cent of the nation's total. However, this figure can be misleading since the non-television figure encompasses direct mail, business and trade publications, outdoor, premiums and display advertising, as well as newspapers, consumer magazines, and radio.

## How National Advertisers Regard Television

Television is the most or the least expensive of all media, depending upon which set of figures is employed to prove the point. Because of television's mammoth available audience, the advertiser's cost-per-thousand viewers can be extremely low when compared with the numbers of readers reached by newspaper and magazine advertisements. Yet the fact remains that advertising nationally on television is an expensive proposition, and has become more expensive every year as TV coverage has grown and as costs of programs and facilities have likewise risen.

Obviously the advertiser has two important aims when he uses television on a national scale. First, he generally wants a large audience, referred to as a "mass audience." This assures him wide circulation of his commercial message. Second, he must have effective commercials in order to sell the audience.

1. *Reaching the Audience.* How big is a "mass audience?" Seventy per cent of sponsored evening network programs reach more than twenty-two million viewers. Thirty-eight per cent reach over thirty million viewers. For a single program worthy of such an audience, the advertiser will probably pay in excess of a hundred thousand dollars, including time and talent charges.

This same amount of money would be ample to produce a Broadway play. However, by applying simple arithmetic one would have to concede that the Broadway play would have to run to standing-room-only crowds daily for more than a hundred years to reach as many people as the advertiser is able to reach with his program on a single night. (Even as early as 1953 it was estimated that more people saw "Hamlet" in one television presentation than had seen all the stage performances of "Hamlet" in history.)

Certain programs attract considerably more than thirty million viewers. Sporting events like the World Series and the Rose Bowl, the political conventions, specials (also known as "spectaculars"), and other big productions draw from forty to fifty million viewers.

Reaching great numbers of people—customers and potential customers—is part of the battle with all national advertisers except those who may choose to sponsor daytime programs, quarter-hour segments, or programs designed for a more selective audience.

2. *Selling the Audience.* There is no doubt that television with its power to combine sight, sound, and motion, has more to offer advertisers in sales impact than any other medium. Bishop Fulton Sheen, an experienced television performer as well as a prominent churchman, has observed: "Our time has been misnamed as the 'atomic age.' It is rather the 'television age.' Television influences human brains a thousand times more than the fission and fusion of atoms!"

While not referring specifically to the commercial uses of the medium, his words are nevertheless consistent with television's ability to sell.

Of course, with all of its charms, television cannot guarantee automatic success. If the advertised product is substandard, television can sell it only once. If the advertiser's technique of selling is substandard, television may not sell it at all.

The television advertiser must compete not only with other brands in his field, but with the commercials of all other products on television. It has been estimated that every viewer—every consumer whose attention the advertiser seeks and needs—sees upwards of nine hundred commercials on his home screen every month!

### How Local Advertisers Regard Television

While his counterpart may talk a weekly budget in the thousands of dollars, the local advertiser generally talks in terms of hundreds or even less. He may buy a single spot announcement on a local station. He may buy several spots a week. Or he may sponsor a local program.

He is, in effect, competing with all other commercials on the air, national and local, for the attention of the viewer.

The local television advertiser has, of course, one decided advantage. He is often able to measure television's effectiveness in a matter of hours simply by counting customers or by consulting the cash register at the end of the day. Indeed he can even test television against newspapers and radio by investing the same amount of money in each at different intervals. For the national advertiser to do this usually requires a complex system of test market operations. Even with the help of these, it is often impossible to measure effectiveness accurately.

Television advertising has produced "miracles" in sales locally just as it has nationally. And, true to the national pattern, there are local advertisers who are convinced that television is not for them.

## Approaches to the Medium

Before actually using television, the advertiser should have (1) a good product, (2) suitable distribution, and (3) a thorough knowledge of the medium. Only then can he make intelligent decisions regarding it.

The national advertiser, for example, may sponsor network or local programs, buy spot announcements, or settle on a combination of both. The local advertiser, too, may sponsor a local or regional program and/or spots. Every possibility involves a different set of facts and circumstances.

## chapter two

# The Network Program

BY linking together a large number of stations throughout the country for the purpose of carrying the same program simultaneously, a television network enables the advertiser to reach many millions of potential customers at one time.

To make an intelligent selection of network, time period, and program, the advertiser must be armed with facts. He therefore relies heavily on his advertising agency and its specialists to present him with the latest information on every phase of the subject, from audience sizes to program availabilities, and to recommend what it considers to be one or more sound courses of action. With this data at hand, the advertiser is better qualified to understand and act on the recommendations.

For purposes of careful analysis, this chapter is divided into two parts—networks and programs. Each of these broad areas rates thorough study.

## NETWORKS

In becoming affiliated with a network, a station signs a contract or "affiliation agreement" for a period of up to three years agreeing to grant the network an option on certain time periods during which the network may carry its commercial (sponsored) or sustaining (nonsponsored) programs. The station receives compensation (approximately 30 per cent of its gross rate) for the commercial network programs it carries. A station is not compensated for carrying sustaining programs and, therefore, may or may not carry these, at its own election.

In buying network time, the advertiser is not required to use *all* of the network's affiliated stations, but the aggregate cost of stations purchased must at least equal a minimum dollar volume established by the network. However, the requirement seldom imposes a hardship on the advertiser since the average network advertiser generally desires broad national coverage. The number of stations necessary to achieve such coverage usually represents more than is required to meet the dollar volume minimum.

It sometimes happens that a network, in attempting to line up a sizeable number of stations, finds that certain stations are unable to carry a particular program due to prior commitments to local advertisers. Perhaps the time period in question had not been previously ordered by the network, or the time is outside the agreed-upon network option time. In this event, the advertiser, through his agency, may contact a different station in each problem city and arrange with the network to include that station in the line-up on a "per program" basis. However, should the affiliated station subsequently be able to clear the time, it still has first claim on its network's program.

## Rates

The advertiser's cost of airing a network television program consists of two major parts. One covers the cost of producing the program; the other covers the cost of the network time. The time costs of the three networks are based principally on the audience each can expect to attract. The base from which networks operate is the nighttime (class "A") hourly rate. A half-hour nighttime period costs 60 per cent of the hourly rate; a quarter-hour, 40 per cent. For an average lineup of stations at night, the advertiser will probably pay a base hourly rate of over $100,000 per broadcast or over $60,000 per half-hour broadcast. (Again, this figure covers time costs only and does not include the cost of the program itself, which may run into a comparable sum, but is usually somewhat lower.)

Rates are lower, of course, at other hours of the broadcast day, at which time the size of the audience is appreciably lower than at night. The hours from 9:00 A.M., to 6:00 P.M., generally constitute class "C" time, costing half the evening class "A" rate. The lowest priced of all time is before 9:00 A.M., or class "D," which is one-third the class "A" rate. ABC, in fact, charges a "D" rate for its entire daytime schedule. The class "B" rate, 75 per cent of class "A," formerly was effective from 5:00–6:00 P.M., Monday through Friday, and at certain hours during the week end, but this rate is no longer in effect.

*Contiguity.* The principle of "contiguity" applies to opportunities available to the multiple-program advertiser who purchases two or more adjacent, or "contiguous," time periods on the same network. To touch on the subject briefly, here are just two of many possible examples:

A nighttime advertiser may buy two half-hour programs "back-to-back," which are considered an hour of time instead of two half-hours. Under the contiguity principle he would thus be charged 100 per cent of the hourly rate, or 50 per cent for each half-hour, as against the 60 per cent he would be charged for each were the half-hours not contiguous.

A daytime advertiser, likewise, may purchase an hour of time and subdivide it into four equal program units, perhaps for four different products he manufactures, and be charged only 25 per cent of the hourly rate for each quarter-hour instead of the 40 per cent he would normally pay for a single quarter-hour.

In certain cases, application of the contiguous rate has been broadened still more, principally in class "C" time during the day, to cover two or more programs which are not adjacent and which, in fact, may be telecast on different days of the week.

The contiguity principle is both flexible and complex, depending upon the network and the general condition at the moment.

*Discounts.* To this point, only the base rates of the networks have been discussed. In actual practice, all networks allow advertisers various discounts which are determined by the amount and frequency of advertising. Each network has its own discount structure and, depending upon the category into which an advertiser fits, he may be entitled to discounts ranging from 5 per cent to more than 30 per cent of his base rate.

The rate and discount structures of the networks are highly complex and are constantly being revised to meet new situations and competition. To list here the myriad provisions as they apply on the various networks would overly complicate the simple point to be made; namely, that each network, like any business enterprise, extends certain advantages to the higher-volume customers.

## Audience Composition

The audience that will view his program is of prime interest to the advertiser for two obvious reasons: (1) He wants to know *how many* viewers he can expect. It is only natural he would desire a high program rating because a high rating means a large audience of potential customers to view his commercials. (How research measures the total audience is explained in the next chapter.) (2) He is interested in the composition of the audience as to sex and age groups. His product or products appeal to a given market—men, women, or children, or perhaps the entire family. If he is selling razor blades, he would not be happy with an audience dominated by women and children, regardless of its total size.

Audience composition is governed to a great extent by the type of program the advertiser sponsors. The particular hour of day or night the program is telecast also has a direct bearing.

The American Research Bureau reports this general average audience composition for daytime hours, Monday through Friday, and evenings throughout the broadcast week:

|  | 10 A.M.—<br>5 P.M. | 5 P.M.—<br>6 P.M. | Evening |
|---|---|---|---|
| Viewers<br>Per Set | 1.7 | 2.5 | 2.5 |
| Men | .2 | .2 | .8 |
| Women | 1.1 | .4 | 1.1 |
| Children | .4 | 1.9 | .6 |

On Saturday and Sunday afternoons, from 2 to 6 P.M., audience composition generally resembles closely that of evening viewing.

The above chart, of course, relates in no way to the *size* of the audience during these hours. It simply reveals who is watching in any one average household. The proportion naturally fluctuates slightly from hour to hour and program to program.

## Time Periods

Once the advertiser is ready to enter nighttime television with a program that meets with his approval, who determines on which night of the week and at what hour his program will be telecast?

If the network owns the program, a specific time spot is often a part of the deal. If not, the agency will set out to acquire a suitable time period. It sometimes works in reverse. A time spot of potentially high viewership may open up even before the program is selected. Upon approval of its client, the agency will secure an option on, or even buy, the time and then recommend an appropriate program to fill it.

The advertiser obviously cannot, as a rule, arbitrarily select any time period he prefers since most high-rating periods are already taken by other sponsors. It is up to the agency to keep abreast of current "availabilities" and thus to be ready to act swiftly on behalf of any one of its clients who may become interested. The agency analyzes each time opportunity in reference to the number of stations likely to be available, ratings of the shows preceding and following, and ratings of competitive programs; then relates this information to the nature of the program to be sponsored and the needs and desires of the particular advertiser.

## Time Buying

In negotiating for program time on the network, the advertiser looks to the agency time buyer, who, besides placing the order for time, maintains a critical eye on all network and station operations. It is essential to know what is available from day to day, what may be available tomorrow, and what can be made available.

Before actually deciding on a given time period, the advertiser must have the following information:

1. Estimated flow of "audience lead-in" from the previous program. A high-rating program preceding the time period in question is generally very favorable, although this is not in itself a guarantee that this large audience will remain for the next program.

2. Ratings and other data on competitive programs on other networks at the same time period. If other programs are getting an extremely high share of audience, the advertiser needs a superior program to lure some of the audience away.

3. Audience to the programs in the following time period. If it is

high, the advertiser can then hope to retain his audience to the end—
even pick up and possibly convert additional viewers who tune in near
the end of his program to be in time for the one following.

4. Tentative lists of station clearances in the formation of a recommended network lineup. The time buyer seeks not only broad coverage
for the proposed program but, in clearing stations, he strives to include
those in the advertiser's important sales markets and distribution
outlets.

5. Estimated time cost. After the decision is made to buy a particular time period, the time buyer places an "order letter" with the
network. This letter is a compilation of the many verbal agreements
made to date. It contains all terms and conditions under which the
purchase is being made, and serves as the agreement between the
agency and the network until the formal network facilities contract is
finally drawn up and signed by both parties.

Among the basic points included in the order letter are these:

1. Name of advertiser.
2. Name of program.
3. Time period.
4. Starting and ending dates (generally fifty-two weeks).
5. Cancellation privileges (generally after twenty-six weeks on a
specified notice).
6. Products to be advertised.
7. Station lineup.
8. Station rates.
9. Costs of program (if network-owned).

### Cost-per-Thousand

One measurement of the value of a network television buy is "cost-
per-thousand-viewers-per-commercial-minute." Taking as an example
the following set of facts, cost-per-thousand is determined in the following manner:

Total U. S. TV homes: 43,000,000.

150-station lineup, covering 95 per cent of U. S. TV homes:
40,850,000.

Program ratings: 30, or 30 per cent of 40,850,000: 12,255,000 TV
homes.

Time cost one half-hour nighttime class "A": $66,000.

Program cost: $50,000.

Time cost plus program cost: $116,000.

Total cost ($116,000) divided by TV homes reached (12,255,000): $.00947 per TV home, or $9.47 per-thousand TV homes.

Total commercial minutes: 3.

Total cost-per-thousand-homes-per-commercial-minutes: $3.16.

Two observations are in order regarding this measurement:

1. Average cost-per-thousand figures differ among the various categories of programs.

2. Cost-per-thousand should never be the only consideration in judging a program's value. Other important factors include the prestige a particular program may carry for the sponsor and its ability to provide the proper "climate" for his commercials.

## PROGRAMS

### Program Formulation

As soon as the advertiser manifests interest in network television, all forces are bent toward securing (1) a desirable program property and (2) a time period that will give the program the wide exposure it needs to be effective as a commercial vehicle.

Programs emanate from many sources. The advertiser may investigate them all before deciding on which to sponsor. They are:

1. The network.

2. The network in association with an independent production company.

3. The independent production company, or "packager."

Approximately half the sponsored programs on networks today are owned and produced by the third group.

Time was when certain advertising agencies functioned as active producers of some of their clients' programs. In 1952, in fact, agencies produced nineteen (or 11 per cent of all) network shows. This holdover habit from radio days helped the advertiser maintain closer control over his program.

However, while the agency must know every facet of program production in order to exercise competent supervision, producing programs was never intended to be one of its basic functions. Today, in fact, not one network program is agency-produced.

Figs. 1 and 2—TV PROGRAM LIGHTING on a grand scale. Above, console controls operation of each of 872 lights in NBC-TV's Brooklyn studio, permitting the pre-setting of lighting for various scenes and changes of lighting within each scene. Below, part of the 872 lighting units. Components of lighting grid can be raised or lowered by electric hoists remotely controlled. *(NBC-TV)*

Nevertheless, agency program experts, because of their experienced knowledge of the client company and their daily contact with the latest program availabilities, are well qualified to recommend the right program to the advertiser. Each year agency people review hundreds of programs in every form, from ideas, outlines, and scripts to pilot films and kinescopes. At the same time they see and evaluate many old shows and reruns. They see the plans for numerous special events such as football bowl games, speedway races, spectaculars, and many others. They are in on a considerable number of planned live, videotape and film programs under development by the networks and independent producers. They keep abreast of all currently sponsored shows in the event any should become available to new sponsors.

It may also happen that an agency will create a program idea which matches none of the hundreds available. In this event, the agency might select a producer in whom it has confidence and assign him the task of developing the idea into an actual program.

Very few, if any, programs are purchased directly from ideas submitted by private individuals.

### The Pilot Film

When an advertiser commits himself to the sponsorship of a new television program, he is probably buying a property he has never seen. In the case of a variety program, for example, the only known quantity at the time of his signing may be a name personality, an outline format, and a producer.

With a new film program, such as situation comedy and drama, the advertiser generally sees a "pilot film," which is simply one literal example of the proposed program produced in its entirety. The pilot often represents the first of the series, which carries with it the job of introducing the characters, establishing their dramatic relationships, and whetting the appetite for further elucidation.

While it is doing all this, the pilot film must stand on its own two feet as an interesting program. It must be representative of the top quality which the writers, directors, producer, and all others concerned can turn out. Judging a series of programs on the basis of one pilot film, in fact, calls for both faith and imagination on the part of the advertiser. The inclination naturally is to want to see more than one sample before investing one or two million dollars in a series of such programs. On the other hand, it would seem unreasonable to expect the packager to provide more than one pilot film, since the one he is showing probably represents a forty- to sixty-thousand-dollar gamble on his part.

## Scripts and Outlines

Provided the pilot film interests the advertiser to the extent of sponsoring the projected series, what is the next step? The packager will then be asked to supply either outlines of future programs or a number of completed scripts, or both. The reason for this step is further insurance against the trap into which more than one advertiser has fallen; namely, buying a series on the basis of one pilot film, only to find that subsequent programs did not live up to the one originally presented.

Regarding this problem, programing expert George Polk adds, "The finest writers and producers may be hired to make a pilot film. We must be guaranteed that the same top quality is assigned to subsequent episodes, once the program is sold."

The many hours devoted to reviewing new programs are of considerable benefit to the advertiser. For this experience, combined with a knowledge of which shows have succeeded on the air and which have failed, better qualifies him to evaluate with some degree of accuracy the relative merits of various program possibilities. It also serves to remove, to some extent at least, part of the guesswork necessarily involved in such a decision.

Such experience is not infallible. It often happens that a program does not live up to its promise. The public taste can be anticipated only to a point. And only after the program is on the air for a time can its success really be judged.

## Program Trends

Another area of interest to the advertiser in his study of program potentialities is current trends in program popularity. For example, he is not likely to be interested in a type of program whose average rating is shown to be in a steady decline. On the other hand, he may put aside his personal aversion to a given type of program if he is convinced it is coming more and more into public favor. He is primarily interested in a property he can live with, one that is popular and offers the proper "climate" in which to present his sales story.

While there is value in retaining the same property over a number of years, the alert advertiser is always on the watch for something better. It is interesting to note that only eleven of more than a hundred sponsored shows survived a recent five-year period. Yet the percentage of sponsors remaining in network TV over the same period was far greater. And very few network time periods, over these same five years, have had to "go begging."

## Types of Programs

The various general categories of evening programs broadcast by the three national networks are these:

1. *Drama,* including general drama, suspense drama, adventure, and western.
2. *Quiz and audience participation.*
3. *Variety,* including general, musical, and comedy.
4. *Situation comedy.*
5. *Sports.*
6. *News.*
7. *Miscellaneous,* including interview, music, etc.

As the advertiser studies the general categories of shows in reference to his own needs, he is bound to have certain strong personal feelings in favor of some and opposed to others. Again, he is concerned with selecting the type of program that will provide an appropriate setting for his corporate name and for his product or corporate commercials. But he remains open-minded until all the facts and figures are gathered.

What is more of a task is the selection of the particular program within a category. When the various groups, for instance, are compared by rating, the picture becomes confused. Westerns may have an average Nielsen rating of 27. However, one show within this category may boast a 41 and another may rate 20. Or, in the suspense drama category, averaging 22, one program may reach 36 and another only 11. The point is, a program must be appraised and purchased as a specific as against a member of a category.

The same principle applies to the cost of the program. It is dangerous to generalize by type because the variations here are even more marked. In the area of suspense drama, while one may expect a new program costing $38,000 to be about normal, the range may be from below $30,000 to more than $50,000.

However, the over-all figures do suggest that an advertiser can expect to pay considerably more for an hour variety show than for an hour dramatic show; and considerably less for a half-hour quiz show than for a half-hour dramatic anthology series.

## Methods of Sponsorship

Another list of variables for the advertiser to weigh in planning his network buy concerns the various ways programs can be sponsored. These are the general methods of sponsorships:

1. *Full program sponsorship* was once the most common form of nighttime television, in which the advertiser sponsors the same program every week. This type represents an average total expenditure in the neighborhood of five million dollars a year for both time and program costs for a half-hour program.

2. *Alternate sponsorship* takes two forms. Two advertisers may share the same program, one being major sponsor on one week, the other on the next. In order for each to gain weekly exposure, the major sponsor may swap one of his three minutes of allotted commercial time to the alternate sponsor so that each will be represented on each program. (Research shows major advantages in terms of greater total audience for advertisers who thus "cross-plug" their messages.) The other form of alternate sponsorship finds two advertisers sharing the same time spot and alternating from week to week with different programs. In either case, this use of television allows an advertiser a steady schedule for two to three million dollars a year, depending on program, network and time discounts earned. Many large users of television prefer two alternating programs in different time periods to one fully sponsored program in order to obtain the largest possible unduplicated audience.

3. *Segment sponsorship* refers to programs which are sold in units small enough to permit several advertisers to sponsor the same show on the same evening. These programs are usually an hour or more in length.

4. *Budget relief,* while not actually a normal form of sponsorship, has developed recently as a method of dovetailing two different adver-

tisers' interests on a seasonal basis. For example, a regular sponsor of a program may be allowed by the network to sell a given number of its programs during a normally quiet sales period to another advertiser who finds the same time of year an active season for promoting the sale of *his* products.

5. *Special events* include election coverage, Academy Awards, the Miss America pageant and other such occasions. The timing of these, of course, is governed by the specific events involved and the length of broadcast. Costs vary tremendously ranging from $200,000 to $800,-000 per show.

6. *Special programs,* also referred to as "spectaculars," may be presented as "one-shots" or as a fairly regular series. These may take the form of dramatic, musical, variety, or even documentary shows and are bigger, more expensive productions than the usual week-to-week programs. Costs of "specials" also vary widely.

7. *News programs* represent probably the least expensive way to be represented in nighttime television.

8. *Participation network programs* are generally relegated to "fringe" hours; namely, before 9 in the morning and after 11:15 or 11:30 in the evening. For one-minute commercial time on a network participating program, the advertiser can expect to pay in the neighborhood of $6,000.

9. *The daytime quarter-hour,* which is basically designed to reach women, may cost the advertiser, for time and program, $25,000 or as little as $6,000, depending upon program, network, and discount structure. Networks allow substantially higher discounts in the daytime than at night, resulting very often in tremendous efficiencies in daytime buys. In addition, the proportion allotted for commercial time is more generous in the daytime.

No one method of sponsorship can be said to be a more sound investment than any other. Again, the nature of the particular program in question and the policies, objectives, and budget of the advertiser help determine the selection of the purchase.

As viewing habits change, so do the habits of advertisers and their philosophies toward sponsorship. When rising costs made the once-a-week program too expensive for some advertisers, they went to alternate sponsorship, with "cross-plug" messages on the alternate weeks. Alternate sponsorship is still popular but some advertisers question whether the once-a-week exposure which "cross-plugging" affords is as valuable to them as the impact *every* commercial enjoys when they retain all commercial time to themselves on their own program, even though they thereby cut down their total audience reach.

## The "Special"

The special, or spectacular, which may cost the advertiser several hundred thousand dollars for a one-time "splash," may seem on the surface to be an extravagant form of advertising. Certainly those unfamiliar with the ways of television find this expenditure the hardest to understand.

Planned months ahead to tie in with a major merchandising promotion, the special can dramatically spearhead the entire effort. A company publicizes its big television event to the trade even before the public hears about it. The entire sales organization coordinates all its activities to take full advantage of the gala occasion. Newspaper and magazine advertising, too, may be keyed to the same promotion. As the program nears, publicity forces go into action to ready the public. The psychological values in such a promotion are many.

The special, in other words, is usually handled differently from the normal program. When timed to coordinate with the sponsor's best selling season—say a month before Christmas—it can pay off big in sales. Part of the build-up, in fact, often involves a concerted drive to increase distribution for the products to be advertised on the program.

The success of this type of show depends on many factors: the appeal of the program itself, the time period during which it is slated to appear, the number of stations carrying it, how it is publicized and how skillfully the commercials are created and executed.

## Daytime Programing

Daytime programs during weekdays naturally attract a high proportion of women. The four most common program types are: (1) general drama; (2) dramatic serials; (3) quiz and audience participation; and (4) general and personality variety.

There is relatively little variation in program cost during the daytime. Likewise, one type of program seems to fare generally as well as another.

On weekends, daytime programing is quite different. Audience competition, as pointed out earlier, is similar to nighttime, not only because more of the family is available to watch but because the type of programing at this time is designed to attract a broader audience. Saturday afternoons, for example, are generally reserved for major sporting events in their respective seasons. Sunday afternoons the networks offer cultural and educational programs of general interest.

The daytime viewing audience climbs steadily higher. Weekdays many package goods advertisers invest much more money reaching women via TV, in fact, than they do through women's magazines.

## Program Openings

In addition to its allotted commercial time—three minutes per half-hour on a class "A" nighttime program, six minutes per hour—the sponsoring company is allowed ten seconds to identify itself with the name of the show at the beginning of the program and ten seconds for further identification at the closing.

Thus, creation of the opening show title is a critical task. Two major jobs must be accomplished within this brief period of time: (1) The sponsor must register ownership of the program. (2) The program itself should be made to look inviting and attractive. Achieving these two objectives in a simple format requires exceptional skill on the part of the copywriter, art director, producer, and others assigned to the task.

If the advertiser so wishes, he may exceed the ten seconds in the show opening, but the *total* time he uses is charged against his allotted commercial time. In other words, if, instead of ten seconds, he decides on thirty seconds in order to describe his company more fully, the advertiser is charged the full thirty seconds and does not receive credit for the ten seconds he would otherwise receive free. A few corporate advertisers with programs running an hour or longer devote a full minute in the opening to a corporate identification of elaborate proportions.

The advertiser is naturally hopeful that when the public remembers his program, his own association with it will also be remembered. "Sponsor identification" is a matter of concern to any company expending millions to provide the entertainment. Whether a gratitude factor exists on the part of the public, more sophisticated in its attitudes now than in the early days of TV, is not definitely known, but research does show that the aura of a sponsored program, which begins with strong identification at the outset, has a positive influence on the effectiveness of the commercials that appear within the program.

A program opening of ten seconds can do little more than dramatically billboard the entertainment that follows and identify the sponsor and one or two of his products. It may further state his corporate theme line. When it exceeds ten seconds, the opening may achieve any of the following objectives over and above identifying the show itself:

1. It may list a number of products manufactured by the advertiser.
2. It may include a short commercial for one of the products.
3. It may enumerate various divisions of the company in order to register the concept of diversification.
4. It may dramatize the meaning behind the corporate theme.

## Program Research

The advertiser is able to track the relative popularity of his program through periodic ratings, which indicate the total number of homes tuned to the program, and the percentage of the total available audience the program attracts.

He may be satisfied with this quantitative measurement alone. Or he may, at frequent intervals, desire a qualitative evaluation of the performance of his program.

While modern program research does not provide all the answers, it does reveal helpful findings in the two basic areas: the entertainment value of the program, and the program's effect on the commercials.

1. *Entertainment value.* "Which are the strong and weak parts of my program?" the advertiser may ask.

The principal method of evaluating a given program is a minute-by-minute profile analysis of audience reaction. One service of the A. C. Nielsen Company measures actual minute-by-minute audience size, based on a sample of more than a thousand homes. (The rating service itself is explained more fully in the next chapter.) If the advertiser subscribes to this service, he learns the pattern of tune-in and tune-out as the program progresses.

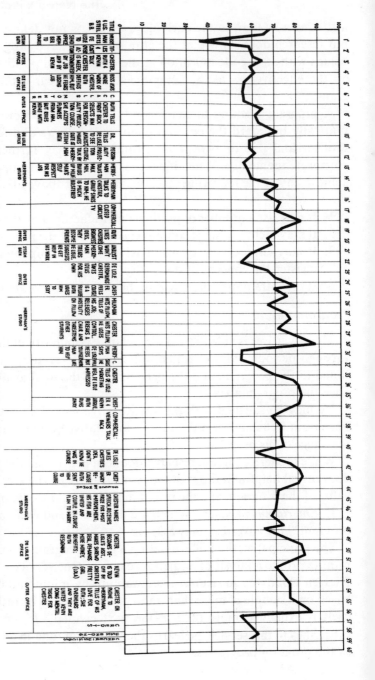

Fig. 3—TV PROGRAM PROFILE reveals high and low points within the United States Steel Hour production, "The Change in Chester." A kinescope projected before nearly 300 respondents allowed researchers to obtain minute-by-minute attitude averages. Corresponding notes along bottom of chart re-cap the various components of the program, including the sponsor messages. The over-all program scored above the average for dramatic shows. The commercials, too, as the chart reveals, did well in holding the audience interest. (Schwerin Research Corp.)

Another *profile* measurement offered by some networks and by certain research organizations and agencies is based on the minute-by-minute reactions of a representative audience gathered in a theater or other large room. As members of the group see the program projected on a screen, they report their attitudes on cue.

By one method the respondent is provided with a sheet of paper with three squares for each minute of viewing. They are labeled "Good," "Fair," "Poor." On signal from the stage, he checks the square which reflects his opinion of the show as of that particular moment.

Another method is more mechanical, but based on the identical principle. Here the respondent is provided with an electrical button for each hand. One represents liking, the other displeasure. He presses the one which expresses his feeling of each small portion of the program.

With each method of the *profile* technique, the minute-by-minute responses of each person are averaged, and a composite profile is charted in curves on the thirty or sixty-minute record of the show. In this manner, the advertiser is able to relate the "hills" and "valleys" to the various components of the show itself and learn thereby which portions pleased most and which pleased the least.

One network has even experimented with the lie detector to measure viewer reaction to program pilots! The subject simply places his hand in a box and the device registers his emotional reactions as the program progresses. Unfortunately, however, it is not always easy to determine whether a change of blood pressure is registering pleasurable excitement, fear, or utter disgust.

Of course, a viewer's minute-by-minute opinion does not necessarily register his over-all opinion of the program. His general feeling toward the show, after all, is what either brings him back to see it again or turns him against it.

It is simple enough to ask for the respondent's general impression and to question him on various aspects of the program. A further extension of this involves the interesting word-association study. After viewing the entire program, the respondent is handed a list of words and asked to check which ones, in his opinion, best fit the program he has just seen. The following words were used in an actual test of a variety program:

# SCORE SHEET

**A.** Now we are about to (view) (listen to) _____
Do you look forward to (viewing) (listening to) it?

Yes.............................................................. _____

Not sure......................................................... _____

No............................................................... _____

| | Good | Fair | Poor | | Good | Fair | Poor | | Good | Fair | Poor |
|---|---|---|---|---|---|---|---|---|---|---|---|
| 1. | ☐ | ☐ | ☐ | 21. | ☐ | ☐ | ☐ | 41. | ☐ | ☐ | ☐ |
| 2. | ☐ | ☐ | ☐ | 22. | ☐ | ☐ | ☐ | 42. | ☐ | ☐ | ☐ |
| 3. | ☐ | ☐ | ☐ | 23. | ☐ | ☐ | ☐ | 43. | ☐ | ☐ | ☐ |
| 4. | ☐ | ☐ | ☐ | 24. | ☐ | ☐ | ☐ | 44. | ☐ | ☐ | ☐ |
| 5. | ☐ | ☐ | ☐ | 25. | ☐ | ☐ | ☐ | 45. | ☐ | ☐ | ☐ |
| 6. | ☐ | ☐ | ☐ | 26. | ☐ | ☐ | ☐ | 46. | ☐ | ☐ | ☐ |
| 7. | ☐ | ☐ | ☐ | 27. | ☐ | ☐ | ☐ | 47. | ☐ | ☐ | ☐ |
| 8. | ☐ | ☐ | ☐ | 28. | ☐ | ☐ | ☐ | 48. | ☐ | ☐ | ☐ |
| 9. | ☐ | ☐ | ☐ | 29. | ☐ | ☐ | ☐ | 49. | ☐ | ☐ | ☐ |
| 10. | ☐ | ☐ | ☐ | 30. | ☐ | ☐ | ☐ | 50. | ☐ | ☐ | ☐ |
| 11. | ☐ | ☐ | ☐ | 31. | ☐ | ☐ | ☐ | 51. | ☐ | ☐ | ☐ |
| 12. | ☐ | ☐ | ☐ | 32. | ☐ | ☐ | ☐ | 52. | ☐ | ☐ | ☐ |
| 13. | ☐ | ☐ | ☐ | 33. | ☐ | ☐ | ☐ | 53. | ☐ | ☐ | ☐ |
| 14. | ☐ | ☐ | ☐ | 34. | ☐ | ☐ | ☐ | 54. | ☐ | ☐ | ☐ |
| 15. | ☐ | ☐ | ☐ | 35. | ☐ | ☐ | ☐ | 55. | ☐ | ☐ | ☐ |
| 16. | ☐ | ☐ | ☐ | 36. | ☐ | ☐ | ☐ | 56. | ☐ | ☐ | ☐ |
| 17. | ☐ | ☐ | ☐ | 37. | ☐ | ☐ | ☐ | 57. | ☐ | ☐ | ☐ |
| 18. | ☐ | ☐ | ☐ | 38. | ☐ | ☐ | ☐ | 58. | ☐ | ☐ | ☐ |
| 19. | ☐ | ☐ | ☐ | 39. | ☐ | ☐ | ☐ | 59. | ☐ | ☐ | ☐ |
| 20. | ☐ | ☐ | ☐ | 40. | ☐ | ☐ | ☐ | 60. | ☐ | ☐ | ☐ |

# SCORE SHEET

Fig. 4—MINUTE-BY-MINUTE audience reaction to a one-hour television program. On cue every sixty seconds, each member of the panel checks "good," "fair," or "poor." By combining all reactions, a composite "profile" chart can be drawn of the entire program. From this, weak and strong sequences can be noted.

| | | |
|---|---|---|
| Adult | Heart warming | Slow-moving |
| Childish | Humorless | Spontaneous |
| Clever | Humorous | Suspenseful |
| Cold | Lacking in variety | Too melodramatic |
| Confusing | Lively | Too rehearsed |
| Disagreeable | Monotonous | Touching |
| Dull | Not suspenseful | Trivial |
| Entertaining | Original | Uneven |
| Educational | Phony | Unromantic |
| Exciting | Realistic | Well planned |
| Fast moving | Romantic | Wholesome |
| Good variety | Silly | |

Thus the viewer is able to express his positive and negative reactions in a free-flowing manner and is not limited to answering specific questions.

All measurements of entertainment value can also, of course, be applied to pilot films and other auditions of new programs before they go on the air. When this occurs, however, the advertiser is advised to exercise extreme caution and not be tempted to predict future success by this research alone. The fact that a program may score well by any or all of the techniques mentioned here is no guarantee that it will either attract a large audience or provide an effective vehicle for moving merchandise.

The time period in which the program is placed has a major bearing on its potential drawing power. So does the weight of its competition on other networks at the same hour. So do the ratings of the show preceding and the show following.

Program research, in other words, is but one indication of a program's future promise and is probably more useful, when all is said and done, in analyzing the strong and weak points of the program tested than in accurately evaluating the program as a whole.

2. *Effect of program on commercials.* Another new kind of program research reveals that marked differences may occur in the relative effectiveness of the same set of commercials tested within the context of one show, then within the context of another.

This new area is called "climate" research; *i.e.,* the effect of the program upon the drawing power of the commercials. While this concept is discussed more fully in subsequent chapters, it bears mention here.

By superimposing a test of commercials on the program-liking score, it was found in one instance that the commercials performed better in a strong program than a weak one. In addition, among the better-liked and higher-rating programs, there is again to be found a range of commercial effectiveness. As more and more data is gathered on this vital subject, it becomes increasingly evident that the kind, or category, of show may be virtually as important to the advertiser as the size of audience. In other words, if show A draws one-third more viewers than show B, but in show B the commercials in question are twice as effective (by research standards) as in show A, is not show B the better buy?

The fact that certain advertisers with high-rating shows are not entirely happy with their sales results, while certain others with lower-rating shows are, indicates that not all products and advertising are compatible with the programs in which they are placed.

However, before the advertiser passes up any chance of a high rating—still the confirmed goal of the great majority of television advertisers—he should see to it that every possible attempt is made to fit his commercials to the general mood of the program. Granted, this is not always practical, especially when filmed commercials are "dropped" into filmed shows. But where such alterations can be made, the commercials will have a better chance to perform at their best.

## Legal Considerations

When a program is selected for sponsorship, the deal in most cases is discussed first only in general terms. But there remains the task of reaching an agreement on the many other important elements of a television transaction and reducing the entire agreement to a written instrument.

It is here that the agency attorney—sometimes in cooperation with the legal department of the sponsoring company—takes over. This type of legal assistance is naturally a specialized one and concerns the culmination of agreements covering talent and program packages as well as network facilities contracts.

The agency attorney must be completely familiar with both the legal and business sides of the television industry. He must know, for example, how to avoid pitfalls which could result in an unexpected rise in the basic price of the program. He must take every precaution to insure that the production company or network has obligated itself to deliver the program in question.

Other problems facing the agency attorney involve talent and technical unions, music licensing, literary rights, indemnities, rights of privacy, residual rights, and many others.

## Publicizing the Program

Favorable publicity for a television program helps to build its audience, and hence its rating. Four methods of publicity are generally employed:

1. The advertising agency's publicity department or consulting publicity and public relations firm disseminates releases to various periodicals and arranges interviews, photographs, and other special material wherever possible.

2. The advertiser's own public relations department distributes the publicity.

3. An outside public relations organization or counsel may be hired by the advertiser.

4. The network's own publicity facilities function on behalf of the program.

The advertiser often sets up a separate publicity budget when he purchases a program. In this manner he can conduct a well-organized and continuing campaign to increase public awareness of his television effort.

Certain shows, of course, lend themselves to publicity more readily than others. Nevertheless, any program worthy of network airing is worthy of publicity. A competent publicity expert is always alert for "angles" which will win space in the editorial columns of newspapers and magazines.

The network's publicity facilities serve many advertisers, which means they can give only limited attention to each program. Often, however, the network sends stations editorial releases and slide film for spot announcements.

Many advertisers also buy "tune-in" advertisements in the radio-television pages of newspapers and TV magazines to help increase the audience.

Whatever method the advertiser employs, certainly a consistent campaign pays off better in the long run than "hit-or-miss" efforts, which stimulate only some individual performances.

"Getting people to tune to his program is an objective in which every advertiser must take the initiative," said agency executive W. Barry McCarthy. "Everyone with a stake in his success—the advertising agency, the network and stations, the program producer or packager—should agree at the outset to a collective plan for promotion in which each will participate. No circus ever sneaked into town."

## chapter three

# Evaluating Program Ratings

"RATING" is a potent word in television.

Since it purports to inform the advertiser of the relative popularity of his program, he is generally happy when his rating is high.

"Why not?" he may reason. "The more people my program attracts, the more people I can expose to my commercials."

"Hold on a minute," cautions another advertiser. "A program that reaches a large audience is all well and good, but is a high rating all I really want? How do I know this particular program is the right one for my product?" Two points of view, which will be discussed later in the chapter. Meantime, there is no denying that ratings and hopes for high ratings are often the basis for business decisions involving many millions of dollars.

## What Is a Rating?

In its simplest terms a rating is the percentage of families watching a specific program or station.

It is obviously impractical, if not impossible, to count *all* the millions of homes viewing a nationally televised program. That is why the advertiser relies on the services of one or more of the syndicated rating organizations to measure the size of his television audience on a continuing basis. Their ratings are determined by learning the viewing habits of a relatively small "sample" of the total available audience.

Each rating service—Nielsen, ARB, Trendex and the others—has its own approach to (1) sample size; (2) sample representativeness; (3) method of gathering its facts; and (4) interpretation of the data. Even here, when two or more rating services happen to be measuring the

# Computation of
## NIELSEN AVERAGE AUDIENCE

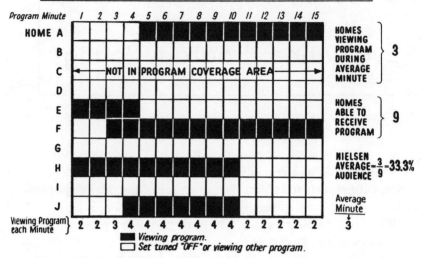

Fig. 5

Fig. 6

# Computation of
## NIELSEN TOTAL AUDIENCE RATING

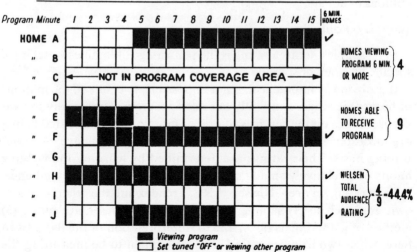

audience of the same program on the same evening, chances are the findings will be very similar. There occur some exceptions, however, where they disagree by several million viewers.

Some services are national in scope, some regional, and some local. The national samples are believed to be designed with the most care, and purport to reflect all elements of the U. S. population in proper proportion.

"When we talk about a 'rating,' " said Mrs. "Teddy" Anderson, manager of Radio-TV Research for Batten, Barton, Durstine & Osborn, "we really don't know what that rating means unless we know whose rating it is and the circumstances under which it was taken.

"This fact has been the basic reason for most of the confusion in the ratings field. It also makes it impossible to conclude that one kind of rating is right and another wrong." This point is all too frequently lost sight of, to the detriment of the whole field of broadcast audience research.

We shall consider separately the most comprehensive of the established rating services.

*A. C. Nielsen Co.* This service, the most widely used in the national field, provides national ratings for all sponsored network television programs. It publishes the national Nielsen Television Index biweekly covering forty-eight weeks of the year; the Nielsen Station Index Reports for local areas each month, and periodic Nielsen Coverage Service studies.

To arrive at a program rating Nielsen studies slightly more than a thousand homes throughout the United States, which are believed to be of the same type and in the same proportion as they exist in the nation's population; that is, big-city, small-town, farm, telephone and non-telephone, all levels of income, family size, education, etc.

Nielsen measures the viewing pattern of these families by means of the Audimeter, an automatic electronic instrument, which is attached to each television set in its panel of homes. The Audimeter records a signal once every minute on a continuously moving photographic film indicating whether the set is on or off, and if on, the station to which it is tuned.

The measurement covers the entire telecast day. Every two weeks Nielsen mails to each of its sample homes a small "magazine" for the film record. Someone in the family removes the old magazine from the Audimeter and inserts the new one. When this is done, two twenty-five cent pieces are automatically released as a "reminder" reward. The full magazine contains from 20,000 to 80,000 individual one-minute records of viewing.

These records are set *tuning* records. They cannot reveal how many in the family are watching—or even if *anyone* is watching. However, the Nielsen Company has analyzed its records and found that, because of the high incidence of dial switching, it is more than likely that, in the large majority of cases, somebody is watching.

Audiences are reported in terms of a per cent tuned among those TV homes able to receive the program signal.

Because the Nielsen panel of homes is intended to project the viewing habits of all homes in the nation, these per cents, or Nielsen ratings, can be converted into the numbers of homes reached. However, when this is done, it is necessary to check the "coverage factor" of a particular program. In other words, two programs could each attract the same proportion of the available audience but one may have a far shorter lineup of stations than the other. In this event, the total number of viewers would be proportionately lower.

The Nielsen Television Index reveals the averages of telecasts during the two weeks covered by the report, except for alternating sponsors or alternate-week programs. Separate-week ratings are supplied for programs specified for analysis treatment by "complete NTI" subscribers.

Nielsen ratings are released about four weeks following the last day covered in the rating report. These are called *total audience* ratings and represent the per cent of Nielsen homes in the program's "station area" tuned to the program for a minimum of any six minutes.

The same report also includes measurements on *average audience,* the per cent of TV homes tuned to the program during the average minute of broadcast; per cent of TV homes in the U. S. viewing any TV during the average minute of each 15-minute time period; per cent of U. S. homes which can view the program; number of homes viewing the program, and share of audience.

The Nielsen technique makes possible certain additional measurements, which are supplied to all subscribers with the "complete analyses" contract; namely, audience turnover, frequency of viewing, audience to commercial, audience profiles (minute-by-minute viewing) and audience by home-characteristics.

*ARB*. The ARB—American Research Bureau—bases its program ratings on viewer diaries placed for one week in 2,200 homes. The homes are selected to represent viewing conditions in all counties in the United States. Completely new samples are chosen for each study.

The diary form contains spaces for programs, stations, and characteristics of the viewers. On it the family is asked to keep a record of its viewing and of which persons are watching any given program.

Well over half of the ARB diaries placed are normally accounted for. And since inactive sets, too, form a part of the broad audience pattern and are taken into account in ratings, special effort is made to follow through with families in the sample who might have been away during the survey week or might have been having their sets repaired and were consequently unable to view television. The results are tabulated and projected nationally, with the ARB ratings then reflecting the total audience for each program covered.

ARB also publishes a national report covering one sample week out of each month.

While ARB's national report has won considerable recognition, its greatest acceptance is in the local field, where it provides reports for up to 150 metropolitan areas.

*Trendex*. The Trendex TV Program Ratings represent a popularity index for evening network television programs, based on telephone-coincidental interviews in twenty cities, all of which are served by three or more TV networks. The term "coincidental" means the interview occurs at the precise moment the particular program is being aired.

Trendex results are projectable to all TV telephone homes in the twenty cities, but not nationally, and are useful in evaluating program strength in areas of maximum competition. They are, in effect, "popularity" ratings as opposed to Nielsen's and ARB's "audience size" ratings.

The Trendex survey, covering telecasts from 8 A.M. to 11 P.M., is usually conducted during the first seven days of each month, with alternate-week shows surveyed the second week of each month.

The reported rating is based on a single telecast except in the case of programs broadcast more than once a week, where the rating is a weekly rating. Respondents are picked at random from residential telephone numbers. To be counted, a set must be in use at the moment of the call. If a program is carried in all twenty cities, the rating base for a half-hour program is one thousand TV homes called; for an hour program, two thousand, etc. Samples for programs carried in fewer cities are, of course, smaller.

Trendex ratings are available approximately one week after telecast. On special order, however, they can be wired the day after telecast, subject to minor changes.

Trendex publishes a bimonthly Television Advertisers Report, containing special breakdowns on audience composition, sponsor identification, program selectivity by program type and by time period averages.

*Pulse.* The Pulse, Inc., produces national reports by combining local market data, but is known primarily for local measurements.

Pulse employs the "roster recall" method, where the interviewer visits the home and questions the family regarding its viewing over a specified period of hours. The interviewer aids the respondent's memory with the help of a roster, which is a three-way guide to station, quarter-hour, and program name.

Pulse surveys are conducted during the first seven days of each month, except holiday weeks, when the second week of the month is used. Selection of homes to be interviewed is by a random process. While the Pulse samples are more representative of the total metropolitan area population than are telephone homes alone, the "recall" method cannot be as accurate as the "coincidental" system for measuring audience size.

### Instantaneous Rating Systems

For years, more than one research organization has experimented with instantaneous electronic equipment which would transmit the record of family viewing over leased lines to headquarters and be immediately tabulated.

ARB has developed one such system, which is in limited operation. Known as Arbitron, this system utilizes devices which record instantly on a central board the number of TV sets turned on at any given time and the channels to which they are tuned.

The machine, a small electronic device attached to the TV set, is activated by an electronic tone signal which can be set to go out automatically at prescribed intervals or can be sent manually at any time. On receipt of this electronic query the machine sends back by

Fig. 7—INSTANTANEOUS RATINGS of television programs light up on the Arbitron Auto-Board while programs are still in progress. Every fifteen minutes the rating information electronically gathered in ninety-second intervals is transferred to pre-printed daily rating sheets, which list program and rating for every telecast in given area. (American Research Bureau)

direct leased wire its own signal designating whether the set is on and, if so, to which channel it is tuned. This electronic reply is picked up by a special computer which digests and interprets the information from all the sets and feeds it in the form of a rating figure to the Arbitron "Auto-Board." At the same time it is fed for permanent recording to a printer resembling a teletype.

A similar system is the Nielsen Instantaneous Audimeter, which automatically compiles homes-using-television and station-audience data each minute around the clock, printing out minute-by-minute and quarter-hour summaries. However, the Instaneous Audimeter has not yet passed far beyond the demonstration stage.

Because of the huge future potential for instantaneous systems, which would provide the advertiser with his program rating immediately after the program is over—or sometimes while it is still on the air—there is much experimentation in progress. It is even possible to build a unit for attachment to the television set which reports by

short-wave signals to central headquarters, requiring no lines whatever. But while it is possible, it is not now practical.

To extend any instantaneous system to a nationwide sampling of
homes and to make it a continuing method of television research is
simply too expensive an operation at this time.

## Criticisms of Ratings

Regardless of their wide usage and acceptance by advertisers, rating systems are constantly under attack.

The *telephone survey,* for example, is criticized on several counts, one
being that it is confined to telephone homes, a condition which may
induce bias. Typically, for reasons of cost, it covers only the non-toll
area, completely disregarding suburban and rural areas. The telephone
interview may encounter difficulty in the early morning and late evening because of resentment on the part of the resident at being dis-
turbed. And many calls are made to business phones that are not
identified as business phones in the directories. And those with un-
listed numbers are likely never to receive a call.

The *recall interview* is criticized because of possible memory failure.
Can people accurately remember the stations and programs they
watched hours before? Does the roster recall method actually help
them remember or instead provide them with convenient answers to
speed up the interview?

The *diary,* one of the more popular methods of measurement, is often
suspect for the following reason: Filling in the station, the name of program, and the number, sex, and age of viewers while each program is in
progress requires time and inconvenience. Entering the information on
a recall basis may lead to inaccuracies and omissions.

The *machine* technique, which automatically records the stations to
which the set is tuned, can measure only whether the set is turned on.
It cannot show the size, age, or sex of the audience. It cannot even
show whether anyone is watching.

In addition, present rating services are criticized on these grounds:

1. Relative smallness of the samples.

2. Lack of agreement among the findings of the various services.
Television critic John Crosby challenged the entire concept of ratings
when he wrote, "The leading scientists of their day were absolutely
convinced the world was flat. The outstanding medieval minds spent

a lifetime trying to figure out how many fairies could dance on the head of a pin. And today we have people, who seem outwardly sane, who believe ratings."

Trade magazines have run articles titled: "A New Ruckus Over Ratings Begins"; " 'We Need Reliable Ratings' "; and "The Answer to the Ratings Muddle."

Regardless of their various shortcomings, ratings do reflect public viewing habits. The most violent attacks on ratings come not so much from advertisers and their agencies as from those individuals who have little or no knowledge of the science of research. The very fact that, by and large, the relative rankings of programs are nearly identical proves there is a sound basis of measurement underlying each of the popular services.

## Improvements in Ratings

The question is not, "Are ratings worth having?" but rather, "What can be done to improve them?"

The Advertising Research Foundation, a nonprofit organization supported by advertisers, advertising agencies, and advertising media, assigned to its Radio-TV Ratings Review Committee the responsibility of developing standards to produce more accurate program size measurements.

The standards set forth in the report define (1) the type and amount of information to be provided; (2) the degree of accuracy required; and (3) the procedures to be followed.

The committee's recommendations follow:[1]

## Basic Information Standards

1. Exposure to a broadcast should be measured in terms of set tuning.

This is the most objective of the various levels of exposure. It is also the simplest and most understandable level of exposure. It is the most inclusive of all exposure measures. It is the only measurement which does not require a subjective evaluation of some kind on the part of the exposed person (which evaluation is different from different respondents under identical exposure conditions). It is thus the only measurement which is unambiguous since it can be interpreted only one way.

[1] "Recommended Standards for Radio and Television Program Audience Size Measurements." Copyrighted 1954 by the Advertising Research Foundation, Inc., reprinted by special permission.

2. The unit of measurement should be the household.

A program audience size measurement reported on a household base has wider application than a measurement based upon individuals. This is because the household is the typical economic unit in marketing; and because the interaction between members of the household plays an important role in influencing most purchase decisions.

3. All sets owned by the household should be measured.
4. The entire reception area should be measured.
5. The measurement should be representative of all households.

... Regardless of economic class, telephone ownership, or any other characteristic.

6. The measurement should report the average instantaneous audience.

... Because this measurement automatically weighs persons or households into the audience in proportion to the amount of their tuning. For this reason, the average instantaneous audience measurement permits uniform comparisons of audience size measurements for programs of different duration.

7. The measurement should express the number of households reached.

Points 8 through 14 list supplementary standards of information "which should be available," but "do not need to be regularly reported." This information includes "total household audience, unduplicated household audience to two or more broadcasts, program audience size measurements as per cent of all households, households using receivers, audience characteristics, program audience size measurements for specific segments of a program, such as commercials, and full network audience by specific time periods."

### Procedure Standards

15. The program audience size measurement should be based upon a probability sample.
16. The program audience size measurement should be based upon the audience during a single week.
17. The measurement should be reported for each commercially sponsored segment of the broadcast.
18. All broadcast hours from 6 A.M. to midnight should be measured.

19.  The measurement should be available at varying frequencies, depending upon the importance of the market.

20.  The measurement should be available within one month of the last measured broadcast.

## Accuracy Standards

21.  There should be adequate control of sampling errors.

22.  The net effect of non-sampling errors should not exceed the sampling error.

No one present method of research meets all of the foregoing requirements, and some experts disagree with certain of the committee's recommendations. But from the standpoint of its value as a constructive force in improving existing audience measurement techniques, it is well worth widespread consideration.

## New Proposals

There is no shortage of new contenders in the ratings field. Periodically, groups try to excite the industry in new measurement ideas they believe will solve the present problems confronting the rating systems.

One of the latest proposals is to employ personal coincidental interviews as a means of securing viewing information. This is not a novel idea. In the past, the method has been found to be too expensive and too difficult to administer because of the problem of gaining admittance to homes.

Another proposed service would be to extend the telephone-coincidental system to cover all sections of the country rather than just a sampling of major markets.

## The "Rating Trap"

It is a rare national advertiser who would not prefer to sponsor a show with a high rating record over one with an average or low rating. Exposing one's advertising message to the greatest possible number of potential customers is a very natural aim.

However, it becomes more and more evident that this criterion alone is not sufficient upon which to base the selection of one program over another. True, it is the program which reaches the viewers, but it is the commercial which sells the products. It is supremely vital that, besides the show's rating or probable rating, its compatibility with the advertiser and with the products he plans to feature be carefully considered.

Batten, Barton, Durstine & Osborn has conducted continuous research studies on the subject of "program climate" for the past two years. Its findings clearly indicate that the identical commercials appearing on two different programs can have an entirely different impact upon viewers. Even with programs of similar rating and audience composition the commercials may impress each audience differently.

In other words, the advertiser who fails to take into consideration the "climate" a program may provide for his commercial messages may fall into a costly trap. Ratings can sometimes be grossly misleading. Having an added dimension upon which to base a decision involving millions of dollars can reduce the risk and increase the eventual rewards for the advertiser, who enters television in the first place with one motive: to sell his products or ideas to the greatest number of people.

## chapter four

# Spot Television

AS contrasted with the network program, which is telecast by many stations simultaneously to reach a large, generally nationwide, audience, "spot" television is local, or non-network, advertising on a station-by-station basis.

While advertisers generally think of the term "spot" as the short commercial announcement on or between local programs, the term, nevertheless, also applies to programs which may be sponsored locally, including live news, weather, sports, women's service, and half-hour syndicated film programs.

Spot broadcasting, as one expert expressed it, is as different from network as newspapers are from magazines. Like a national magazine ad, a network purchase assures the advertiser of a mass audience with each single effort. Like newspapers, spot TV enables the advertiser to *spot* his campaign to fit his needs, affording him greater flexibility in that he may vary his markets and stations, his frequency, his time periods, even his duration. Most times his commitments in spot are considerably more flexible than in network. He can "move in and out" of markets, depending upon what his sales strategy might dictate.

More than one major product has been born, raised, and matured on spot campaigns alone. However, commitment to a network program does not preclude an advertiser's purchase of spot TV in certain areas to supplement his network and other-media efforts at strategic seasons of the year.

## Status of Spot TV

The Television Bureau of Advertising estimated that advertisers invested $511.7 million in total gross time purchases in spot TV in 1958.

Each of one hundred brands spent over $1 million. Forty-two of them spent over two million each. (Total network TV spending for the same year was estimated by other sources at approximately $560 million.)

Highest spot TV spender was Procter & Gamble Company, investing $33.8 million on behalf of thirty-seven brands. Next in order came Lever Brothers Company, $16.5 million; Adell Chemical Company, $12.3 million (the entire amount for one brand, Lestoil); General Foods Corporation, $11 million; Colgate-Palmolive Company, $10.9 million; Brown & Williamson Tobacco Company, $9.4 million; Continental Baking Company, $9.2 million; and Warner-Lambert, $8.8 million.

Foods and grocery products formed the largest category of spot TV spending by almost a three-to-one margin over the next product category—cosmetics and toiletries. Other groups in their order of spending were as follows: ale, beer, and wine; drug products; tobacco products and supplies; confections and soft drinks; household laundry products; gasoline and lubricants; consumer services; clothing, furnishings, accessories; automotive; household cleaners, cleansers, polishes, waxes; dental products; watches, jewelry, cameras; household equipment, including appliances; household paper products; pet products; household furnishings; transportation and travel; building material, equipment, fixtures, paints; general household products; sporting goods, bicycles, toys; TV, radio, phonograph, musical instruments; agriculture; publications; amusements, entertainment; garden supplies and equipment; notions; stationery, office equipment; hotels, resorts, restaurants. (Several product types were classified as "miscellaneous.")

## Spot Buys

Spot buys fit into three general categories:
1. The spot announcement.
2. The local live program.
3. The syndicated film program.

All, are placed directly on local stations. Their frequency and time of broadcast are suited to the needs of the individual advertiser.

# THE SPOT ANNOUNCEMENT

## Forms

The most common use of spot television is the *announcement*. When placed *between* programs, announcements are often referred to as "spots." When slotted *within* programs, they are commonly called "participations."

Spot announcements are sold in four lengths:

The *one-minute,* placed on or between local programs during the daytime and late evening. Because less than a minute of time is available between evening programs in prime time, the advertiser must sacrifice a certain amount of audience size in order to gain a full minute in which to sell his product or service. Therefore, minutes are usually available only during "fringe" hours on network stations or in prime time on independent stations.

The *twenty-second chainbreak* and the *ten-second "I. D.,"* are placed back to back between sponsored programs, including high-rating nighttime network shows, affording the advertiser the opportunity to capture large audiences. As might be expected, the "I. D." time period costs approximately half that of the chainbreak.

The *thirty-second announcement,* a new length of announcement now being accepted by more and more stations, is simply a single commercial sold in place of the chainbreak and the I. D., for which the advertiser pays time charges about equal to the total cost of the shorter two.

## Costs

While spot announcements are relatively inexpensive, considering the fact that no program cost is involved, they can represent a substantial expenditure of money. For example, five nighttime chainbreaks in eighty markets with a potential coverage of 90 per cent of U. S. TV homes would cost an advertiser approximately $100,000 or more, and continuing for ten weeks would exceed the million-dollar mark. However, an efficient use of I. D.'s in only forty markets with a potential of 75 per cent of U. S. TV homes, would cost less than $50,000, and for ten weeks would amount to less than half a million dollars. (Daytime spot announcement costs are listed as approximately half the evening rate, but in actual practice average considerably less.)

## Rates

Stations post various rate classifications for various times of the day. Starting with the highest rates, they are generally identified as class "AA," class "A," class "B," etc. There is no standardization among stations as to the time brackets each class covers. To compare accurately one station's rate with another's, it is necessary to compare *time of day* rather than rate classification. For example, on one station class "AA" might run from 8 to 11 P.M. On another, class "AA" might run from 7 to 10. A comparison on the lone basis of "class AA" time will, therefore, be misleading.

Although the one-minute announcement affords the advertiser more commercial time, the twenty-second chainbreak announcement usually costs as much or more when placed adjacent to high-rating nighttime shows.

Discounts on television time are not confined to network advertisers. Spot users, too, may qualify, depending upon the amount of business they place on the station. Each station has its own formula for the granting of the "frequency" discount, generally basing it upon the number of units run during a contract year. A typical formula might be: 26 times, 5 per cent discount; 104 times, 15 per cent; 250 times, 25 per cent. A station may also offer a "package plan" discount, based upon frequency within a week, often called something like a "five-plan" or "ten-plan."

Local program time, too, may qualify the advertiser for discounts, but most stations do not apply a discount to a combination of program and announcement units.

## Copy

The question is often asked: "Is a spot announcement created and written differently from a program commercial?" The answer logically should be positive, although the same set of film commercials is often used to serve both purposes. The actual theories behind the two forms of messages are these:

A commercial appearing on a program has every right to "get down to business" from the very first scene without need to "manufacture" attention at the beginning. The advertiser, after all, is paying for a program to surround his commercials with a large audience.

A spot announcement, on the other hand, often falls *between* programs, when the viewer may tend to become distracted in conversation or duties elsewhere in the home. The commercial must, therefore, command attention from the start in order to hold the audience, for it has more competitive influences surrounding it.

Both theories are probably true. Yet *any* commercial should be interesting from the first scene to the last. And, judging by the tremendous success spot announcement campaigns have brought to so many advertisers, fewer people are leaving the room between programs than one might suspect.

There is a difference between starting a commercial in an interesting way and starting a commercial with pure entertainment. The former method is always sound; the latter only sometimes reliable.

## Production

Most national advertisers and some local advertisers schedule *film* commercials to run in the spot announcement periods. Other national advertisers supply scripts for *live* presentation or "fact sheets" for local personalities to follow in delivering the commercials.

A third method, in which production costs are kept at a minimum, involves the use of still photos and artwork, including drawings, graphs, maps, charts, and other illustrations commonly referred to as "graphics." Following are the three ways such material is reproduced for television:

1. *The title card* is mounted on a sturdy board and placed, often on an easel, directly in front of the camera. The card, measuring 8 by 10 or 11 by 14 inches, should, of course, be prepared horizontally to a three-by-four ratio to conform to the shape of the television screen. When several such cards are bound together by looseleaf rings and allowed to drop so that the camera focuses on one at a time, they are known as *flip cards*.

2. *The balop or telop card* is handled not in the studio but in the projection room by a Balopticon projection machine or similar device. The result is often a slightly sharper image than a card used in the studio. Furthermore, the balop does not tie up a studio camera. Balop size is 4 by 5 inches over-all, with a scanned area of 3 by 4 inches and a safety area of 2½ by 3¼ inches centered in the scanned area.

3. *The transparent slide,* usually measuring 2 by 2 inches, is likewise handled in the projection room and does not require use of a studio camera. However, since a few of the stations are equipped only to project a larger size slide, it is wise to check slide specifications in advance.

Since *action* is a basic virtue that sets television apart from all other forms of advertising media, commercials which lean on flip cards,

Fig. 8—TELOP 1: "Fans, if you listen to the lingo of a ball player long enough, you'll hear him refer to a teammate as a 'junk man.' Know what that means?"

Fig. 9—TELOP 2: "Why sure! A junk man is a pitcher who has no fast ball, but serves up a big assortment of soft curves, knucklers, and what-have-you."

Fig. 10—TELOP 3: "And his lingo for a great smoke and a *genuine* cigarette? What else but Lucky Strike!" (Etc.)

Where many commercials are needed over the course of a season, as in cases like regular sponsorship of ball games, telops added to the "bank" of film commercials provide variety at relatively little extra cost. The above example shows the first three of six telops comprising one forty-second between-innings commercial. Voice-over was by live play-by-play announcer.

balops, or slides for their video support cannot possibly carry the impact of a live, in-person or motion picture film commercial.

## THE LOCAL LIVE PROGRAM

When an advertiser sponsors local news, weather, sports, or other programs, he is tying his interests to the appeal of local live personalities. A national or regional advertiser may sponsor one type of program in one market, another type in another market. In this manner he generally receives more than a minute of commercial time, and benefits further from becoming better and better known as the program sponsor.

There is somewhat of an overlap in the first two classifications—spot announcement and local live program—in that an advertiser's one-minute spot announcement is often placed within a program, thereby casting him in the role of "participating sponsor."

The next chapter describes local live program opportunities in greater detail.

## THE SYNDICATED FILM PROGRAM

### Advantages

The half-hour syndicated film program can be a product of the same high-quality production effort that goes into a network program. But it is placed on a station-by-station syndicated basis rather than on a network. Time costs are based on the size of the market in which it is placed.

Syndication, therefore, affords an advertiser the opportunity to buy programs on less than a national hookup either for economy's sake or for marketing reasons. For example, because of the nature of his product, he may desire to eliminate the warm weather markets. Or, for competitive reasons, he may want only a few of the top markets.

The advertiser whose distribution is regional finds the syndicated film program ideal since he can sponsor the same program in more than one market, but only in those markets where his product is sold.

Many national advertisers use syndication as a definite marketing tool, most often to supplement their network fare. *Sponsor* magazine's *TV and Radio Basics* gives these reasons: "(1) Syndicated programing lends itself well to regional distribution and merchandising situations. You can spot your emphasis where you want it. (2) Syndication is an excellent way of programing desirable non-network areas. (3) Advertisers sometimes sell products under different labels in different parts of the country. With spot programing, you can pitch your commercials locally. (4) A syndicated program, well merchandised, is a good way to firm dealer relationships. (5) Sponsoring a program rather than spot announcements gives identification to a specific brand within the community. (6) It is a good method with which to test market a product. (7) It is a good way to strengthen weak market positions."

### Examples

Typical of the syndicated show are such perennials as "Highway Patrol," "Annie Oakley," "Sea Hunt," and, of course, the famous "Hopalong Cassidy" series.

Most of the films produced for syndication tend to follow the themes of adventure, crime, comedy, or dramatic anthology simply because these have proven the most successful in drawing an audience.

Not all film programs which are syndicated were produced for that purpose. Many shows now sponsored on local stations are reruns of former network properties, such as Burns and Allen, "Susie," (re-titled version of "Private Secretary"), "San Francisco Beat" (re-titled version of "Lineup"), and "Our Miss Brooks."

Not all syndicated films are single-sponsored. The station may schedule a "strip," or daily showing, of popular reruns, for example, for the benefit of participating sponsors, where no single advertiser owns the property but rather participates along with others in the form of one-minute announcements.

### Growth

Film syndication has been a rapidly expanding business over the past several years and continues to grow today. While Hollywood feature films still retain considerable interest and attraction, syndicated films, now estimated as a one-hundred-million-dollar business, have become more and more an integral part of the marketing plans of TV advertisers.

To meet the increasing demands for new properties, scores of production companies have enlarged their offerings. Some of the better-known companies are ABC Film Syndication, Associated Artists Programs, California National Productions (a division of NBC), CBS TV Film Sales, Desilu, Gross-Krasne, MCA-TV, MGM, National Telefilm Associates, Official Films, Screen Gems, Television Programs of America, United Artists, and Ziv Television Programs. Some of these firms produce films for network use as well.

The New York market alone airs more than one hundred syndicated films weekly; Los Angeles, over eighty; and Washington, Milwaukee, Detroit, Chicago, and San Francisco, in the vicinity of sixty.

### Time Clearances

The largest syndication sales, dollar-for-dollar, are made directly to sponsors rather than to stations. Advertisers, then, have the problem of finding good local time periods during which to schedule their programs. And a problem it is. In New York, for example, network option time extends from 7:30 to 10:30 P.M., with some network shows extending until 11. The advertiser must then seek prime time on a non-network station or earlier or later time on a network affiliate.

There is no formula for suitable good time beyond approaching each station directly or through the station representative; or, possibly, through the syndication company itself, which in turn, contacts one or the other.

Working closely with his dealers and distributors in each area can stimulate enthusiasm at the local level, and sometimes provide the advertiser with a further contact in dealing with the station for suitable time.

### The "Film Network"

In this connection, a newer use of television has come to be known as the "film network." Best known of such operations is the NTA Film Network.

NTA is a film distribution company which, in addition to selling feature films and certain half-hour programs to advertisers, has financial agreements with more than a hundred stations throughout the country to clear certain time periods.

NTA affiliates represent a cross section of the NBC, CBS, ABC and independent stations. Times available for the NTA programs vary with the program purchased, the market, and other factors.

The NTA package actually consists of feature films, a number of half-hour TV film series, and reruns of hour network shows scheduled for five-times-a-week daytime programing.

## Role of the Station "Rep"

Most of the nation's TV and radio stations rely on groups of representatives to relay their spot time availabilities to advertising agencies and to advertisers. These groups are known as station "reps." For acting as intermediary between the distantly separated parties, they receive a commission (in the neighborhood of 10 per cent of the stations' charges) from the time purchased.

"Reps" perform a valuable service. It would be a mammoth, nearly impossible operation for the agencies to keep in daily contact with the more than five hundred television stations—even with the top fifty. Likewise, the stations themselves would find selling local spot time to national advertisers an extremely expensive and chaotic proposition if they were each forced to maintain a sales staff in the major metropolitan areas where the time-buying decisions of most national advertisers are made.

## Role of the Time Buyer

As in the case of the purchase of network programs, the agency time buyer is a key man in buying spot time on local television stations. He must have a working knowledge of the coverage patterns of various stations, their rates, expected audience, etc. He must know local conditions, including station management, programing policies, and general facts concerning each specific market. In analyzing the value of each station, the time buyer turns to various audience-measurement services for such information as the number of sets in use during any particular time of day, the average number of families tuned to the station at a given time, ratings of preceding and following programs adjacent to the time period or spot under consideration, and the audience composition in terms of men, women, and children.

He must consider all these various factors in the light of the advertiser's budget, marketing objectives, and his distribution and merchandising plans. Over and above all this, he must understand the advertiser's selling strategy, as expressed in his commercials.

It is up to the agency time buyer, in other words, to deliver the most and best audience for the least amount of money.

Once the advertiser has approved a campaign and a budget, the time buyer contacts the station "reps," secures time availabilities,

## TELEVISION AVAILABILITIES

BUYER: John Smith
AGENCY: Black & Brown, Inc.
ADVERTISER: Universal Gum
PRODUCT: Buz Gum

MARKET: Birmingham, Ala.
STATION: WBRC-TV
NETWORK: CBS   CH.: 6   Rate Card #10

Rating - Nielsen (November)

| PRECEDING PROGRAM | DAY(S) & TIME(S) | TYPE | FOLLOWING PROGRAM | 1x | Costs 6 Plan | 9 Plan | 12 Plan |
|---|---|---|---|---|---|---|---|
| G.E. Theatre 44.3 | Sun. 8:30 PM | 20 | Alfred Hitchcock 39.7 | $250.00 | | | |
| Red Skelton 33.1 | Tues. 9:00 PM | 20 | Garry Moore 31.3 | 250.00 | | | |
| Pursuit 31.0 | Wed. 8:00 PM | 20 | The Millionaire 43.6 | 250.00 | | | |
| The Millionaire 40.8 | Wed. 8:30 PM | 20 | I've Got a Secret 36.9 | 250.00 | | | |
| Playhouse of Stars 43.6 | Fri. 9:00 PM | 20 | The Lineup 45.1 | 250.00 | | | |
| Red Skelton 33.1 | Tues. 9:00 PM | 10 | Garry Moore 31.3 | 125.00 | | | |
| December Bride 36.6 | Thurs. 7:30 PM | 10 | Yancy Derringer 43.8 | 125.00 | | | |
| 26 Men 41.2 | Fri. 10:00 PM | 10 | U.S. Marshal 30.5 | 125.00 | | | |
| Have Gun, Will Travel 41.9 | Sat. 9:00 PM | 10 | Gunsmoke 47.9 | 125.00 | | | |
| Our Miss Brooks 13.7 | M,Tu 12:30 PM | 60 | As the World Turns 16.3 | 80.00 | $56.00 | $52.00 | $44.00 |
| As the World Turns 15.4 | M,W,Th 1:00 PM | 60 | Petticoat Party Line 10.2 | 80.00 | 56.00 | 52.00 | 44.00 |
| Petticoat Party Line 10.2 | Fri. 1:30 PM | 60 | Brighter Day 16.2 | 80.00 | 56.00 | 52.00 | 44.00 |
| Secret Storm 16.6 | Th,W,Th 3:30 PM | 20 | Edge of Night 17.0 | 80.00 | 56.00 | 52.00 | 44.00 |
| PARTICIPATIONS Mon. thru Fri. | | 60s | | | | | |
| In "Our Miss Brooks" 13.4 | 12:00-12:30 PM | | | 80.00 | 56.00 | 52.00 | 44.00 |
| In "Petticoat Party Line" 10.2 | 1:00-1:30 PM | | | 80.00 | 56.00 | 52.00 | 44.00 |
| In "Amos 'n Andy" 22.4 | 5:00-5:30 PM | | | 90.00 | 63.00 | 58.50 | 49.50 |

Submitted subject to prior sale, DATE 12/10

Peter Green

THE KATZ AGENCY, INC.

Fig. 11—TIME BUYER CONTACTS "STATION REPS" for TV spot availabilities. "Reps" must know name of product (to avoid adjacent commercials of competing products), lengths of time periods needed, and, in general, the times of day the spots should run. The above sample shows availabilities for a hypothetical product. Each horizontal line describes the time location of an available spot period, with the length of spot listed under "type." (Note the shorter twenty-second chainbreaks and the ten-second I. D.'s cost more since they are nighttime spots, commanding larger audiences.) The first column of prices applies to the one-time rate. Daytime availabilities here earn discounts on 6-, 9-, and 12-plans. Although the higher-priced spots do not qualify for discounts on this chart, they may, nevertheless, apply as units toward the plan.

orders the best spots, or time slots, and places contracts with the stations he has selected.

## Merchandising Services

How important are merchandising services, contest, and promotional mailings in influencing an agency to place a spot schedule on one station in preference to another?

*Advertising Age* polled a group of media directors of top agencies on this question and found that such factors are most often secondary. Virtually every station is selected on concrete, factual bases—rates, coverage, proper adjacencies, etc. "Sure," one said, "we look for merchandising help from a station—but only *after* we have checked its other values. Merchandising is strictly a marginal appeal, not a direct influence."

Stations, nevertheless, continue to make a major point of additional ways they can help advertisers buying spot or program time to merchandise their efforts. The next chapter lists scores of merchandising ideas offered by the stations themselves to help make the advertiser's dollar work even harder.

## Late-Night Viewing

Late evening feature films have been relatively popular for years, but not until recently has the average advertiser realized the size of the audience to be reached after 11 P.M.

Blair-TV-represented stations in ten major markets underwrote a survey by The Pulse, Inc., which revealed that approximately 75 per cent of the television audience watches at 11 P.M., or later. The average TV home watches 3.5 nights per week with an average of two viewers per home.

Equally significant, these "night owls" are family people, with more than 70 per cent of the households consisting of three or more persons. "Economic status of the late-night television viewer closely parallels the television audience make-up during 'prime' hours and substantiates the sales productivity of late television time periods."

These results are not so startling when one considers the additional attention both stations and networks have given these late hours in the form of better programing.

*chapter five* _____

# Local Stations

LOCAL stations are the *heart* of television. Local programs emanate from the studios of local stations. Network programs could not reach an audience without local stations to carry them. Spot announcements of both local and national advertisers are transmitted by the local station. *All* television advertising, in the final analysis, then, is *local*.

No two of the more than 500 local television stations in the United States are completely alike. A few operate with a single live camera. Some have more than twelve. A few stations are on the air less than ten hours a day. Some telecast almost twenty hours. Some are affiliated with networks. Some are not. A few stations are staffed by only eight or nine people. Some employ more than two hundred. Whatever its size and characteristics, the station, identified by both call letters and a channel number, is the means by which television entertainment and commercials reach the viewer.

The local station depends for its livelihood on the sale of time, either for programs or spot announcements, to local and national advertisers. If it is affiliated with a network, the station also receives income from the sponsored network programs it carries.

Its time rates are generally based on the size of the population area it covers. In markets of more than one station, the advertiser is naturally interested in the relative popularity of each station's fare at various hours throughout the broadcast day and evening. Many rating services operate locally to provide both advertisers and stations with viewing information.

## Local TV Advertising

Local advertisers, it has been estimated, spend nearly three hundred million dollars a year in television to sell merchandise and build consumer good will. Impressive as this may appear, however, it still represents less than 10 per cent of the total being budgeted by local advertisers in all media.

This startling fact can be viewed in two different lights. One, television has not yet become a major factor in the advertising plans of the local advertiser. Two, the growth potential of this already powerful medium is tremendous. Television, a giant in the national picture, now seems to be gaining momentum on the local front as well. For here, too, the local advertiser is able to apply over-the-counter salesmanship to more customers in a single day than his sales force reaches in half a lifetime.

## STATION MANAGERS SURVEY

Because the individual local television stations vary in their facilities, their rates, their services, and their philosophies, it is no small task to obtain a broad view of the local picture.

Yet the life and habits of local stations are of intense interest to a number of parties: the national advertiser, the local advertiser, advertising agencies, and the stations themselves, who can evaluate themselves by better understanding the pattern of others.

To answer this need, a comprehensive survey was conducted in the summer of 1958.[1] Detailed questionnaires were sent to managers of 484 television stations, seeking information on classification data, facilities, and services, commercial practices, types of advertisers and their schedules, and programing trends. One station manager called this "by far the most penetrating survey ever taken."

Had 30 per cent of the stations answered the questionnaire, researchers would have been satisfied they had obtained a more-than-adequate sampling. To this questionnaire, however, 331 of the 484 stations responded—an astounding 68 per cent return!

Because of the completeness and timeliness of this important information, the next major section of this chapter is devoted to the enlightening results of this survey.

[1] By Batten, Barton, Durstine & Osborn.

## Hours per Day of Station Operation

As the following summary reveals, two-thirds of the TV stations in this country operate 16 hours or more every day.

| | |
|---|---|
| 1–10 hours | 11% |
| 11–15¾ hours | 21% |
| 16–16¾ hours | 13% |
| 17–17¾ hours | 26% |
| 18–18½ hours | 23% |
| 19–19½ hours | 4% |
| No answer | 2% |

## Hours of Network Programs Carried per Week

Of the stations reporting, 49 per cent are affiliated exclusively with one of the three major networks:

| | |
|---|---|
| CBS | 21% |
| NBC | 16% |
| ABC | 12% |

Forty-eight per cent reported various combinations of dual or multiple-affiliation.[2] Only nine of the 331 stations who answered the questionnaire, or 3 per cent, were not affiliated with any network.

Among the exclusive affiliates, nearly three-quarters of the CBS stations carry between 40 and 80 hours of network programs per week; 59 per cent, 60 to 80 hours. Sixty-seven per cent of the NBC affiliates transmit from 60 to 90 hours per week. ABC stations, on the average, carry fewer network hours: 73 per cent, from 20 to 40 hours per week; an additional 7 per cent carry between 40 and 50 hours, the highest number mentioned.

Totaling the "exclusives" with the "multi-affiliated" stations, the network hours per week pattern is as follows:

| | |
|---|---|
| Under 10 hours | 33% |
| 11–50 hours | 29% |
| Over 50 hours | 32% |
| No answer | 6% |

[2] NTA (National Telefilm Associates) included by some stations as "network." (See Chapter 4.)

## Number of Live Cameras

Three-quarters of the local stations own from one to four live cameras. Thirty-nine per cent reported two cameras; 16 per cent, three; 13 per cent, four; 7 per cent, five; 4 per cent, six; 3 per cent, seven. Eight per cent have only one camera. A few of the larger stations reported more than a dozen. The average station can do a most adequate local programing job on two or three cameras.

## Film Projection

Relatively few stations have 35mm film projection equipment. More than 90 per cent reported 16mm only, which, again, offers sufficient quality for reproducing both programs and commercials.

## Remote Equipment

Fifty-eight per cent of the stations own or have access to remote equipment, including mobile units, enabling them to pick up live programs at points outside their regular studios.

## Rear Screen Projection

"R. P.," a production effect which provides backgrounds or portions of backgrounds by projection of slides or motion picture film on a screen behind the subject, is available in seven out of ten local stations, a surprisingly large proportion.

Rear screen can be an extremely dramatic and effective device when used, for example, to project a still of the advertiser's store front or interior behind the live announcer as he sells a live product on-camera. The business locale of practically any advertiser can thus be made a part of the commercial "set" inexpensively.

## Studios

Fifty per cent of the nation's television stations have two studios; 33 per cent have one; 12 per cent, three. Very new stations have more. (See Appendix.)

## Size of Station Staff

Staffs of local stations range in size from less than ten people to more than 200. Thirty-five per cent employ between 11 and 50; 44 per cent, 50 to 100; 12 per cent, 100 to 160. (See Appendix.)

*Merchandising Help*

Stations were asked: "What types of merchandising help does your station offer local and national advertisers?" The services varied, of course, with each station. The following list, a composite of the total replies, forms a valuable check list for any advertiser interested in availing himself of the merchandising services of local stations.

Mailings
Trade calls at point of sale
Display material
Setup of displays
Display case at studio and lobby displays
On-the-air promotion
Merchandising magazine
Personal call on key buyers and chain executives
Bus cards
Newspaper ad space
Billboards for programs
In-store demonstrations
Grocery, drug trade newspapers
On-the-air product interviews
Appearances at dealer meetings by local personalities
Taxicab displays
Personal letters
Bulletins to wholesalers
Merchandising memos
Consumer panel surveys
Station giveaways
Jobber contracts
Mobile unit
Special telegrams
Contests
Shelftalkers
Show cards for windows
Movie screen ads
Jumbo postcards
Bonus spots
Sampling
TV timetable

Film strip at local theaters
Dealer contests and promotions
In-store preferred shelf space
Personal letters
"Whatever we can think up"

This much is certain: there is no shortage of ideas when it comes to helping the advertiser merchandise his products locally. What is less clear-cut is the policy of many stations toward charging for such services.

An extremely important factor is, of course, the size of the schedule purchased by the advertiser. A station is naturally inclined to do a more elaborate merchandising job for the more frequent advertiser.

### Stations Producing Film Commercials for Local Advertisers

More than two-thirds of the local television stations produce film commercials for local advertisers.

Forty per cent of those who do said they charged advertisers a *minimum* average of from $10 to $45 per one-minute film commercial, a proportionately low figure that could obviously hold true only outside union jurisdiction. Another 23 per cent set the minimum average cost per film commercial at $50 to $85; 7 per cent from $90 to $105. Only 8 per cent reported a minimum figure of more than $110, the highest being $300.

*Maximum* cost of a one-minute film commercial produced by the station for the local advertiser ranges from $16 to $1,500. Most of the maximum figures mentioned range from $50 to $300.

### Stations Creating Commercial Copy for Local Advertisers

Not only do most stations prepare the advertising copy for local advertisers, but the copy is often created before the campaign is sold. Approaching a potential advertiser with the script or storyboard of a sample commercial invariably makes the salesman's job easier than when he has to sell only the *concept* of TV advertising to the prospect. Even a low-cost film commercial, created and produced on a purely speculative basis, is not beyond the means of the alert station seeking a good prospect.

The survey showed that 86 per cent of the stations regularly prepare copy for local clients. Three-quarters of these, in fact, prepare more than half the local copy used on their respective stations.

## Spots Sold by Local Stations in Class "A" Time

All stations offer for sale both 10- and 20-second spot announcements to local and national advertisers. The 20-second "chainbreak" announcement and the 10-second "I.D.," spot, in which the station also identifies itself by reciting its call letters, is the traditional pattern within the thirty seconds of time available for local sponsorship between sponsored programs.

Recently some stations began offering this thirty second period to advertisers as *one* commercial, replacing the 20- and the 10-second spots. Thirty-eight per cent of the stations report this new length is now available. Another 38 per cent reported they do not sell this length of spot. Twenty-four per cent did not answer the query, indicating perhaps a "wait-and-see" policy, to be clarified when the relative demand is determined.

In about two-thirds of the cases, any advertiser buying the 30-second length must pay the sum of the 10-second and 20-second rates. Twenty-three per cent of the stations offering the 30-second availability, in fact, charge *more* than the sum of the other two. Eleven per cent charge less.

## New Development on I. D. Specifications

The 10-second I. D., the shortest commercial in television, has enjoyed a most interesting and successful history. Some large advertisers have based their entire television campaigns on this length alone. Sometimes called the "name and claim spot," it allows the advertiser strong registration of his product name and his basic theme line.

Originally, the 10-second I. D. was a shared affair. The picture portion of the commercial, from beginning to end, went 75 per cent to the advertiser and 25 per cent to the station call letters. Shared I. D.'s are still on the air, but a national spot advertiser running I. D.'s on many stations simultaneously must pay extra production costs for the imprinting of the individual station call letters.

An outgrowth of this has been the "split I. D." Here the advertiser is entitled to 100 per cent of the picture portion for seven seconds. The station then occupies the full screen for the remainder. While the advertiser here gains the full screen area for his video message, he must then surrender 30 per cent of his visual to the station.

The newest form of I. D., and by far the most advantageous to the advertiser, gives the product 100 per cent of the picture portion for the full 10 seconds. Only the last 2½ seconds of audio are devoted to oral station identification. When asked if they would accept this new form of I. D., 79 per cent of the stations replied in the affirmative, indicating that soon virtually all stations will standardize. When this happens, the less-effective "shared" and the "split" will certainly be obsolete.

### Local Rate vs. National Rate

Most stations charge national advertisers more for the same spot time period than they do local advertisers. There are two reasons for this, one involving commissions the stations must pay on national business: to their station representatives or "reps," and to advertising agencies; the other being that many local retail businesses cannot benefit from the total coverage area of the station. Sixty-three per cent of the stations reported they do have a local rate as distinct from national; 36 per cent said they do not; 1 per cent, no answer.

Those with a local rate were then asked, "Approximately what percentage is it of your national rate?" Two-thirds reported percentages ranging from 61 to 89. Conversely, then, the typical station's national rate is between 11 per cent to 39 per cent more than its local rate for spot announcements. Many stations gave qualified answers, stating that the difference in the two rates varies with the time of day.

### Average Number of Spot Announcements per Week

How many announcements per week are purchased by the typical *local* spot advertiser? Stations reported as follows:

| Spots Per Week | Stations[3] |
| --- | --- |
| 1–5 | 42% |
| 6–10 | 47% |
| Over 10 | 14% |
| No answer | 5% |

How many announcements per week are purchased by the typical *national* spot advertiser?

| Spots Per Week | Stations[3] |
| --- | --- |
| 1–5 | 54% |
| 6–10 | 38% |
| Over 10 | 7% |
| No answer | 5% |

[3] Column adds to more than 100% because of multiple mentions by some stations.

*Types of Local Business Concerns Advertising on Television*

Who are the local TV advertisers? Are department stores, traditional users of newspapers, still "cool" to television? What about banks, lumberyards, movie houses, real estate brokers, automobile dealers, dairies, restaurants? Which business concerns are mentioned as most frequent users of the medium?

The survey revealed surprising and exciting information. Station managers were presented a list of thirty kinds of local business and asked to check which ones advertised "regularly," "occasionally," or "never" on their stations. Local soft drink bottlers were mentioned by more stations as "regular" local advertisers than any other category of business.

The others, in the order of their frequency of mention, were these:

Banks, dairies, auto sales and service, grocery stores, bakeries, appliance stores, local utilities, oil companies, home furnishings, local breweries, department stores, jewelry stores, cleaning and dyeing establishments, drugstores, shoe stores, local manufacturers, movie houses, restaurants, floor covering stores, lumberyards, real estate, hardware stores, meat markets, discount houses, nurseries, produce markets, beauty parlors, mail order houses, and coal companies. The one most mentioned under the category of "other businesses" was farm products and services. In fact, besides the thirty listed, sixty-eight additional types of business were mentioned by one station or another as "regular" TV advertisers. (See Appendix.)

It would be difficult, judging by this survey, to think of many categories of local business that are not now, somewhere, represented on television. The fact that 51 per cent of the stations listed department stores as "regular" advertisers and 44 per cent called them "occasional" advertisers indicates that television has come of age as a retail medium.

When asked if the same pattern of local TV advertising had changed from a year ago, 66 per cent of the stations saw no significant change. Among those stations that did notice a change, 8 per cent noted the entry of department stores into the medium as the major change. However, this alone could hardly be considered a trend.

Station managers were next asked, "In your opinion, what types of local business concerns should use TV advertising, but are not doing so?"

No fewer than eighty types were mentioned, for the most part duplicating the previous listing of "regular" advertisers, indicating that the problems of one station are not necessarily the problems of another. However, in this case each category, with one exception, was listed by so few stations that one might conclude there was hardly a hold-out business type among them.

The exception was department stores. After rating twelfth on the roster of "regular" advertisers, department stores were listed by 49 per cent of the stations as a local business "that should use TV advertising but are not doing so."

The conclusion is fairly obvious. Department stores are "getting their feet wet" more and more in local television. Some have even entered the medium in a big way. But most are still not using TV as their major medium and some perhaps never will. The station manager naturally sees a great potential in a large store. But a television commercial does not offer the completeness of a full-page newspaper ad, and certain department store executives have viewed the change as difficult to accept after half a century of success with newspapers.

*Television Age* sees the trend of department stores toward TV gaining momentum. "The traditionalism that has long been the highest hurdle in the path of television's pursuit of the department store advertising dollar is finally—and rapidly—breaking down in the face of all the incontrovertible evidence that video reaches not only a numerically far greater audience than newspapers but also one which represents the bulk of today's buying power—the younger family group which has grown up in the radio and TV eras of mass communications."

Reported *Printer's Ink*, "A pioneer in such TV advertising is the J. S. Brandeis Co. of Omaha, largest department store in Nebraska. On Easter Monday the firm began a series of one-minute commercials on KMTV, seven a day, five days a week, advertising all kinds of retail merchandise from backyard barbecue sets to ladies' ready-to-wear. Each 'TV special' is identified on the air with a number.

"Viewers may phone their orders to the store directly, or they may purchase the merchandise by using mail-order blanks available in booklet form from the TV station. The campaign is less than three weeks old, and the station is filling booklet requests at the rate of 700 a day."

### Reasons for not Using TV

When asked, "What is the reason for not using TV most often given by local non-TV advertisers?" 63 per cent of the stations answered, "the high cost of both time and production." The next most frequent answer, by 12 per cent of the stations, "experience with, and confidence in, newspapers." A lack of knowledge and general unfamiliarity with the medium was mentioned by 9 per cent; coverage too great to be economical, 8 per cent. (See Appendix.)

Regarding the "high cost" objection, forces promoting the wider use of television advertising answer with a variety of arguments. Said one, "Even in a small market, a $50 to $75 TV spot which commands the personalized attention of only 10,000 viewers represents truly high productivity for a low-cost piece of advertising."

Most TV stations now have their "10 plans" and their seasonal package plans. These are only two ways in which they allow the advertiser attractive discounts when he buys announcements in groups rather than one at a time. On a cost-per-thousand basis these local packages are well within the reach of most local businessmen.

### Per Cent of Revenue from Local Advertisers

Most television stations derive less than half their total revenue from local business. When asked for percentages, the stations replied as follows:

| Percentage of Income Provided By Local Business | Stations |
|---|---|
| Under 20% | 7% |
| 20%–40% | 44% |
| 40%–60% | 23% |
| Over 60% | 17% |
| No answer | 9% |

"Is this percentage of local business increasing or decreasing?"

| | |
|---|---|
| Increasing | 61% |
| Decreasing | 18% |
| Staying about the same | 12% |
| No answer | 9% |

The conclusion should not necessarily be drawn, however, that local stations in the future will depend less and less upon income from national advertisers. The particular survey jibed with certain national cutbacks which did not reflect local business conditions in all communities.

Answered one station, "We anticipate a return to a normal of 20 per cent local next fall." The "norm," however, seems to be a bit higher.

## Local Personalities Selling On-Camera

Most television stations feature one or more male or female personalities who not only conduct programs but also demonstrate and endorse products with most gratifying results.

National advertisers are not averse to "using" this local talent; many indeed have with considerable success. Nevertheless, probably the great majority of national advertisers, in conducting an extensive spot campaign on stations throughout the nation, find it more expedient today, if not more effective, to film a series of spots in three or four basic lengths and send the prints to stations, where the commercials are telecast in their controlled, pre-approved form. In this way, advertisers are certain of a "perfect performance" whenever and wherever the films are shown.

The question then arises: Is the national advertiser not "missing a bet" if he fails to take full advantage of the local personal touch? "The most underrated buy in TV today is the strong local sales personality," said one station. "We are well known," said another, "having also been in radio here for years. If we say it's a good buy, our audience has faith in our word."

On the other hand, for a national advertiser physically to arrange local live treatment for his commercial in multiple markets is no simple undertaking. Film at least assures him that (1) his product will be properly lighted and presented, (2) his copy story will be delivered in a sound, consistent manner, and (3) any tricky components, such as a jingle, will be well handled. Furthermore, on 20- and 10-second nighttime periods between programs, a local personality would have too little time to do an adequate job. Many stations, in fact, do not offer live commercial facilities during these hours without additional high cost, if at all.

There is no question that film spots make the job of preparation easier for both the national advertiser and the station. Once he approves a "batch" of film spots, the advertiser can sit back and rely on his advertising agency to send prints to the stations and on the stations to transmit the commercials in the periods purchased.

What makes the scores of comments by stations on this subject so significant is the fact that the stations themselves stand to gain little or no immediate additional income from handling national spots on a live basis—except in cases where slightly elaborate production values are required. They are generally willing to go to the extra trouble to dramatize to the advertiser that all selling is *local.*

A national advertiser interested in applying the local touch to his spot opportunities could experiment in the following manner:

1. Select a group of three or four markets where all one-minute spots are performed on a live basis by a respected local personality.

2. Select a comparable group of markets in which film spots are run in the normal manner.

3. After a period of 13—or better, 26—weeks, attempt to compare the results of the two efforts by (a) checking on sales, or (b) surveying a cross section of viewers of the stations in each group of markets for their awareness and comprehension of the sales messages.

Perhaps the best-known of all local personalities on television is Ruth Lyons, who has conducted her "50–50 Club" on WLW-T, Cincinnati, for more than twelve years. In observing the event, *Television Age* quoted her as follows: "The most important consideration is always the audience. Never fool them, never talk down to them. Be forthright in your approach, and they, in turn, will support your sponsor's products and activities.

". . . The next most important consideration is the dealers who serve the audience. We must always recognize our responsibility—to the audience and the dealers—to advertise the best possible product with the best available distribution so that we may do a commendable job for the sponsors."

Quality of product, by the way, is just as essential to the success of a local television campaign as it is to a national campaign.

## chapter six

# How to Create Television Advertising

WHATEVER else may occupy the television advertiser, nothing is more important nor more basic to a successful campaign than *good commercials*. The commercial is all-important in that it is the advertiser's selling message to the viewer. It is his advertisement on the air. With each showing it reflects not only on his product but on his entire company.

So, regardless of how or how often the commercial is going to appear, it must rate top priority. To describe the story of its development, which along the way requires a number of special skills, it is fitting first to describe the key person involved in its creation.

## THE TELEVISION COPYWRITER

The commercial which Bulova Watch Company sponsored on WNBT (now WRCA-TV), New York, July 1, 1941, signaled more than the hour of day. It signaled the beginning of commercial television in the United States, an era that was to breed in great numbers an entirely new species of creative advertising person—the television copywriter.

The early TV copywriter had to struggle from scratch, exploring and experimenting as he went; but the newness of the medium and the absence of many other commercials on the air were in his favor.

Today's copywriter, armed with a knowledge of the basic techniques, experience, and facts from research, faces a still bigger problem—competition. Not only is the product or service he is advertising likely to be competing with other products and services in the same medium, but his commercial is bidding for the attention of the viewer who, with all of his other distractions, is now seeing approximately thirty television commercials during the course of an evening.

## FOUR STEPS TO TV SELLING

Behind every successful effort in television advertising is a *plan*. No two plans are alike because no two products are alike and no two advertisers are alike. But every plan for every advertiser should evolve from these four critical steps: (1) The Basic Theme; (2) The Copy Plan; (3) The Campaign; (4) The Commercials.

### 1. The Basic Theme

All sound advertising is based on two principles: unity of thought and frequency of impression. The latter is achieved by a budget sizable enough to provide for repetition of the commercial message. Unity of thought is expressed by the basic theme, which should be emphasized consistently in all media used by the advertiser.

The basic theme line is a short phrase giving the consumer a reason to buy the product or service. The word "slogan" is often confused with "basic theme." Not all slogans are basic themes. If the slogan is an active one which the advertiser makes the basis for the major part of his copy story, then it is indeed a basic theme. If, on the other hand, the slogan is simply an appendage to the commercial but does not relate to the main sales story of the commercial, then it is a slogan only. Frequently, when an advertiser decides on a new basic theme, his former one is relegated to the status of slogan and used in a supplemental way. Or he may drop his former theme entirely.

Ideally a basic theme should live on and on for months and years. Only by "sticking with it" will the advertiser reap its benefits in sales.

*Requirements.* To be effective, a basic theme should possess as many of the following qualities as possible:

*a)* It should be simple and easy to remember.

*b)* It should be as short as possible.

*c)* It should be specific.

*d)* It should be original.

*e)* It should describe the most important consumer benefit.

*f)* It should urge the customer to act.

Unity of thought expressed in a strong basic theme is the foundation for successful advertising in television and in all media. All copy points, all selling arguments, all evidence and demonstration should pay off again and again with the one basic theme. As Carleton Spier, one of advertising's most respected men, puts it: "Advertising built on one basic theme cuts faster, bites deeper, pays off better in sales— just as a tree falls more quickly when every blow is directed at one spot."

*Building the Basic Theme.* A sound basic theme is much more than just a clever phrase. It must be carefully and thoughtfully developed in order to do the best possible job for the advertiser. Many considerations are involved in its development.

First, the copywriter must know all there is to know about the product he is advertising.

Second, he must be familiar with competitive products. He must know how they compare, feature by feature, with his own.

Third, he must look for points of difference between his product and those of competition. He should ask himself, "What big advantage does my product have over the others?" If the answer is "None"—and it often is—then he should rephrase the question: "What *small* advantage does my product have over the others?" Big ideas are built on small advantages in advertising today because competition forces all products to improve constantly. Uniqueness and exclusiveness are extremely valuable assets when they concern salable features. "Only Apex Has . . ." is ideal in a basic theme if what only Apex has is worth having.

Arriving at a strong basic theme involves, in short, much fact-gathering, patient analysis, and shrewd thinking. In the case of the television copywriter, he must keep the peculiarities of his own medium in mind from the outset. Other factors being equal, he wants a basic theme he can dramatize and demonstrate. For in television the basic theme truly becomes alive.

*Standards.* A basic theme, as mentioned, should be identical in all media. But in the instance of the advertiser who invests much of his budget in television, the theme should be judged not by print standards but by television standards. This may appear obvious to the reader; but unfortunately it is not obvious to some of today's biggest television advertisers, who insist on approving new themes in advertisements before even considering how they will perform in commercials.

The basic theme conceived with television in mind will, almost without exception, adapt well to advertisements and radio commercials. Where the reverse procedure is followed, the advertiser may not be making the most of the television medium. The reason is that writing for print and writing for television require vastly different styles. Even a phrase as short as a basic theme line can be strong in an advertisement and weak on the picture tube.

## 2. The Copy Plan

The basic theme line and the copy plan are actually formulated at one and the same time. The copy plan is simply the copywriter's written philosophy outlining the strategy the advertising should follow. Intelligent selling requires sound tactics and clear objectives. His thoughts therefore are organized to allow the copywriter to proceed on more than impulse or cleverness.

While the basic theme line is the ultimate expression of the idea, the copy plan represents the copywriter's and the advertiser's mutual agreement, in view of all facts and conditions, on how the product or service shall be most effectively advertised.

*Scope.* A copy plan may be covered in one or two paragraphs, but more often it is written into several pages. It should provide positive strategy for every medium in which the advertiser is active or in which he may plan to become active.

The ideal copy plan should include complete analysis of facts in these areas:

*a)* The product or service to be advertised.
*b)* Competitive products or services.
*c)* Competitive advertising and marketing strategy.
*d)* Nature of the market, including characteristics of consumers.
*e)* Determination of the strongest selling appeals.
*f)* Consideration of media to be employed.
*g)* A plan of action.
*h)* The basic theme.

Once the copy plan is set, all advertising should adhere religiously.

While the copy plan and basic theme are relevant to all media, their importance to television cannot be overemphasized. Today too many copywriters experienced only in printed advertisements are influencing the copy strategy for television commercials. Invariably in such cases the first consideration becomes "Will this make a good ad?" rather than "Will this make a good ad *and* television commercial?" The trend, fortunately, is slowly changing. More and more, television, by proving its ability to move goods at a record pace, is making its presence felt at the outset of advertising planning.

### 3. The Campaign

Even before he creates his commercials, the copywriter should know the type of campaign in which they will be used. For the campaign is the pattern, the course of action, the battle plan, which dictates to a degree the general type of commercials needed.

The television campaign may take several forms. It may include full or partial sponsorship of one or more local or network programs. It may include both programs and spot announcements. Or it may consist entirely of spot announcements—in one local area, in several key areas, or nationwide. If the campaign calls for spot announcements, the commercials may be of various lengths or all of one length. These facts the copywriter needs from the beginning.

*Product Image.* Just as the basic theme line should be repeated over and over from one commercial to the next, so, too, should commercials for the same product or service in the same series bear a consistent "look." One commercial—and particularly a campaign of commercials—should be so designed as to go beyond immediate selling. After seeing a company's advertising for a period of time, the viewer begins to get an "image" of the product, a sense of the product's personality. Every product has one whether it attempts to establish it or not. By steering the campaign in a given direction the advertiser can, and should, control this image to serve his best interests.

For example, if the young housewife constitutes the major market for his product, he will do everything possible to help the young housewife actually identify herself in every commercial. More important, the advertiser takes great pains to keep his product from becoming identified with one sex, age group, or income group when he feels the appeal of his product should be much broader. The mood, the tone, the physical look of the commercials themselves have much to do with influencing the image the public will draw of the product. Over and above its objective to effect immediate sales, the commercials should reflect a pre-planned product image.

This may seem an almost impalpable requirement. But it must be remembered that television, with all of its other unique characteristics, is the most personal form of advertising. Its impressions are believed to penetrate far deeper than those of any other medium.

Small wonder that more and more television advertisers are conducting product image surveys to find out how consumers *really* feel about their product. Some, to their horror, are discovering they are dispensing a wholly different image of their product from the one they had intended. One, who believed his campaign was projecting a high-toned and dignified image, found that viewers actually regarded his product as "cheap" and "for lowbrows."

*Other Factors.* The commercials, of course, comprise only one part of the campaign. Time buying, programing, merchandising, and special promotions—these, too, help round out the effort. Every phase requires the creative planning of a specialist. And the people concerned must coordinate their plans toward the one big goal: a hard-hitting, hard-selling television campaign to win more and more customers.

## 4. The Commercials

Television commercials come in assorted sizes, types, and purposes. So many variables are there from one TV advertising campaign to another that commercials virtually defy classification.

Physically, commercials are presented on film, "live," or on video-tape.

Most commercials for network and national spot use are shot on 35mm film and projected locally on either 35mm or 16mm reduction, depending upon the facilities of the particular station. The 35mm film is more expensive to shoot and affords the advertiser better quality. However, commercials shot on 16mm are satisfactory.

Live commercials, as the term implies, are transmitted to home receivers the moment they are presented.

Commercials on videotape, the newest form, are shot by live television cameras and the same techniques as live therefore generally apply.

Film, live, and videotape are covered extensively in later chapters.

*Uses.* Broadly speaking, television commercials are used in either of two ways:

*a)* On programs.

*b)* As spot announcements.

One advertiser may devote his entire television budget to the sponsorship of one or more programs, either locally or on the network. Another may concentrate his full effort in spot announcements only; that is, between programs, or as one of many different advertisers within the same "participation" program. Another may sponsor a program and buy spot announcements as well.

*Commercial Lengths.* The length of a television commercial is governed by where it appears.

*a.* In programs. The accepted time standards for advertising copy, as set forth by the National Association of Broadcasters, are listed in Part I of the Appendix.

The three minutes allowed in a half-hour nighttime program may be broken up in any manner the advertiser desires, but four commercials are usually considered the maximum. Where products are advertised, three one-minute commercials are the most common format. Or, in the case of four commercials, a typical arrangement is as follows: forty-five seconds, sixty seconds, sixty seconds, fifteen seconds. Actual time allotment depends upon the nature of the copy story to be told and how many products are being featured in the various commercials. The type of show also may dictate to a certain extent the commercial format.

If the half-hour evening program is alternately sponsored—that is, two different advertisers paying for alternate weeks—the advertiser generally takes two sixty-second periods for commercials on the night he is the major sponsor and gives up the third commercial position to the alternate advertiser for a "cross-plug" commercial. The reverse is true, then, the following week.

Because of television's high costs, most programs are alternately sponsored. The "cross-plug" message, which affords each advertiser weekly exposure of his commercial, does not have to be a full sixty seconds. It may be forty-five seconds or even shorter, according to the agreement worked out at the beginning of the season between the advertisers themselves. Some prefer not to "cross-plug" at all, each taking the full three minutes on his own program, then waiting two weeks for the next opportunity.

Program commercials of a corporate, or institutional, nature often require more than sixty seconds. In such cases, the advertiser may concentrate his time by running fewer, but longer, commercials.

*b.* In spot positions. Spot announcements, which appear on local stations, can be purchased in any of four lengths: sixty seconds, thirty seconds, twenty seconds or ten seconds.

The one-minute variety is available during the daytime, early evening, and late evening, assuming that the station carries network programs during the prime evening time. Such programs, including a five-second network preview announcement at the end, are timed at twenty-nine and a half or fifty-nine and a half minutes. In the thirty-second interval between programs, the local station sells a twenty-second "chainbreak" and a ten-second "I. D.," or "station identification announcement," in which the station recites its call letters after the brief commercial.

## Creating the Commercial

After the basic theme and copy plan are determined—after the "product image" the advertiser wishes to impart is clearly in mind—the all-important commercial is about to take form. The copywriter, with all pertinent facts in mind, sets out to create a masterpiece that will be judged not by the beauty of the words and the drama of the pictures but by the results the commercial achieves.

Professional television copywriters follow five precepts in building commercials that sell:

### Be-Attitudes for the Copywriter

*Be personal.* Remember you are talking to the consumer about *his* problems. He is much more interested in himself than in anything else.

*Be interesting.* This does *not* mean you must entertain. Just don't be dull. Grab the consumer's full attention in the first four seconds.

*Be informative.* Once you have answered the consumer's need, describe the product. Not too many points about it. Pound away at the most important.

*Be believable.* Television viewers have become most alert to phony demonstrations, unreasonable exaggerations, and unnecessary superlatives.

Fig. 12—LONG SHOT (LS)

Fig. 13—MEDIUM SHOT (MS)

Fig. 13A—MEDIUM CLOSEUP (MCU)

Fig. 14—EXTREME CLOSEUP (ECU)

*Be yourself.* Try to give your commercial a personality, a tone, a look of good taste that will create a subtle halo effect not only for the product but for the company behind it.

## The Script

Before he puts a word on paper the copywriter should formulate a broad idea of the commercial in his mind. He must "see" it and "hear" it before he writes it—not so much specific words as a mental progression of picture images.

Writing the television commercial script consists of a double job: (1) creating the pictures, or "video"; (2) creating the words and sounds, or the "audio." The two should be created simultaneously because the viewer sees and hears the commercial simultaneously.

Following is a list of general but vital principles to guide the copywriter in creating an effective commercial script:

1. Be sure the video and corresponding audio relate. Don't be demonstrating one sales feature while talking about another.

2. While the audio should be relevant to the video, don't waste words by describing what is obvious in the picture. Rather, see that the words interpret the picture and thereby advance the thought.

3. Rely on the video to carry more than half the weight. Being a visual medium, television is more effective at showing than telling.

4. Use short, everyday words in the audio. And remember there are still many good everyday words that are not used every day in commercials.

5. Avoid static scenes. Provide for camera movement and changes of scenes.

6. Don't cram the commercial with too many scenes lest the viewer become confused. No scene should time less than four seconds. A one-minute commercial should contain no more than a dozen scenes.

7. Superimpose in lettering the basic theme line at least twice over scenes in the commercial, including the final scene, if practical.

8. Be sure transitions are smooth from scene to scene. Conceiving the commercial as a flowing progression of scenes makes it easier for the viewer to follow. Proper use of opticals (defined and discussed in a later chapter), too, can add to the smoothness.

9. Remember that television is a "medium of closeups." Avoid

long-shots. Even the largest television screens are too small for extraneous detail in the scenes of the commercial.

10. Be sure that backgrounds in the various scenes are kept simple and uncluttered. They should point up, rather than detract from, the subject matter.

11. Don't expect to write the final script at first try. Professional copywriters often rewrite their own scripts many times before they are satisfied. The important thing is to put the idea on paper before it escapes.

12. When timing the commercial, don't just read it. Act it out. The action usually requires more time than the words indicate. A good rule is purposely to time the commercial short, as it invariably runs a few seconds longer in actual production.

13. After the first draft is written—or as it is being written—make drawings of the video portion. Stick figures will do, since the purpose of this step is to help the copywriter better visualize his own script before proceeding to the first revision.

14. As soon as possible, talk the script over with the art director, then the producer. Get their ideas. Then, if necessary, rewrite it once more.

## The Copywriting Secret

In television as in any profession experience is the best teacher. Experience comes from much practice.

The secret of the top copywriters in television today lies in the art of self-criticism, the ability to improve the script through a series of rewrites to the point of satisfaction.

The true mark of great copy is not always found in the commercial that sells the most goods. Some products are naturally more interesting than others. They are more wanted, more in demand. The true test comes in creating the commercial that will sell the types of products that must fight amidst strong competition on the television channels and in the market place.

Perhaps the greatest strain put upon any copywriter is the constant striving to be fresh and original in his approach to the commercial. Weaker souls proclaim, "Everything has been done before," and this is difficult to refute. However, the extent to which old ideas can be "twisted" to appear new and to which entirely new ideas can be created depends solely upon the creative capacity and the resourcefulness of the man or woman assigned to the job. Good ideas are still abundantly available to the television copywriter who will sweat a little harder.

## Keep It Simple

Robert L. Foreman, a leading authority on television advertising, reported in *Sponsor* in 1951 an experience which still contains a most timely message for copywriters.

The reason so much TV is ineffective these days is simply that it contains too many thoughts, too many gimmicks. The reason for this is usually caused by the fact that the folks who are creating TV copy approach their jobs in the traditional way; that is, by "lifting" a print campaign and sliding it over into television as undisturbed as possible.

Let's say you've got a modest 100-line advertisement replete with headline, subhead, main picture and caption, two thumbnail sketches, body copy, coupon, slug with theme line and a box that says, "Compare these seven features." Not too much even for 100 lines. But by TV standards this same amount of ideas and wordage would take a full seven minutes to expound—and then you'd have created nothing but chaos.

Recently on a package goods account I faithfully translated a newspaper ad packed full of copy and copy points into a one-minute television storyboard. Then I presented the storyboard, reading the audio as I went along, to the account man and the print writer. This demonstrated clearly that we'd have to sacrifice at least four of the side ventures in the ad and concentrate solely on the theme line and elucidation of it. The subordinate issues were unanimously left on the cutting room floor in order that we could devote all our time and the full potential of TV's impact to the basic reason-why.

The result, I feel certain, will be as satisfactory as any this client has achieved because the copy is strictly geared to the medium and will roll right along over the audience's one-track mind and never deviate.

## Script Forms

The script for the television commercial, be it for live or film production, may be written in either of two basic forms. While there is a difference of opinion in the trade as to which is more practical, each contains the same words and each serves the purpose well. They are these:

*a) Two-column script,* with video occupying the left-hand vertical column, usually typed in capital letters, and audio in the right-hand column. The writer should match every video paragraph to the audio paragraph that fits it. The two-column script has the advantage of giving a continuous flow of either video or audio for those who may wish to examine each separately. Its disadvantage lies in the difficulty of trying to receive a total impression of the commercial by studying both columns simultaneously.

*b) Shooting script,* as the term implies, is the form film production companies prefer to work with as it forces every scene and every piece of audio to be separated as a unit. In the shooting script the full width of the page is used for both video and audio. Some copywriters, too, prefer to follow this style from the moment they begin to write. The disadvantage, if any, is the "stop-and-go" reading habit one must develop as he reads video and audio, scene by scene. This is not a handicap, however, for those experienced in the medium.

Either of the two script forms is satisfactory. Whichever he chooses, the copywriter should pay particular attention to the video directions, seeing to it that he spells out in specific detail the description of each scene in order to avoid any misunderstanding as to the visual content.

## Storyboards

A storyboard is simply a script with pictures. A series of rough sketches is made for each paragraph of video. Under or beside each drawing the copywriter places the words describing the video. The audio words, of course, appear directly opposite. The storyboard may take any of the following forms:

1. *Chart,* where all frames, or pictures, are displayed in sequence and totally visible at one glance. The size of the individual frames varies, depending upon the size of the group to whom the storyboard will be presented. The frame measurement is generally 4½" x 6" or larger. While the "chart" storyboard frame for a one-minute commercial, is sometimes bulky to transport, it has the advantage of giving a clear, over-all picture of the commercial as a whole while also depicting the individual steps.

2. *Thumbnail,* where the frames measure less than two inches in width, and are arranged in a vertical column, four or five drawings to an 8½" x 11" page, the corresponding audio appearing to the right of the respective drawings. This size, of course, is convenient for carry-

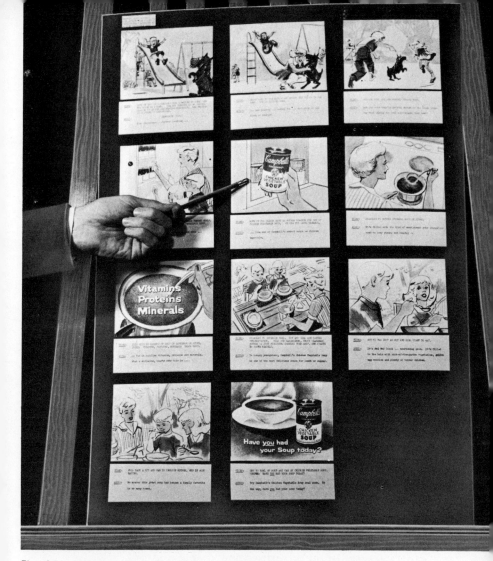

Fig. 15—EXAMPLE OF CHART-TYPE STORYBOARD for one-minute film commercial. Note, too that storyboard can specify literally the style of lettering to be used in "supers."

ing and for study. Also, the artist can draw these smaller frames more quickly, but is not always able, within this confined area, to express in such detail the visual concept of the commercial. While this type of storyboard is certainly better than no storyboard at all, it is inferior to the larger size.

3. *Accordion-Fold,* where the frames resemble those on the chart-

type storyboard but are pasted, one to a page with the corresponding audio copy, then bound into overlapping pages. The commercial elements are then studied singly. After frame-by-frame study, however, the entire "book" can be opened so that all frames are then displayed in one horizontal line. Obviously, if the storyboard requires many frames, opening it up in this manner may present a problem in that it may stretch half the length of a room.

4. *Notebook,* where, like the accordion type, the drawings are arranged one to a page and bound into a "book." However, the frames here cannot conveniently be revealed side by side. Revealing one frame at a time allows for better concentration by those not familiar with the concept, but, again, it is valuable also to be able to see the frames simultaneously in order to get a general "feeling" of the commercial as a whole.

Storyboards are not an absolutely essential step, but they add efficiency to the job—especially in the case of the film commercial—in these two ways: (1) They make possible a meeting of the minds among the copywriter, the advertiser, and the producer on precisely what each scene in the commercial is intended to depict. (2) They become a working tool for the production unit during the shooting sessions.

### How to Present the Idea

A script, or even a storyboard, is a far cry from the final production, especially when the commercial is going on film. The copywriter can visualize it because he conceived it. But the advertiser, who is to pay thousands of dollars for its production and many, many thousands more to buy air time to expose it, may well have a difficult time understanding the full meaning of the commercial in its crude state. This is especially true of the advertiser new to television.

It is important, therefore, for the copywriter to know how to present the storyboard in a way that will stimulate the advertiser's imagination to the point of grasping a mental picture of the final commercial.

If by "the advertiser" is meant one person or a small group, the copywriter holds the storyboard on a table or easel and begins by describing the pictures from beginning to end. He makes it clear that the storyboard itself consists only of drawings but that the finished commercial will be in motion.

After fully describing the visual sequence, the copywriter returns to the beginning of the commercial and reads the complete audio portion, pointing to the corresponding pictures as he goes. In this manner the advertiser can first develop a "feel" for the pictures, then is able to relate to them what the announcer will say or what the singers will sing. Were the copywriter not to follow this system and instead describe both video and audio of each scene as he proceeded, the presentation would then become choppy and hard to follow.

If the meeting is a large one, which often is the case with large companies, the copywriter can use any of a number of visual aids to help him in his presentation. In this manner he projects the image of each storyboard drawing on a large screen. Advertising agencies often follow this method in presenting commercials in large meetings. The various frames from the storyboard can be reproduced on slides, on 16mm slide film or 35mm slide film.

The sound track is then either read live by the person presenting the idea or recorded in advance in rough or finished form and played as the pictures are shown, one by one.

The more elaborate the presentation, the easier for the advertiser to understand the idea. And the more expensive to prepare. Reproducing drawings for projection may cost from one to two dollars per frame for black-and-white and more for color. The sound track may run into even more money—from a few dollars for the "homemade" variety to several hundred, depending upon its complexity.

In rare cases, agencies actually put motion into their presentation. If the commercial so lends itself, a rough version of it may be shot on 16mm motion picture film or on kinescope with live cameras and presented in this more nearly complete form. This, too, may involve an outlay of several hundred dollars. But to some television advertisers this extra step is well worth the insurance it offers them. This rough version can also be used for testing purposes before the final film commercial is produced.

Some agencies own or rent facilities to present commercials or parts of commercials to their clients in live form. With a live television camera or two on the premises, the presentation can be carried from the agency studio by coaxial cable to a monitor in another room in the agency or to another building, where the client can pass on its content. However, most commercials do not lend themselves to this kind of "rough" presentation.

*Creativity*

It is only proper to conclude this chapter where it began—with the television copywriter. It is his or her own capacity for original thinking that determines, in the long run, how effective television will continue to be as a medium of advertising.

Because of its intimate nature and its powerful impact on the buying emotions of the public, television demands and consumes advertising ideas at a rate faster than any medium in history. Consequently, those who hide behind the ideas of others, who play it safe by following literally the generalities revealed by research, who apply what worked last week to this week's problems, are not keeping pace.

The true creative mind, on the other hand, thrives and grows with practice and pressure and competition. It knows no limits if properly encouraged and granted the right to explore and experiment and develop. In fact, on the air today is many a commercial that has worked out successfully because the advertiser had faith in a new—perhaps even untested—idea.

Television is no longer new—no longer young—not even adolescent. Television is mature and so are the people who watch it. To reach and convince these people requires a shrewd mixture of sound advertising planning and a touch of the daring.

Alex F. Osborn, whose many books on creative thinking have inspired scores of today's leading copywriters, warned: "Too many of us look upon imagination as something that will run itself—like a stomach or other organ which works automatically under the effortless guidance of the sympathetic nervous system. Accordingly, we let our imagination push us around. Unless we do something about pushing it around, it will not only shortchange us, but will grow less and less usable."

It has also been said, "To those who create, creativity is not only necessary; it is also challenging, inspiring, mystifying, gratifying; it is boundless in its scope, in its areas to investigate and conquer."

The biggest problem today, however, is not *finding* or *developing* creative people. It is *protecting* them. As an industry, advertising has grown far beyond the point where sound creative work is considered its only function. There is research. There is merchandising. There is marketing. There are many other allied functions, as well, each one a specialized facet in the complex process of moving goods to the consumer. The creative service is still present, but its basic importance is not always recognized.

There is a need these days for more agency managements and advertisers to listen seriously to the copywriter who says, "This may sound like a crazy idea, but—." There should be a strict penalty for those who keep saying, "It will never work," because now and then it *will* work.

What about "brainstorming," where many people collectively try to create ideas on a given problem? Properly conducted, this form of group thinking can be extremely helpful. But those who lean on it as a substitute for individual thinking are destroying the heart of the advertising process. "A group can spark an idea," said Dr. Gregory Zilboorg, "but only an individual can have one."

What makes a person creative? According to most experts, it is the ability to relate two or more things that were not previously related. It is the art of solving a problem in a way it has never been solved before.

"The way you make a creative man creative," declared W. John Upjohn, "is to let him be creative."

A copywriter named Charles H. Brower, who also is president of one of the world's largest advertising agencies, sums up his feelings with these words:

"These people, the kind that produce basic selling ideas, are precious today. Unless we do something to protect and help them, they will be as extinct as the Passenger Pigeon in another ten or twenty years. I think we ought to do as much for them as the government does for the Whooping Crane—protect them and their nests against the encroachment of rampant industrialization."

## chapter seven

# Creating and Producing the Film Commercial

MOST national advertisers produce most or all of their commercials on film. This does not mean that live commercials are not sometimes more effective—nor that videotape will not affect this proportion—but up to now, film has been the convenient and economic decision in most cases.

It is the intent of this chapter to state the case for film. Live and videotape commercials will be treated in subsequent pages.

### Advantages of Film

These are the major advantages of film:

1. Film allows a faultless performance, thereby enabling the advertiser to see and approve the finished commercial before it appears on the air.

2. Film offers more perfect lighting of scenes, more sharpness on tricky camera angles.

3. Film saves the advertiser money when he amortizes the production costs over repeated uses of the same commercials. Re-use payments for talent are his only significant additional costs.

4. Film allows greater scope within the commercial by making it practical to shoot in many locations, including exterior scenes.

5. Film removes the risk from product demonstrations. If a door fails to open, if a glass of beer fails to develop the proper head, or if an announcer "flubs" a line, the scene may be re-shot.

6. Film makes possible such techniques as animation and stop-motion.

7. Film provides the widest selection of "opticals," or transitional devices, that join one scene to another.

8. Film production can be scheduled to fit the availability of the talent.

## The Copywriter's Task

To create an effective film commercial for TV, today's copywriter must be armed with a variety of facts and experience. Being able to write clear, concise copy and to think visually is only part of the requirement. He must be familiar with film production, including the various techniques at his disposal, if he is to do a professional creative job. He must be aware of the countless film approaches already in use by other advertisers. He must possess a sense of showmanship. Above all, he must know *advertising,* including the basic principles confirmed by up-to-date research.

Proper background and careful preparation are essential because the commercials he creates must compete with hundreds of others for the attention of every steady viewer every day and night. His commercials must impress at the moment they are seen. The impression must linger on.

The mounting competition among products and among commercials is resulting, in fact, in better-conceived, harder-selling film commercials each year. Testing procedures definitely confirm this. And, as creativity has increased, so, too, have the mechanics of film making, giving the copywriter every imaginable opportunity to express himself to the ultimate.

## Basic Techniques

One basic fact makes all the techniques of motion picture film easy to understand:

There is no such thing as a "motion picture."

Live action, for instance, is photographed as a fast series of still pictures. When the film is projected, the stills are shown separately, but at a speed faster than the eye can discern, giving the *look* of motion.

The same principle applies to animation and stop-motion except that here the camera must stop for the filming of each individual frame.

Fig. 16

1. *Live-Action*. Probably 90 per cent of all commercials on television contain at least some live-action; that is, a reproduction of objects and people as they actually are in real life.

It is a rare commercial that does not contain a live shot of the product, for this is literally what the advertiser is asking the consumer to purchase.

It is a rare commercial that does not depict the product in use, for this is the advertiser's opportunity to demonstrate its advantages over competition.

It is a rare commercial that does not show at least one person or part of a person enjoying or reacting to the product, although such scenes require able direction lest they appear trite and "phony."

Since television is "a medium of closeups," live-action photography for film commercials is shot mostly at medium or close range. This allows the viewer to concentrate attention on one element at a time with a minimum of distraction.

Live-action film for television commercials can be shot, of course, either in a studio or "on location" in any locale the script designates. The copywriter may, for example, specify studio footage showing the product in use, plus exterior, or outdoor, footage showing additional uses or tests. Or a traffic scene may be needed to establish a sales point near the beginning of the commercial, with indoor shots continuing from there. Whatever the need, film can go anywhere. It is up to the copywriter, however, to plan his commercial to a set budget and avoid extravagant scenes which do not tangibly enhance the sales message.

In addition to voices on the sound track, all talent whose faces appear in the live-action film commercial except those classed as "extras" are paid Screen Actors' Guild session fees and repaid as the commercial is repeated. As explained later, the use of many actors can be an extremely expensive proposition. Consequently, a special effort should be made to use only the talent needed and no more.

2. *Animation*. As opposed to real-life situations, animation consists of artists' drawings set to motion after the slow and painstaking process of single-frame photography.

The most commonly used animation for television film commercials is the "cartoon," a technique older than "Felix the Cat."

While it may not always penetrate the viewer's mind as deeply as live-action photography, the animated cartoon has many points in its favor as a technique in advertising:

*a)* Its appeal is universal. Animation is a favorite of young, old, educated, and uneducated.

*b)* It stimulates favorable discussion of the commercial among viewers the "morning after."

*c)* It wears well. A commercial featuring animated cartoons can usually withstand repetition even better than a straight live-action commercial.

*d)* It creates a warm, friendly atmosphere for the product and for the advertiser.

*e)* It permits exaggeration of the product's features. A boy can suddenly grow from four to fourteen feet tall after eating a certain cereal with small likelihood of Federal Trade Commission interference.

*f)* It works well with music, notably singing jingles.

*g)* It offers the greatest latitude of originality of approach.

Many cartoon commercials contain live-action inserts to add credibility and viewer-identification. But this is not essential.

The animated cartoon should never substitute for live-action when a product lends itself to dramatic, convincing demonstration. But the two techniques blend well together, and the exact proportion of the blending differs in each case, depending primarily upon the copy story of the particular product.

*Cautions.* As a film technique for advertising, the animated cartoon has managed to survive and grow in usage despite the reservations and doubts of certain so-called experts. Their criticism can be generally considered as cautions worth noting.

*"Animation sacrifices credibility."* Possibly so in some cases, but to what extent is a question. It is inconceivable that a shrewd touch of animation would make an audience *disbelieve* the claims of the advertiser.

*"Animation happens too fast for the viewer to follow."* Only when the copywriter goes overboard with too complicated a "plot." It is also true that, when seen for the first time, an animated commercial may not implant so many specific sales points in the memory of the viewer as a live-action commercial. But animation improves with age, often leaving a fresher impression than live-action on each repeated showing up to the point where repetition is no longer advisable.

*"The viewer can see 'the other fellow' in a cartoon situation, but he finds it difficult to picture himself."* Only partly true. While he may not always identify himself as the character in the commercial, the viewer nevertheless involves himself in the situation if the situation itself is built on a believable basis. As for the drawing of the cartoon characters, there is a difference of opinion as to how grotesque the styling can become without losing a tie with the viewer. What should be remembered, however, is that animation as a technique is more symbolic than literal to begin with. Any advertiser prone to worry about viewer-identification can always avoid it and use live-action.

*"Animation is no cure-all."* Correct. In fact, the use of more than a few seconds of animation is probably wrong for more than half the average product film commercials. In more cases than not, the product advantages are sufficiently strong to demand straight live-action presentation. Animation is more in order and more worthy of consideration for the types of products whose superiority over competition is practically nil, newer-type products desiring to call attention to their advertising as well as their names, and very well-known products whose virtues are already famous.

*Degrees of Animation.* Animated cartoons come in various degrees of "finish." *Full animation,* such as most animated cartoons shown in movie theaters, is the most expensive form because there is more movement per second; and the more movement, the more man-hours required to draw and photograph. A one-minute commercial may call for more than a thousand separate drawings!

In the earlier days, full animation, for those who could afford it, was considered the ultimate. But most copywriters and art directors settle for, and prefer, a more limited form today because full animation tends to give the viewer more motion than he is able to absorb in sixty seconds.

*Limited animation* is a broad term that encompasses an elaborate treatment one step below full animation down to a very crude style with little movement. Between these two extremes lies the degree of animation that is perfectly adequate for most commercials. It is still expensive. Its execution still requires high artistic talent. But its simplicity makes all movements more relevant to the copy story.

*Semi-animation* is barely animation at all. A single simple movement, such as an arm waving back and forth, is added to still artwork.

Titles can pop on and off. It is a noticeable improvement over the slides used by many smaller advertisers in that it lends some motion to the commercial.

*Other Uses for Animation.* Not all animation, of course, is cartoon. The technique is especially useful in the formation and transformation of lettering within the commercial, in "building" the package, and in creating countless interesting effects that point attention to the product. As an example, the copywriter can call for the basic theme line, lettered full-screen, to "animate," or change, into the product. One never tires of watching "The Wines of California" grapes squeeze themselves into wine pouring into a glass.

Legends, or "supers," on the screen are important for emphasizing certain copy points. Animation can make lettering pulsate, sparkle, even become entirely new lettering in one smooth, continuous motion.

Animation is useful, too, for the demonstration that may be too complex for live-action. Bufferin has animated a "mechanical man" to demonstrate the speed of the product going to work in the blood stream. Du Pont used the technique as a brief insert in a live-action commercial to simplify the explanation of how the sun converts salt water into pure drinking water.

## Supplementary Techniques

Besides live-action and animation, film offers the copywriter other techniques which he employs less frequently but often with great success. Among them are:

3. *Rotoscope.* This is an involved process combining live-action photography and animation within the same picture. Example: The Campbell Kids (animated) dance on a buffet table, then "push" an actual dish along and stop in front of an actual pitcher of soup. The real and the fantasy are one in the same picture.

But, as in the case of full animation, the technique can be confusing to the viewer if too many elements are moving at the same time. Seldom is an entire minute devoted to this elaborate technique alone.

4. *Stop-Motion.* Veteran viewers still talk about Lucky Strike's famous "marching cigarettes" commercials of the early 1950's. This striking effect was achieved by means of stop-motion, the process whereby three-dimensional live objects are filmed one frame at a time in much the same manner as are the individual drawings in animation.

Figs. 17 and 18—STOP-MOTION requires intricate handling of subject matter between each frame of shooting. Virtually invisible wires connect each package with jig (above), which, in turn, helps keep the packages in registration while they are being manipulated. Effect here is a series of packages "dancing" to music (below). (Sarra, Inc.)

By this technique a product can move under its own "power." A package of cigarettes can rise, float in the air, turn itself around, march, or exercise any movement called for. A virtual parade of products can walk by the camera. Doll puppets can be made to perform in a very life-like fashion.

5. *Still Photographs and Artwork.* This clean, simple technique is a wise choice for the advertiser with a very limited budget. The pictures themselves do not move, but the camera does. It may, for instance, travel in to a closeup, "pan" a wide piece of artwork or pull back to a wider angle. Add to this the proper opticals and the commercial will have a surprising amount of pace and interest.

## Opticals

The effective television commercial almost always consists of more than a single scene. Even if the set remains the same, the commercial may be shot from various angles and distances. It is important therefore not only to plan scenes in a logical order, but to lead the viewer out of one scene and into the next as smoothly as possible.

Opticals are the transitional devices which blend the scenes together. In live television opticals are achieved electronically as the commercial is in progress. In film commercials, opticals are added during editing; that is, after the film footage has been shot.

When opticals are correctly used, the viewer does not notice they are there. Because he is so accustomed to watching television and the movies, however, he would miss them if they were absent or incorrectly selected.

There are actually scores of opticals available, but only a few get the most usage in commercials. These the copywriter should know thoroughly, for each has a definite purpose:

CUT—The direct "cut" takes no editing beyond the splicing of two scenes together. One scene is cut off and the next scene begun faster than the eye can see. The "cut" denotes simultaneous action in the two scenes it joins. *Example:* The announcer is shown holding the product. As he speaks, the film suddenly "cuts" to the next scene: a closeup of the product in his hand. No time has elapsed between scenes.

DISSOLVE—Here one scene quickly fades out while, at the same time, the next scene fades in. This gives the effect of one scene

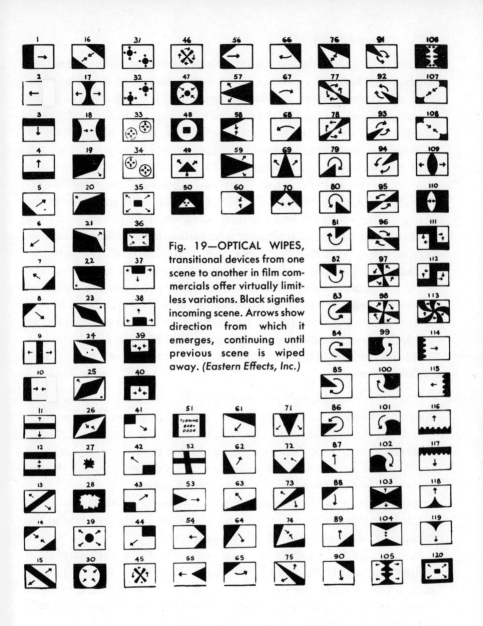

Fig. 19—OPTICAL WIPES, transitional devices from one scene to another in film commercials offer virtually limitless variations. Black signifies incoming scene. Arrows show direction from which it emerges, continuing until previous scene is wiped away. (Eastern Effects, Inc.)

quickly blending into or overlapping the next. The "dissolve" generally denotes a passage of time or a change of mood or copy point between scenes. *Example:* The camera is on closeup, as in the second scene above, and the film then "dissolves" to the next scene: a housewife using the product in her home. (If the next scene had been the announcer holding the product again, the optical would, of course, have been another "cut.")

WIPE—As in the cases of "cut" and "dissolve," the term "wipe" is almost self-explanatory. The effect is literally the wiping or pushing of one scene off and the next scene on. This is achieved by a vertical line moving from one side to the other, a horizontal line from top to bottom or vice versa, or by countless geometric patterns. The "flip wipe" physically turns the picture over to a new scene. The "wipe" generally denotes the transition from one scene to a parallel scene. These may be demonstration sequences. Example: A housewife is using the product in her home. The scene now "wipes" to another housewife using the product. This may, in fact, wipe to a third housewife. The "flip wipe" is often used to join "before" and "after" scenes.

The "before-and-after" effect can also be attained by means of the "match dissolve." In this transition, one subject is held static from one scene to the next, but the remainder of the scene is changed. *Example:* A man is relaxing in his easy chair in the comfort of his living room as the announcer is extolling an air-freshener product. As the "fresh as out-of-doors" point is made, the scene "dissolves" to a woodsy exterior, with the man still seated in his easy chair in the same position within the frame. In other words, he remained constant as the remainder of the scene dissolved to a new scene.

Also under the heading of "opticals" comes the very important "super" or "superimposure." This gives the effect of lettering being placed over a scene. Nearly every commercial contains one or more supers. Vital copy points, especially the basic theme line, are "supered" over scenes of the commercial for added emphasis.

### Special Effects

"In film," asserted Bernard Haber, a top agency film producer, "we can create absolutely any picture or any image or any effect. All we have to do is put our minds to it.

"We can drive a new car past the Arc de Triomphe without leaving New York or Hollywood. We can show Jack Benny talking to Jack Benny. We can shoot a 'ship on the high seas' inside a studio. Regardless of what the copywriter dreams up, there's a way of doing it on film."

Special effects, the generic term for achieving unusual scenes by unusual production methods, remove practically all restraints and limitations, giving the copywriter more scope than he will ever need.

Driving a new car past the Arc de Triomphe is a combination of live-action filming of the car against a rear-screen projection slide or motion picture of the background. The total effect is that of shooting on location.

Jack Benny talking to Jack Benny is simply a combination of two negatives of the comedian printed into one picture.

The ship that never left the studio is no bigger than a toy, "fighting" the waves in a tank hardly larger than a bathtub.

Hollywood feature movies have made extensive use of miniature shooting for many big, elaborate scenes at a huge saving of money. Entire backgrounds can be filmed in three-dimensional miniature and combined optically with either miniature or life-size foreground objects in such a way that the two bear a perfect size relationship, giving the impression that all elements were in one scene at the time of shooting.

Few film commercials have yet taken full advantage of miniature effects, probably because few require such elaborate scenes. As competition grows for the viewer's eye and ear, however, the trend may well be in this direction, for by combining miniature backgrounds with life-size subjects, the producer can simulate beyond detection scenes of grandiose proportions.

By use of the prism camera lens, film can achieve multiple images, blending one into the next. By means of mattes, film can achieve clean-cut multiple images.

"Traveling mattes" in the optical printer can combine two pieces of action film to create the illusion of an object, such as a refrigerator, floating in a "foreign" background, such as Times Square.

Action can be reversed by special effects if the copywriter, for instance, wishes to dramatize an erroneous solution to a problem, return the subject to the starting point, and begin again.

One picture can be inset into another within the same frame. Or action of a moving picture can be "frozen," or held, by repeated printings of the same frame. Action can be increased by "skip-frame" printing.

Whatever the need, film can do it. "Magic," one expert calls it, "but a very practical magic."

## Which Technique to Choose

Bearing in mind that the first step to an effective commercial is an effective selling idea, the copywriter is then faced with a problem of almost equal importance: how to express the idea in a way that will capture attention and effect positive motivation on the part of the viewer. No idea, however basic and exciting, can ever be effective if it is not conveyed to the customer's mind by means of the proper vehicle.

This is why film techniques other than live-action available to the copywriter should not be disparaged by referring to them as "tricks." Or, if they are tricks, then the word should be spoken with respect. The printed advertisement should have more of them!

Where does the copywriter start, once he knows all the facts about the product, what competition is doing, and what his basic theme line shall be?

There is a saying among copywriters that the stronger the copy story, the fewer the tricks required to put it over in a film commercial. Any product which has a distinct, demonstrable advantage over all competition is likely to demand the straightest live-action approach to tell its story. In this instance, stepping far beyond live-action—that is, beyond actual shots of the product in use and the product being demonstrated—would be unnecessary, impractical, even suspect. In other words, any amount of animation or stop-motion, except perhaps to bring on the lettering or basic theme line or to simplify the demonstration would be out of place.

At the opposite extreme is the type of product—often a low-price package item—that is extremely well known but reasonably similar in make-up to its competition except for the important difference of taste. A candy bar is one example.

A straight, serious live-action approach from the beginning to the end of the commercial is probably insufficient. Taste is assuredly one of the strongest reasons for a consumer to select one brand over another. But it is unfortunately one of the most difficult points for television or any other medium of advertising to prove or demonstrate.

It is entirely logical, then, for the copywriter to explore every available technique in order to build a commercial that (1) registers strongly the name of the product; (2) repeats the basic theme line as many times as possible; (3) calls attention to the advertising itself with the hope that people will keep "playing it back" in their minds long after exposure to the commercial.

With these factors in mind, the copywriter may consider animation, stop-motion or a novel, offbeat live-action approach along with a jingle—techniques which enforce, underline, and dramatize exciting copy claims which by themselves are not "world-shakers."

Between these extremes—straight live-action treatment for the product with exclusive features of direct interest to the viewer and the more novel treatment for the product with far less to say—comes the broad area where picking the right film technique is not so easy.

Within this middle ground is found the average product on television today. Here the relative strength or weakness of the copy story bears no set relationship to the technique the copywriter may choose. Some cigarettes follow a serious live-action approach. Others use some animation. One dessert may concentrate on real-life table settings with a generous amount of appetite appeal. Another may go with a series of amusing cartoon commercials. Beer commercials, too, range from one end of the spectrum to the other. With products like these, every campaign is treated for all it is worth, each one fortified with the strongest words and techniques possible to tell its story.

This constant searching for the original, the different, way to advertise on television—and there will always be a new way—forms the big challenge for today's TV copywriter.

Where does the copywriter start? He looks at what competition is doing. He looks at what research has taught him, but this will not give him the big idea. He looks at the techniques available to him, but he cannot possibly use them all. He looks at the production budget and wishes it were higher although it is probably high enough. He looks out the window, up at the ceiling, down at his typewriter. He then takes a pencil and starts drawing a few stick figures on paper. He tears off a few sheets and throws them in the wastebasket, but they are not wasted. The idea will finally come, although seldom without strenuous mental exercise.

### Role of the TV Art Director

The agency copywriter may claim, but does not always deserve, full credit for some of the fine commercials on television today. Working with him is a creative specialist whose talents are too often taken for granted. That person is the television art director, who converts the script into a storyboard with a series of drawings in order that the client and the film production studio can better visualize the total concept.

The art director also styles artwork, animation, and lettering to be used in the commercial. Occasionally he suggests the design for live sets. But, above all, his most valuable talent is his ability to contribute basic visual ideas to the television campaign.

The copywriter may complete a sample script before conferring with the art director. In this case, the latter, rather than automatically sketching what he sees, will often suggest changes and improvements. A friendly discussion of this nature cannot fail to result in a better final product.

It is not unusual, in fact, for the art director to come up with the main visual idea. This is especially true of animation, a field in which agency art directors have become most proficient craftsmen. While the outside film company will actually draw the final frames, the art director often literally styles the characters to be used.

Because he is so thoroughly qualified to judge the quality of the job in progress, the art director also works closely with the producer in the actual production of animated commercials.

### Production Costs

Production costs vary widely, depending upon which techniques the copywriter employs, and the degree of quality and workmanship the commercial demands. For national advertisers and those local advertisers situated in areas of union jurisdiction, the film cost ranges, including sound track, session fees for talent, and a 10-per cent contingency fund, but not including the 15 per cent agency commission nor city sales tax, if any, are as follows:

*One-minute live-action film commercial,* from $2,000 for the simplest one-set commercial to $20,000 for an extremely elaborate production which may involve many studio sets plus perhaps exterior shooting on location and a large cast. The average for all one-minute live-action commercials on the air is approximately $4,500.

*Twenty-second live-action film commercial,* from $2,000 up if the footage is not "lifted" from the minute version. Certain minimum costs must be met, no matter what length the commercial may be. However, if the twenty-second commercial is built from footage already shot, then the major outlay is for editing and sound track, in which case the commercial may be made for from $300 to $750.

*Ten-second station-identification commercial* (I. D.), from $800 to $1,800 if produced separately or as low as $150 if, as in the case of most "twenties," the footage is "lifted" from other lengths. If station call letters are to be added to the "I. D.," approximately $60 must be added for each different set of call letters. If many stations are to be used, the advertiser usually omits all call letters and uses the full screen for seven of the ten seconds instead of the shared screen for the full ten seconds. Some stations now allow advertisers full-screen area with no call letters for ten seconds, which is obviously the ideal plan as far as the advertiser is concerned.

The advertiser invariably saves per unit when he produces several live-action film commercials simultaneously because much footage is interchangeable. The copywriter's knowledge of production costs thus helps him pre-plan carefully to save the advertiser money whenever possible.

*One-minute animated commercial,* from $2,500 for the most limited type to $14,000 for full animation, including sound track. National average: about $8,000. Animation is sold by the foot—from $55 to $140 per foot, not including sound track. The 35mm film totals ninety feet per minute.

It should be noted that many animated one-minute commercials do not contain a full minute of animation. Often advertisers using this technique insert a portion of live-action footage between the animated opening and closing. This does not necessarily reduce the cost, however, since the live-action shooting requires a minimum outlay of approximately $2,000 and usually more.

*Twenty-second animated commercial,* from $1,800 to $4,000 if the footage is not "lifted" from the minute.

*Ten-second I. D.,* $900 to $2,500.

*Rotoscope and stop-motion* are the most expensive of all techniques. A full minute of either may cost as high as $19,000, seldom less than $8,000, including sound track. Again, a sequence of live-action may be inserted, and this time have a lowering effect on the over-all cost. The final cost of rotoscope and stop-motion, as well as animation, depends upon the number of units in motion simultaneously and the elaborateness of the sound track.

*Semi-animation* and *still photographs and artwork* are the lowest in cost because most movement is the camera itself rather than the subject. A one-minute commercial by these techniques ranges from $700 to $2,200.

## Costs of Color

Although there are still relatively few color receiving sets in the United States, the advertiser may have occasion to sponsor a program in color or to buy spot time adjacent to a color program. In either case he may well desire to produce his commercial in color.

His film production cost is up to one-third higher.

## Competitive Bids

The advertising agency, after securing the advertiser's approval of the commercial, generally hands the storyboard to a number of film production companies, each of whom is invited to submit a proposed production cost. At the same time, the agency producer confers with each company on various details called for in order that every bidder interprets the copywriter's concept in the same way.

It would then be a simple matter to award the contract to the lowest bidder, but this is not always the case. The experienced agency producer, who knows personally the abilities of the individuals within the production companies, wants to know the names of the crew each company would assign to the project. He considers his delivery deadline and, in turn, queries the bidders as to their schedules in order that he will be assured of prompt delivery. He weighs all bids against his own estimate of what the job should cost and against his professional estimate of what quality each company would provide for the price mentioned. He then, with approval of his superior, recommends to the advertiser which bid should be accepted.

### Delivery Time

Normally, from the date the production company takes over to the date of delivery of the final film, the following time is required to produce the commercial:

*Live-action,* three to five weeks. *Animation,* four to eight weeks. *Rotoscope* and *stop-motion,* six to ten weeks. *Semi-animation* and *stills,* one to three weeks.

What if the advertiser needs the commercial to meet an air date in a much shorter time? Most live-action commercials can be produced in a few days, but at considerable extra cost for overtime. Animation, rotoscope, and stop-motion can also be speeded up, but cannot be completed in a matter of days.

### Commercial Cost vs. Program Cost

There is no denying that commercials cost advertisers large sums of money. Besides agency personnel, scores of people are involved in the production of each film commercial—producer, director, assistant director, unit manager, cameraman, assistant cameraman, script clerk, several electricians, prop men, set designer, sound man, sound recorder, casting director, costume designer, make-up artists, musical director, special effects man, film editor, laboratory personnel, to name only a *few.*

Considering the fact that the average network advertiser may be spending millions each year for one television program, the question continues to be asked: Is he spending enough on commercials? Surely competition among commercials on the air, all clamoring for the viewer's attention, steadily raises the required standards.

It is estimated that advertisers spend between 5 and 10 per cent of their total television expenditures for production of commercials. There is a wide difference of opinion as to whether this amount is sufficient. Certainly a sound selling idea does not always require expensive production to put it over. On the other hand, it is often to the advertiser's advantage to look "big-time" in his commercial messages, and for this the budget must be generous.

The mistake advertisers most try to avoid is the spending of millions on a network show, getting top ratings, and then losing their impact with commercials that do not deliver the customers. Weak concept is just one possible cause for failure. Skimping on production is another.

It is evident, however, that most national TV advertisers are not penny-wise and pound-foolish about commercials. They fully realize that the commercial represents their sole reason for being on the air, and that their success or failure depends not entirely, but to a large extent, upon how efficiently the commercials perform. Show or no show, "the commercial's the thing."

### Short Cuts in Production Costs

Regardless of how much an advertiser can, and should, spend to create commercials that sell, there also is a need to "watch the dollars" and save money wherever the saving will not harm the commercial's ability to sell. Many advertisers must operate on a limited budget regardless. Local advertisers, for example, are seldom in a position to spend thousands of dollars on one commercial.

It can be helpful to all advertisers, large and small, program and spot, to examine additional ways in which money can be saved in producing television film commercials. This list supplements the low-cost techniques already mentioned:

1. *Keep the cast simple.* Talent payments are not a major factor at first use, but repayments are.

2. *Repeat the commercials.* The advertiser is likely to tire of seeing the same set of commercials repeated long before the public does. A good commercial bears much repetition. In the first place, the same viewers do not see it every time it is telecast. Secondly, repetition is one of the basic rules of advertising. When commercials are repeated, the production cost is thereby amortized to a smaller and smaller amount.

3. *Investigate stock footage.* There are sources where stock footage—that is, film already existent—can be purchased by the foot. Of course, the entire commercial cannot be built from such film, but certain establishing shots such as long-shots of crowds, sporting events, buildings, and other general subjects can often be purchased more cheaply than specially shot. Two cautions: stock footage, while plentiful, can also be elusive. Spending days looking through thousands of feet of film to find the exact scene required can be expensive. Also, if there are people shown in the scenes selected, they cannot be used in the commercial without their permission and without meeting union standards.

4. *Shoot entirely in closeup.* Some first-rate commercials of national advertisers are built entirely around closeups of the product, hands demonstrating it, lettering popping on, and other interesting effects that require no background studio set, no animation, and a simple one-voice sound track.

5. *Simplify the sound track.* When featuring a jingle, five or six voices are not always necessary. In some cases, groups of singers are carried away by their own harmony and fail to register clearly and audibly the important selling points of the product. A solo can often be just as effective—and much cheaper.

Costly techniques are valuable when they perform a service, but wasteful when they are not really needed. Every penny saved is either money in the bank for the advertiser or money that can be applied toward additional time periods for better coverage of the market.

## Film Sizes

Nearly all television film commercials for national advertisers are photographed on 35mm film, the same size used for Hollywood feature films. More expensive than 16 mm, 35 mm offers these advantages:

Better picture; better sound; easier to edit; better quality opticals, and special effects. When reduced to 16mm, as it must be for projection on many stations, 35mm is still superior to film shot originally on 16mm.

However, being lower in cost, 16mm is more within the reach of many local advertisers and its quality is more than adequate.

## Stages of Film Production

The most detailed storyboard cannot possibly convey a completely accurate image of the final film commercial. Consequently the advertiser who approves the storyboard and then sits back and waits to see final film may be in for a few small surprises and perhaps some additional expense he had not planned on.

It is probable that a few minor changes are in order during the filming session—not necessarily because the storyboard was in error, but because certain improvements and simplifications become more obvious on the set. In live-action shooting, a camera-angle is the best example. The storyboard may call for a head-on shot of the product. On the set the director may find an angle-shot to be more dramatic. In television the chance to be creative should never be curbed.

Many times, too, the final film conforms literally to storyboard directions and no significant changes are required.

In many cases it behooves the advertiser to see the film at least once during its stages of development. The earlier after shooting corrections or revisions are made, the lower the cost.

Approximately seven minutes or more of film footage are shot to produce the average one-minute live-action commercial. This allows for several "takes" of each scene so that the best may be selected for inclusion in the final commercial. The total footage is sent to the laboratory and developed virtually overnight. So within a day or two after shooting, the "rushes" or "dailies"—all the filmed footage—are ready for viewing.

From this footage are picked the scenes to be used in the commercial. These scenes are then spliced together without opticals and without sound track into a "rough cut" or "work print." The advertiser can view this rough version of his commercial, in which not only the opticals, but also any "supers," or lettering over scenes, are absent. There is still time at this point to second-guess on the selection of scenes at no significant cost.

The next step is to hear the sound played against the picture. The sound track is retained on a separate piece of film. In order to hear it in synchronization with the picture, it is played as an "interlock." Opticals and supers are still missing. This is the final stage where last-minute changes may be made inexpensively.

At this point the various elements are joined in the laboratory; picture, sound, opticals, supers. The resulting film is an "answer print," or "composite print." The British call it the "married print." Once this has been approved, the shading of all scenes is re-checked and the "release print" is issued for use on the air.

What about amination? Before the many final drawings are "inked" for final shooting, a series of "rough" drawings are made and photographed in order that the basic action, size of characters, and timings can be checked. This stage is known as the "pencil test" and allows the advertiser to make revisions before the major portion of the production money has been spent.

*Servant, not Master*

The more one delves into it, the more one is likely to became awed at the apparent complexities involved in creating film commercials. Yet the observation stressed earlier can only be stressed again: The basic principles of film are simple to understand.

What is more important, film is just one tool the advertiser may use to express his selling message in an effective manner. It is not the technique, after all, that determines the campaign—it is the basic advertising idea behind it. The idea is where the commercial begins and ends. Film, with its infinite powers of dramatic expression, must remain the servant of the idea.

### TV FILM CONVERSION TABLE NO. 1

| Time Period (in seconds) | Frames | 35mm Film | 16mm Film | Maximum Words |
|---|---|---|---|---|
| 1 | 24 | 1½ feet | 24 frames | 2 |
| 2 | 48 | 3 " | 1 ft. + 8 frames | 4 |
| 3 | 72 | 4½ " | 1 " + 32 " | 7 |
| 4 | 96 | 6 " | 2 " + 16 " | 9 |
| 5 | 120 | 7½ " | 3 " | 11 |
| 6 | 144 | 9 " | 3 " + 24 " | 13 |
| 7 | 168 | 10½ " | 4 " + 8 " | 16 |
| 8 | 192 | 12 " | 4 " + 32 " | 18 |
| 9 | 216 | 13½ " | 5 " + 16 " | 20 |
| 10 | 240 | 15 " | 6 " | 22 |
| 15 | 360 | 22½ " | 9 " | 33 |
| 20 | 480 | 30 " | 12 " | 44 |
| 25 | 600 | 37½ " | 15 " | 55 |
| 30 | 720 | 45 " | 18 " | 65 |
| 35 | 840 | 52½ " | 21 " | 77 |
| 40 | 960 | 60 " | 24 " | 88 |
| 45 | 1080 | 67½ " | 27 " | 99 |
| 50 | 1200 | 75 " | 30 " | 110 |
| 55 | 1320 | 82½ " | 33 " | 120 |
| 60 | 1440 | 90 " | 36 " | 130 |
| 90 | 2160 | 135 " | 54 " | 195 |

## chapter eight

# Creating and Producing the Live Commercial

THE trend in television commercials has been toward film because of its convenience, its long-range economy, and its built-in safety features.

Yet some major advertisers still prefer to present their sales stories "live." A number of others would probably insist on live, over film, were they able to justify the separate production budget necessary for each airing of each commercial.

As with film, live production provides the advertiser with exciting opportunities to convey his selling message to the American public. The oft-heard comment to the effect that live is the more limiting of the two cannot be denied. Yet not all copywriters have really learned how to take full advantage of the many exciting possibilities live has to offer.

## Mechanics of "Live"

Film reproduces past action and makes it appear present. A live commercial is happening at the moment the viewer sees it. In nontechnical terms, the image is captured by the live television camera, transmitted by cable to the control room, then to master control, and finally to the transmitter, where it is sent out over the air.

In most cases, more than one camera is used in a live commercial. As the various cameras stand focused on various elements of the commercials, the director sees the images, each on monitors in the con-

Fig. 20—TYPICAL TV CONTROL ROOM includes the following equipment for the handling of live commercial or program production from adjoining studio: (1) master monitor, used primarily by the engineering department to check video quality and levels; (2) extra large line monitor for portraying to the technical director and production personnel the picture being transmitted to the air; (3) monitors (labeled Camera 1 through Camera 8) for showing what is being picked up by the available cameras in the studio; (4) and (5) preview monitors for showing any program which is being fed into this studio for integration (may be live, film, or videotape); (6) technical director's switching console, used to switch cameras and for film feeds, as required in the production, and equipped with faders and other devices to secure special optical effects; (7) technical director's seat; (8) program or commercial director's seat; (9) associate director's seat. Beyond window at right is audio control room. (ABC-TV)

trol room, and indicates the one to be on the air at each moment during the commercial. Often, when one camera is active, another is moving to a new "station" within the same studio to prepare for a subsequent scene. The copywriter must be familiar with this operation in order that his script will allow time for cameras to be in their proper positions for every scene.

With sufficient rehearsal, most live commercials today are almost as smoothly produced as those on film. The announcer is generally provided with "cue cards" or other devices to insure against lapse of

Fig. 21—MASTER CONTROL, a maze of buttons and monitors, is nerve center of network telecasting. By pushing, on cue, button on panel in front of him, engineer selects program feed that is to go out over the network. Engineer on phone in background is in touch with various studios and can advise on the quality of their respective pictures. *(NBC-TV)*

memory. Technical personnel are richly experienced. Chances of anything going seriously wrong are slight.

### Advantages of "Live"

For the local advertiser the live commercial may be ideal for either spot or program use. For the national advertiser the more practical choice for spot use is film, which allows him to amortize the production costs of each commercial. In programs, however, the decision may go either way.

These are the major advantages of live production:

1. Because the commercial is occurring at the moment he sees it, the viewer is likely to attach more immediacy to the sales message.

2. A live commercial allows the advertiser complete flexibility. On short notice he may announce a new product or change the selling appeal of an existing product. The live commercial, in other words, can be as timely as news itself.

3. A live commercial can be more easily integrated with the program content in cases where integration is considered desirable.

Only the circumstances surrounding each particular campaign can help the advertiser decide whether his commercials should be live or on film. Each time he is confronted with the problem, these are some of the questions to be answered:

Is the copy story likely to change on short notice?

Does the commercial require a demonstration? If so, is it simple enough not to involve risk or failure?

How many of the company's products will be advertised on the program?

How would the relative production costs of live and film compare over a season's time?

Is integration of commercial with program practical?

Is the program itself live or film?

Will the star of the show participate in the commercials?

Do any of the commercial elements require especially tricky lighting?

Can the commercial be produced in one studio, or are other locations required?

Will the commercial be effective without animation or other such techniques?

Is more than one program involved, where commercials can be interchanged?

## The Copywriter's Task

If any one advantage of live television can be singled out as most important, it is the element of timeliness. The copywriter creates each commercial for a *specific occasion*. He has every opportunity, consequently, to capitalize on its news-making value. By acknowledging current conditions and problems, or by referring to the plot or situation within the show immediately preceding the commercial, the copywriter can always make the live commercial appear fresh and timely. Or, even disregarding specific references to time, he may start selling from the opening word and still rely on the spontaneity of the live commercial to have a positive effect upon the attitude of the viewer.

Research has never been able to attribute more believability to live than to filmed commercials. Yet proponents of live firmly contend that the viewer is more inclined to involve himself in the message when he knows he is seeing and hearing it as it is being delivered. Somehow, the live commercial seldom has the "polish" of its film counterpart, and this quality, too, may register on the viewer.

## Basic Approaches

All live commercials come under the heading of the one basic live-action technique. It is the purpose here to cover the various successful approaches to this technique advertisers follow in order to inject the most possible impact into their selling messages. No one of these approaches can be called more effective than another since it is the product type and the advertiser's individual copy story which indicates, and sometimes dictates, the approach to be used. The general nature of a particular program, too, may influence the commercial treatment.

Following are the live-action approaches:

1. *Straight Announcer.* Here the announcer appears on-camera in most or all scenes throughout the commercial. This direct, personal approach to selling simplifies the commercial by narrowing attention to a relatively small physical area.

The straight announcer approach is probably the most common of all approaches. Reminiscent of the early pitchman, who captivated onlookers and sold stacks of merchandise by his own personal persuasiveness, the announcer appeals directly to the viewer and sometimes conducts a demonstration and submits other evidence to support his claims for the product.

Not all scenes necessarily show the announcer on-camera, but, when he is off-screen, his presence continues to be felt.

2. *Star of the Show.* Participation by the star of the show is known to add to the interest-value and often the selling power of the live commercial. The master of ceremonies, for instance, can so integrate the advertising message into the content of the program that he continues to command the viewer's attention and confidence even when he "changes hats" momentarily to deliver the commercial. Advertisers seldom turn down the opportunity of using the stars to deliver at least part of their sales messages when such arrangements can be made.

Local stations, too, feature personality programs where the principal star or host adds much credibility to the copy story by personal handling. This star participation, in fact, is one of the main reasons advertisers are attracted to this type of program.

It often happens that the program principal, while he may not participate in the commercials, does "set up" the message with a transitional lead-in sentence or two. This, too, is of value to the advertiser as it both implies big-name endorsement and serves to keep the viewer attentive.

Star of the show can also refer to the dramatic star, but here, of course, his participation, if any, best occurs at the end of the story lest an interruption of the plot prove distracting to the viewer.

3. *Closeups.* For years on network television, Kraft Foods have set high standards in live commercial presentation by concentrating on inviting closeups of cheese recipes. These "service" commercials have shown housewives how, step by step, to prepare new and interesting dishes by use of Kraft products. The announcer is never seen.

Closeups make large images of small objects. And large images are always commercially impressive. Keeping the product close to the viewer from beginning to end also tends to remove the barrier between them, thereby making the messages more intimate, easier to understand.

In addition, the closeup approach invariably reduces production costs since the entire commercial can be presented on table-top without need of studio sets.

4. *Extravaganza.* At the opposite extreme from the simple closeup approach is the spectacular treatment, in which the live commercial may consist of many sets, orchestra, dancers, announcer, and any other features needed to build the message into a veritable event.

Live commercials for automobiles sometimes pursue this elaborate approach, especially to announce new models on live programs. The extravaganza approach is useful in bringing prestige to the product, and in pointing up such features as style and design.

5. *Combination.* Not all approaches to live commercials can be arbitrarily placed in only one category. For example, the extravaganza may feature a straight announcer throughout. Closeups may dominate a commercial which shows the announcer at the outset and at the conclusion. The star of the show may share the selling chores with an announcer.

Indeed the combination can include both live and film within the same commercial.

*Special Visual Effects*

As with film, live production provides countless unusual visual effects which allow the copywriter to reproduce almost any image that comes to mind. He can reduce the announcer to six inches high and place him on the shelf of a refrigerator. He can multiply an actor into many identical images. He can have rain, snow, fire, or fog. He can also pick from a full selection of sound effects.

The trickier the commercial, the more complicated, and sometimes the more expensive, the production. While most advertisers do not make a steady diet of offbeat "gimmicks" within their live commercials, there often are one or more special effects that prove extremely appropriate in helping to dramatize particular points of copy.

Unlike film, where special effects are added in the laboratory after the basic film is shot, live effects are incorporated during the actual performance of the commercial.

The list which follows includes some of the better-known visual effects for live television. Before specifying any particular one, however, the copywriter is well advised to check its availability and price at the station or network that will carry the commercial.

*Filter Lens*—A colored filter can cause an actor, properly made up, suddenly to appear older or younger.

*Diffusion Lens*—Mounted in front of an ordinary lens, it is frosted around the outside, with a small, clear round hole in the center, permitting the object being televised to be framed in a round picture area in the center of the screen.

*Iris Effect*—The picture area, reduced by a diminishing circle, may be closed in, or opened out from the center.

*Wipe Amplifier*—A special piece of electronic gear permits portions of pictures from two different sources to appear on the same screen. The picture from one of the sources may be made to grow smaller and be displaced by the picture from the other source, giving the effect of wiping one picture off as the other wipes on. The wipe may occur horizontally, vertically, diagonally or in various shapes.

*Matting Amplifier*—Where normal superimposition of one camera's image over another's reduces the brightness quality of both images, the matting amplifier produces the "super" effect without loss of quality to either image. One live image may thus be matted upon another, telop on live or live on film.

*Prisms*—Mounted on the lens and rotated by the cameraman, prisms can produce such effects as two images rotating around one another; three images rotating around a center point; even five images rotating around a center image.

*Electronic Ripple*—Horizontal lines of the picture wave back and forth laterally. Most frequent use is to distort the picture deliberately for a dream sequence or a transition effect.

*Reverse Scanning*—Horizontal reverse scanning results in a reversal of the picture horizontally. The effect may be compared to printing a negative from the wrong side. The vertical reverse turns the picture upside down.

*Rear Projection and Front Projection*—Film, slides or "effect wheels" can be projected on a screen situated beside or behind the subject, making possible backgrounds which either cannot be physically duplicated with scenery or would be prohibitively expensive to construct. The effect of looking out of a "moving" automobile and watching the scenery pass by is provided in this manner. The "effects wheels" can simulate rippling water, twinkling stars, rising flames, moving clouds, panoramas, moving country scenes, fireworks displays and waterfalls.

*Electronic Background Insertion*—This recently-developed process is roughly comparable to the motion picture process of traveling mattes for backgrounds. It permits foreground action to be live, but on a substantially empty set. The background action is provided by slide or motion-picture film and the two are electronically combined into a composite picture of such perfection that even the most skilled eye has difficulty detecting any trick. Here again, money can be saved in scenery construction. And the copywriter enjoys complete flexibility in the selection of locales.

*Chroma Key Process*—Developed for use on its color programs, NBC's color key electronic inset makes possible, for example, an actress to be seen, in quick succession, waving good-by from a passenger liner leaving New York, dodging traffic in Piccadilly Circus, lunching at a Parisian sidewalk café, watching the Trevi Fountain in Rome, sightseeing in Tokyo and, finally, arriving at Los Angeles International Airport. Any movie or still depicting any background can now replace location shooting and set-building with the aid of a small box of electronic equipment about six inches wide, six inches high, and just over a foot long.

Fig. 22—SPECIAL EFFECT shown here is combination of wind machine and secret-formula snow machine to create a realistic, blowing snowstorm. *(NBC-TV)*

*Telop Rain Machine*—This device fits on the top stage of the telop machine and reflects small, rapidly moving light flecks on the output of the telop machine, which in turn is superimposed over the live scene where the rain is required. Used in conjunction with sound effects, and with a small spray for securing droplets for closeup purposes, the effect is amazingly realistic.

This is by no means a complete list of the various unusual visual effects the copywriter can call upon for added production values in the live commercial. There are types of mechanical setups which can be physically moved into the studio, and operated in conjunction with permanent equipment.

One of these is Cellomatic, which is able to achieve the effect of limited animation by clever superimpositions of transparencies. At the base of the machine are twin light sources from which light is reflected through mirrors up through transparencies, further through lenses and then to a screen, where the image is picked up by the live television camera. By using both light sources, type can be "popped" or wiped on a background picture; one photograph or piece of art-work can dissolve or wipe to another; dotted lines can be made to "animate" across a map. The possibilities are many.

## Opticals

Certain transitional devices have already been mentioned in previous paragraphs. However, as is true in film, the most commonly used opticals in live are the "cut" and "dissolve." Both are handled in the control room, where all cameras respond to the touch of a key. When a cut is called for, one camera is simply turned off and another simultaneously turned on. The dissolve, too, is accomplished electronically. One camera is made to fade out at the same time another is fading in.

## Which "Tools" to Use

Products differ, competition differs, advertisers and their policies differ, prices differ, copywriters differ, production facilities differ, and so do the production personnel charged with the responsibility of executing the live commercial. As a result, no two commercials are ever created under precisely the same conditions. No ironclad rules can be formulated with any expectancy of universal application.

There are two theories among advertising people regarding the handling of live commercials.

One insists that, to "cash in" on the sense of immediacy experienced by the viewer when he or she watches a live commercial, the copywriter should pursue a simple, straightforward treatment and thereby exploit the reality of the occasion. Dependence on special effects to any extent, they contend, may tend to break down an intimate advertiser-customer relationship which live television, by its very nature, makes possible.

The other school argues in this manner: The average decision to produce commercials live is not necessarily based on any inherent advantage of live over film, but rather on such factors as whether the program itself is live or film and whether the product story is constant or changing. Therefore, when the copywriter faces the prospect of live commercials, a situation over which he seldom has any control one way or the other, he should approach his task precisely in the same manner as he would were his commercials going on film; namely, with the firm intention of using every possible tool at his command that will help him create the hardest-selling commercial.

The latter theory seems to make more sense and is definitely more reflective of conditions as they actually exist. The success of a commercial, after all, depends more on the basic idea behind it than whether it is geared for the live camera or the film camera.

### Steps in Production

From concept to execution the live television commercial calls on the talents of many specialists and requires careful planning and coordination every step of the way.

Covering all functions in their chronological order, the following steps are based on a typical routine set up to produce a group of two or three commercials for a nighttime network program. To make the sequence of events complete, the starting point will be the moment the copywriter receives his assignment to create the scripts.

1. Agency copywriter and producer confer on general approaches. The copywriter then writes the scripts.

2. Copywriter confers with TV art director, who may offer further ideas and draw storyboards. (Storyboards are not necessary where live commercials already conform to a general pattern or a series.)

3. Copywriter re-checks scripts with producer so that both agree on all details.

4. Scripts are submitted to client. If changes are requested, the scripts are revised and resubmitted for approval. At this time the client also approves a tentative budget.

5. The approved scripts are then returned to the agency producer, who takes charge and coordinates all production activities from this point on.

6. The producer calls a meeting of the writer, art director, and the person who will direct the commercials in the studio. (Some agencies assign a free lance director. Others designate the agency producer to act also as director.) The purpose of the meeting is to discuss the various commercial elements and reach agreements on interpretation.

7. Producer and director confer with scenic designer on the types of sets required.

8. A second production meeting includes the scenic designer, who submits sketches of the sets for approval of the producer and director.

9. Producer and director conduct one or more casting sessions to select talent for the commercials.

10. Final production estimate is determined, and cleared with the client.

11. Producer and director meet with network personnel to discuss special effects, if any, and other technical problems which may exist.

12. Producer and director call a meeting of the cast to discuss the commercial scripts and interpretation of the copy.

13. The group next meets in a rehearsal studio, where the floors are taped or chalked to guide the cast in a "walk-through" of the commercials. This rehearsal is conducted without scenery and equipment.

14. Producer and director visit scenic studio to check progress of the sets.

15. Producer and director meet with network personnel, including technical director, lighting director, associate director, and stage manager.

16. On the day preceding telecast, scenery is moved into studio. Lighting is set up and tested.

17. At the first camera rehearsal, on the day of telecast, all shots

are planned and set, final lighting adjustments made, scenery and props checked.

18. A final run-through is scheduled later in the day.

19. Dress rehearsal of the commercials is coordinated with the dress rehearsal of the program, ending at least one hour before air-time.

20. From thirty minutes before air-time until air-time, cameras are focused on the test pattern to make certain they are operating properly. Final notes are made and discussed with the cast if necessary.

### Costs

To produce a live "participation" commercial integrated with a program on a local station or even on a network the cost may be negligible. On the other hand, the production operation just described step-by-step may cost the advertiser anywhere from $2,000 to $8,000, depending upon size of cast, number of sets, range of facilities, length of rehearsal time, and other factors. It is not unusual for commercial production costs to run well into five figures for a longer program.

A typical budget for a half-hour evening show with two minutes of commercial time (the third minute going to the alternate sponsor for his "cross-plug" commercial) may break down in the following manner:

| | |
|---|---|
| Talent (including director's fee) | $1,700 |
| Scenery, set design, trucking, props, costumes | 2,000 |
| Network facilities, including camera rehearsal, studio usage, special effects, and camera equipment | 2,500 |
| Artwork and photographs | 300 |
| Miscellaneous | 200 |
| Total | $6,700 |

When the commercials are produced by an agency, the agency adds the customary 15 per cent commission to the total.

No two production budgets are ever alike because of the endless variables. Each network has a different rate structure for live production.

### The "Risks"

Only at certain times must a risk be reckoned with in live commercials. In fact, most commercials involve no risk at all.

In the area of product demonstrations, the advertiser seeks insurance against possible product failure before the camera. A refrigerator door, for example, which may operate properly for a lifetime in the security of a family's kitchen, has been known to "stick" when "frightened" by a TV camera! Beer has gone "flat" when poured on live television. Anything *can* happen—but seldom *does*. These are the factors which tend to make the live presentation safer every year:

1. Adequate rehearsals assure a more perfect end product.

2. For difficult product demonstrations, advertisers use film or videotape inserts.

3. The advertiser who has been featuring substantially the same demonstration over a long period of time has the "odds" in his favor. In the remote event that his live demonstration should happen to go wrong some night, the resulting publicity generally adds up in his favor in the form of audience sympathy and sense of humor.

"The point to remember," said Everett Hart, one of TV's busiest live commercial producers, "is that the days of 'hit-or-miss' are over. The experience and skill of the professional specialists involved today makes the live commercial a strong, sound vehicle of advertising."

## chapter nine

# Videotape

A REMARKABLE electronic process that converts a television picture and accompanying sound into electromagnetic impulses on recording tape is the third method by which the advertiser may communicate his message via television to the viewing public.

The use of videotape, in fact, reaches far beyond the area of commercials. Complete network and local programs can now be recorded in advance of telecast.

The program or commercial in this case is performed before *live* television cameras. Both picture and sound are recorded on one two-inch-wide tape and, with no processing of any kind, the tape can be played back immediately after recording. It can be played back at least a hundred times without wearing out; or it can be erased, or demagnetized, and used again and again. The videotape picture, as seen on the air, is technically so perfect that the viewer is unable to distinguish it from live.

### Advantages

Videotape by its very nature fires the imagination of the advertiser, the copywriter, the producer, and all concerned with commercial creation. For here is the timeliness and spontaneity of live combined with the security and much of the smoothness of film.

Where film requires processing—"rushes" cannot be checked until a day or two after shooting—tape can be played back immediately to show how the performers came across and whether staging, lighting, and other elements were at their best. If the total performance is found

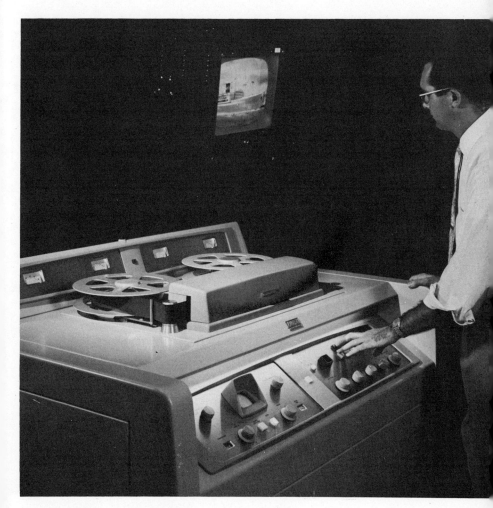

Fig. 23—AMPEX VR-1000 Videotape Recorder console.

to be below standard, the tape can be erased and the commercial shot again.

Even after film "rushes" are approved, editing and further processing may consume weeks of valuable time. Tape, being instantaneous, can be approved and put on the air in a matter of minutes.

Fig. 24—EXTENSIVE USE OF SETS, controlled lighting of products and fault-less camera work were assured before telecast . . .

A further advantage of tape may eventually be a saving of production money for the advertiser. The convenience and speed of video-tape suggests short cuts of many kinds, including the shooting of several programs or commercials in a single day.

Fig. 25 — . . . when Westclox commercials, featuring Dorothy Collins, were shot
on videotape for use on "Wonderful Town."

## Development

The first commercial videotape recorder was introduced by Ampex
Corporation in April of 1956, although RCA, Bing Crosby Enterprises,
and others had been developing their own systems. Ampex's basic con-

Fig. 26—VIDEOTAPE encourages copywriter and producer to take full advantage of live-camera techniques. *(Jay Seymour Photo)*

tribution was to make a slow speed videotape recorder commercially available for black-and-white recording and reproduction. In the light of the Ampex developments, RCA and Ampex worked out a cross-licensing agreement whereby RCA's color system was made available to Ampex while RCA made use of the Ampex recording head and both companies now produce recorders capable of operating in black-and-white or color.

Videotape has been in daily use by the major television networks since November 1956, and television stations began installing the new device about a year later.

In early model recorders it was necessary to play the tape back on the same head that recorded it because of variations in the individual heads. In the new models, however, it is possible to play the tape back on any machine since the tapes and heads are now interchangeable. High-quality copies can be made simply by feeding the output of one machine into another.

## Splicing

At first, tape was most difficult to edit. If a mistake occurred in the taping of a commercial, not only the faulty scene but the entire commercial had to be re-shot from beginning to end.

The problem was to develop a method which would quickly and accurately locate the precise splice line, make an even cut, then rejoin the cut ends into a continuous sequence. And the splice had to be made within very close tolerances.

Today modern tape splicing makes it possible to re-shoot any portion of a sequence and insert the scene into its proper place, thereby reducing the over-all time required for production.

Editing taped commercials into taped programs also has become a practical reality.

## Effect on Film

While with videotape the commercial copywriter and the program producer can call upon every device known to live TV—the use of many cameras, slides, lap dissolves, superimposures, matting amplifier and all the others—the total effect remains that of a well-produced live coumercial and no more.

Certainly, where money can be saved as a result, a certain number of advertisers will favor tape over film. Nevertheless, many believe that film will continue to be a major factor in the production of television commercials.

Film, after all, still offers effects and images not obtainable either

Fig. 27—ENLARGED PORTION of recorded videotape. Video information is contained in vertical lines. Control track, across bottom, is magnetic equivalent of film sprocket holes, assuring playback at exactly the same speed at which picture was recorded. Editing pulses on control track are spaced every quarter-inch, or 1/60 of a second. Each represents the completion of one scanning cycle. Third informational component of tape, sound track, runs across top but cannot be seen in this magnified section. (Ampex Corp.)

live or on tape. Animation, for example, is a film technique which has risen in popularity over the years. Stop-motion, too, has its place in the more elaborate types of commercials and remains a technique which only film can achieve.

The fact remains, however, that some major film production firms now operate tape equipment and have made ready to serve the advertiser, *whichever* vehicle he chooses for his commercials.

### Effect on Live

There is no question that live programs and commercials, particularly on network television, will become fewer and fewer since tape offers the advertiser a picture of equal quality plus a performance approved in advance of broadcast.

However, in the types of live programs where the advertiser is able to achieve close integration with show personalities, the commercial may lose more than it gains by going to videotape unless the program does, too. In addition, the simpler "stand-up" live commercials, tried and tested over many airings, are not necessarily in need of tape to guarantee quality performance. Here the decision may rest on the economic advantage of producing several taped versions at one session, thereby reducing the production cost per unit.

### Program Uses

Videotape opens a whole new field of program production techniques. No longer, for one thing, must a live program be played in continuity. Where in the past an abrupt change of scene involving an actor had to be planned so that he would have time physically to change costume or move from one studio location to another, key portions of the drama may now be pre-recorded on videotape and dropped into an otherwise live television program without a noticeable difference in picture quality.

Similarly, location exteriors can be taped and inserted into a studio-originated program, again with no quality difference. In addition, difficult scenes involving special effects can be pre-taped so that the producer knows the sequence will work on the air.

It is also possible, of course, to tape a live show in its entirety and run it again as often as desired, provided legal and union considerations are satisfied. The networks use this means to repeat programs in various time periods.

In fact, because network shows can now be aired at the same time across the country, buyers of syndicated film shows may soon find it difficult to clear prime time on many network-affiliated stations. On the other hand, the syndicators themselves are interested in tape as a possible means of saving production money. Many feel that tape and film can exist side by side, while others insist that ultimately tape will replace film.

### Local Station Uses

Strictly local uses of videotape by stations will eventually be many. For example, in this manner stations will be able to repeat live programs.

Those broadcasters who are sometimes plagued with the problems of presenting controversial people in news and interview programs can record the program in advance and review it carefully before broadcast.

Some stations may record their regular week-end shows during the week, thereby utilizing talent and facilities not hitherto available during the week end itself.

Certain remote events often happen at a time not convenient for immediate scheduling. The remote unit can then transmit special event programs to the studio-based tape recorder for playback at regularly scheduled hours.

In addition, local stations can use videotape to remove the performance risk from live commercials. It is also likely that many locally originated programs of wide interest may be picked up for regional or national distribution.

Regardless of the large investment necessary, more and more stations are installing videotape facilities in order to gain greater production flexibility and greater programing effectiveness.

## chapter ten

# How to Demonstrate on Television

THE greatest single advantage television enjoys over every other medium of advertising is its inherent power to demonstrate. Sight, sound, and motion together comprise the enviable combination that makes possible living, moving proof of a product's superiority.

From its earlier days, when a small, rather frail girl displayed the ease of unfolding a Castro convertible sofa four times her size, on down through its few but eventful years to date, television has created new desires and new sales by exhibiting products' features in a straightforward, hard-selling manner never before equaled in any major medium of advertising.

Because the demonstration has become so commonplace in television commercials, however, the advertiser must recognize that today's public views the medium through a much more critical eye than formerly, and frequently manifests disbelief as well as belief in what it sees.

Many laundry soaps and detergents, for example, make a major copy point of whiteness and brightness of the wash. Many of them— too many of them—try to demonstrate such a claim by showing *whiter* sheets and *whiter* shirts and *whiter* diapers than those washed by competitive products. After watching a parade of such demonstrations over the course of a few evenings, many a housewife throws up her hands and doubts them all.

When a floor wax or cleaner tries, through visual "demonstration," to make her believe *her* floor will look like the floor in the commer-

Fig. 28—POLAROID'S LIVE DEMONSTRATION has been a famous technique for years. The very risk involved has added credibility to the live commercials. Jack Paar is one of many celebrities who have successfully proved the reliability of this product before the responsive television audience. *(NBC-TV)*

cial if she will only use the product—even though she has used the product and knows otherwise—is she not perhaps becoming a little hardened to some of the "miracles" she sees in television demonstrations?

Fortunately, most advertisers have learned that demonstrations must be honest to be believed, and they must be believed if they are to sell. Not only their consciences, but their sense of good business, tells them that gullibility disappeared as an audience characteristic back in the days when wrestling was television's favorite attraction.

## When to Demonstrate

Nearly every product has some demonstrable feature. Whether or not that feature or any feature should be demonstrated within the television commercial, however, is quite another matter. To help him decide, the advertiser can ask himself these questions:

Will the demonstration be interesting to the viewer?

Will it be dramatic?

Will it be sufficiently simple for the viewer to comprehend?

Will it be believed?

Will it convey a convincing consumer benefit?

Will it be remembered?

The answer to all of these questions should be affirmative if the demonstration and, consequently, the commercial are to be successful. Finding the best feature to demonstrate and the most effective technique may take some ingenuity, considering the abundance of obvious demonstrations on television today.

## Where to Begin

There can be no universal set of rules to apply to all products when it comes to planning the television demonstration simply because no two products are alike. However, these hints are well worth considering at the outset:

1. Examine carefully the demonstrations used by competitive products. Plan to be different if you cannot surpass them decisively at their own game.

2. Keep the viewer in mind at all times. He will watch and listen only as long as the demonstration offers him some reward for using the product.

3. Pick only one feature to demonstrate in one commercial. Allow sufficient time for its performance and its moral to "sink in."

4. When possible, select a demonstration the viewer can do himself if he should so desire. Chances are he won't trouble to, but such a possibility makes any demonstration more credible.

5. Keep the demonstration simple. If this is impractical, use a technique like diagrammatic animation to simplify a more complex feature.

6. Consider carefully the element of risk involved in demonstrating before the camera. The sturdiest product can fail to function properly at the critical moment. If the commercial is on film or videotape, there is, of course, no risk at all since the scene can be re-shot until perfect. If the commercial is live, the demonstration must be carefully handled. Many advertisers employ film inserts of their demonstrations within their live commercials to reduce the danger of possible embarrassment. However, if the live demonstrations are performed on a regular basis, a loyal audience will not condemn a product on one failure.

### Types of Demonstrations

It is difficult to categorize TV demonstrations since some may fall under more than one classification. However, by recognizing various general types, the copywriter can thus organize himself to explore a number of promising areas before he decides on the best possible demonstration for his particular product or on no demonstration at all.

Generally speaking, demonstrations in television commercials can be classified as follows:

1. Dramatic Performance
2. Service
3. "Before-and-After"
4. Side-by-Side
5. Symbolic
6. Humorous
7. Technical

1. *The Dramatic Performance Demonstration.* In live-action an automobile leaps through the air and lands safely to dramatize its sturdiness of construction. A man shaves a two-week growth of beard to prove the speed and efficiency of an electric razor. A waterproof watch

is attached to an outboard motor, spun under water, and brought to the surface still keeping perfect time. A spike is driven into a tubeless tire, then withdrawn as the air stays in. A radio, pushed off the top of a step-ladder, lands on the floor without damage.

The severe test is the most basic sort of sales approach, having its roots in the interesting, persuasive routine of the sidewalk and car-nival pitchman. Research shows that such a demonstration, because of its shock value, impresses viewers, and tends to penetrate their memories.

Nevertheless, the success or failure of the dramatic performance demonstration really depends on the method by which it is staged. "How do I know they didn't start out punishing one product and then change the scene and substitute a new product just like it?" the viewer may ask.

There is a way to avoid arousing such suspicion; namely, by keep-ing one camera, wherever possible, *continuously* following the critical action of the demonstration. If, instead, the camera shows one scene, then cuts to a different angle, the viewer's mind, trained by watching movies throughout his life, automatically tells him something is awry. He senses a trick.

In other words, it is not enough for the advertiser to *be* honest in the demonstration portion of the commercial. He must also *look* hon-est in the way he presents it.

The only other possible area of viewer suspicion lies in the ques-tion, "How do I know they're not showing me a product specially re-inforced to stand this punishment?" There is not much the advertiser can do to alleviate this doubt beyond phrasing the audio in such a manner as to reassure the audience that the product shown in the video demonstration is exactly the same as that sold in the store. Chances are, his word will be accepted.

2. *Service Demonstration.* Some products are made attractive simply by showing the "amazing" way in which they work. For instance, the camera which shoots, develops, and prints a picture within sixty sec-onds is a "natural" to demonstrate before the audience. So is the tele-vision set that can be operated by remote control from an armchair. But only a modest percentage of products are sufficiently unique to depend upon this approach alone.

Within this category also come those demonstrations which show new uses for an existing product. Watching a chef prepare a familiar food in exciting new ways can stimulate a woman's imagination, a man's appetite, and sales as well. A package of aluminum foil, a roll of cellophane tape, a hair spray—these, too, can demonstrate "service" ideas that will promote new uses and new interest in the product.

Watching an announcer install floor tiles provides a strong "come-on" for "do-it-yourself" fans. This excerpt from an Armstrong Excelon Tile commercial illustrates that advertising which offers viewers "something extra" can gain more attention, more response:

| *VIDEO* | *AUDIO* |
|---|---|
| OPEN ON CLOSEUP OF AN-NOUNCER. ON CUE HE SNAPS FINGERS AND SPEAKS. | ANNOUNCER (ON-CAMERA)<br>It's a snap to install your own plastic tile floors. All you need is . . . |
| HE SNAPS FINGERS AND PAIR OF WHITE ARTWORK SCISSORS POP ON (SUPER). | . . . a pair of scissors . . . |
| HE SNAPS FINGERS, AND WHITE ARTWORK BRUSH POPS ON. | . . . an ordinary brush like this . . . |
| HE HOLDS UP EXCELON TILE. ON CUE, REVEAL: "EXCELON TILE, BY ARMSTRONG." | . . . and Excelon Tile, by Armstrong—the modern vinyl asbestos tile designed for you to install yourself. |
| WIDEN TO REVEAL ANNOUNCER ON PARTIALLY COMPLETED FLOOR. HE CUTS TILE WITH SCISSORS. | Use the scissors to cut the tile wherever there's any trimming to be done. |
| HE PUTS DOWN TILES, PICKS UP BRUSH AND HOLDS IT TO CAMERA. | Use the brush to brush on the cement that'll hold the tiles in place. Isn't that easy? |
| CUT TO WIDER SHOT OF AN-NOUNCER INSTALLING A CUSTOM | And here's the easiest part of all . . . putting down the tiles. Just |

| *VIDEO* | *AUDIO* |
|---|---|
| DESIGN. HE LAYS ONE REGULATION-SIZE TILE, THEN INSTALLS PIECE THAT WE WATCHED BEING TRIMMED IN #5. INCLUDE AN OPEN BOX OF TILE. | lay them down like this, in your own custom design. |
| DISSOLVE TO STILL PHOTO OF PLAYROOM WITH A FLOOR FEATURING DESIGN IDENTICAL TO THAT WHICH ANNOUNCER HAS JUST INSTALLED IN #7. | ANNOUNCER (Voice Over) Isn't that attractive? You'll be proud when you install your Excelon Tile floors. You'll save money, too, because Excelon is one of the lowest-cost vinyl tiles you can buy. |
| DISSOLVE TO MEDIUM CLOSEUP OF ANNOUNCER AGAINST BLACK. POP ON, IN SYNC: WHITE ARTWORK SCISSORS, BRUSH. ON CUE, SUPER: "EXCELON TILE, BY ARMSTRONG." | ANNOUNCER (On-Camera) It's easy and it's fun to design and install your own modern vinyl tile floor. Remember—all you need is a pair of scissors . . . a brush . . . and Excelon Tile, by Armstrong. |

3. *"Before-and-After" Demonstration.* This demonstration brings into play one of the oldest and soundest principles of basic advertising—problem-solution.

"Why put up with hard-to-clean pots and pans like these?" asks the announcer over the scene of a stack of greasy pots and pans. A woman picks up a pot and goes into action with a certain scouring product. "Look at that grease disappear *now!*"

Herein lies a danger. Just how clean should the pot become? Chances are, the commercial will make it look like new in a matter of seconds. And unbelievability again rears its head.

Whenever he starts with a familiar problem, the copywriter stands a better-than-average chance of commanding the viewer's close attention. Once he has it, however, he must make certain the solution he offers does right by the product and right by the viewer. He has no alternative but to *convince* the viewer that the same solution depicted in the commercial will also result in the home. Obviously he is not going to show a half-cleaned pot in the "after" shot of his demonstration. But must it really sparkle as if it had just come from the factory? Reasonable judgment is the antidote to thoughtless exaggeration.

A nail enamel turns "dull, lifeless" fiingernails into beautiful nails within one continuous camera shot. A cracked ceiling becomes both new-looking and soundproofed as a man's hand staples up new acoustical tiles. Application of a depilatory removes hair from a woman's legs. Here, too, life is made better—the viewer is made happier—with results proven through forceful presentation.

In this type of demonstration it is not always possible to follow the complete sequence from "before" to "after" in one continuous camera motion. Passage of time required to achieve the result often calls for a "dissolve" or other optical that will tie together the earlier and the later scenes. For example, in the believable "before-and-after" demonstration in the following Wisk commercial, the complete washing cycle must occur between the application of Wisk to the spot in the fabric and the spotless fabric hanging on the clothesline. Here an optional "wipe" is used to denote the elapsed time.

| *VIDEO* | *AUDIO* |
|---|---|
| OPEN ON LONG ESTABLISHING SHOT OF MOTHER, DAD, JUNIOR, AND SIS (WITH DOLLY) AT PICNIC SPOT. THEY ALL ARE IN LIGHT, BRIGHT CLOTHES. | (MUSIC: Happy picnic theme) MOTHER (Voice Over) I never dreamed any detergent could beat my old one for getting all the family wash its cleanest—but *this* one can— |
| SUPER CLOSEUP CAN OF WISK WITH TITLE: "BLUE LIQUID." | (MUSIC: Sting) . . . blue liquid Wisk. |
| CUT TO MEDIUM SHOT OF MOTHER UNFURLING PICNIC TABLECLOTH. | (MUSIC: Gliss) ANNOUNCER (Voice Over) Wisk not only gets things spotless white . . . |

| VIDEO | AUDIO |
|---|---|
| CUT TO MEDIUM SHOT OF DAD IN BRIGHT COLORED SPORT SHIRT, OPEN AT COLLAR. HE IS LIFTING HIS SON UP OVER HIS HEAD. | (MUSIC: Gliss)<br>. . . not only gets things brand-new bright . . . |
| DISSOLVE TO CLOSEUP OF LITTLE GIRL. SHE SPILLS RELISH ON THE TABLECLOTH. | (MUSIC: Gliss, then playoff)<br>Wisk easily handles tough jobs beyond the cleaning range of laundry powders. |
| DISSOLVE TO CLOSEUP CAN OF WISK ON WASHER IN LAUNDRY ROOM. SUPER: "FULL-RANGE DETERGENT." | That's why it's called the full-range detergent. |
| CUT BACK TO LONGER SHOT OF MOTHER POURING WISK INTO CUP. FOLLOW AS MOTHER PUTS CAN DOWN ON EDGE OF WASHER. | MOTHER (On-Camera)<br>You can prove it any washday. You pour the Wisk you need for the whole wash. |
| CUT TO CLOSEUP OF CLOTHES IN WASHER. | MOTHER (Voice Over)<br>Put the routine things in the machine. |
| SHE PICKS UP SOILED TABLECLOTH. SHE APPLIES WISK TO STAINED AREA. IRIS DOWN TO HIGHLIGHT APPLICATION. | Then you take the problem stain and apply a little Wisk . . . |
| SHE FOLDS TABLECLOTH TO SPREAD WISK OVER THE ENTIRE STAIN. SHE THEN OPENS CLOTH. | . . . making sure Wisk covers the entire stain—to concentrate its cleaning power right where you need it. |

| VIDEO | AUDIO |
|---|---|
| OPEN UP IRIS AS SHE DROPS CLOTH INTO WASHER AND POURS IN THE REST OF THE WISK AFTER IT. | Then in with the other things—and add the remaining Wisk. |
| DISSOLVE TO SHOT IN OPEN WASHER WITH SUDS AGITATING. | Liquid Wisk goes right to work on all the family wash. Its bluing action . . . |
| WIPE TO EXTERIOR CLOTHESLINE SHOT, INCLUDE TABLECLOTH, DAD'S SHIRT, ETC. SUPER: "SPOTLESS WHITE, BRAND-NEW BRIGHT." | . . . gets everything spotless white and brand-new bright. |
| ZOOM UP CAN OF WISK FROM INFINITY, DISSOLVING OUT SUPER, DISSOLVING IN "FULL-RANGE DETERGENT." | ANNOUNCER (Voice Over) So use the full-range detergent—blue liquid Wisk. |

Not to be confused as a "before-and-after" demonstration or as any demonstration at all are the personal reaction shots so common, and often so necessary, to certain television commercials. When a woman is shown fretting over a big laundry job ahead of her, then later in the commercial (thanks to the fact that she used the product) she is discovered happily playing golf, the personal "before-and-after" effect does not consitute a demonstration.

The same applies to "taste." If a thirsty character suddenly drinks iced tea and looks refreshed, this may be sound selling but again it is not demonstrating. Sometimes these scenes work, sometimes they look "phony." "Taste" is too personal a sensation to *prove,* but if the commercial can motivate the viewer to *try* the taste, then the product has a chance of winning a new customer.

4. *Side-by-Side Demonstration.* Here is where television advertising really shows its teeth. The side-by-side test, designed to demonstrate the superiority of one brand or product-type over another, is one of

the most commonly used of all devices. Here is the "hard-boiled" school of advertising, which demonstrates not just how the product works, not just how it makes life better, but specifically and graphically in what way it surpasses competition.

"First," says the announcer over the scene of a car swaying over as it turns a corner, "let's see what it's like in a car *not* equipped with our suspension system." The scene changes to the car being advertised. "Now see the difference!" The car takes the corner smoothly, with little or no sway!

More than one hair spray has employed this type of demonstration, showing one model losing her lovely curls because she uses the "wrong" spray, then another whose curls stay in because she used the "right" spray. Many hand lotions, face powders, and other cosmetic products also rely on the side-by-side demonstration to put more bite into their messages.

Cigarettes, detergents, waxes, drug products, television sets, appliances, auto safety glass, facial tissues, home permanents, even brassières are represented among the myriad of products demonstrating by comparison.

A sink is cleaned—half with one scouring powder, half with the advertised brand. A floor is likewise treated with two waxes to show the comparison.

Usually the side-by-side demonstration is performed in live-action, whether the commercial is live or on film. Exceptions occur when the comparison is of a technical or personal nature. For example, the famous series of Bufferin commercials show the throat, stomach and other innards, for obvious reasons, in animation.

| *VIDEO* | *AUDIO* |
|---|---|
| OPEN ON LIMBO SHOT OF TWO CYMBALS AS THEY COME CRASHING TOGETHER. | (SOUND: Cymbals crashing together) |
| AS CYMBALS OPEN, MAN'S HEAD APPEARS BETWEEN THEM. CYMBALS COME TOGETHER AGAIN, CLAMPING MAN'S HEAD ON EITHER SIDE. HE WINCES FROM | ANNOUNCER (Voice Over) When you have a headache that clings (SOUND: Clang) and clangs (SOUND: Clang) and clangs (SOUND: Clang) . . . |

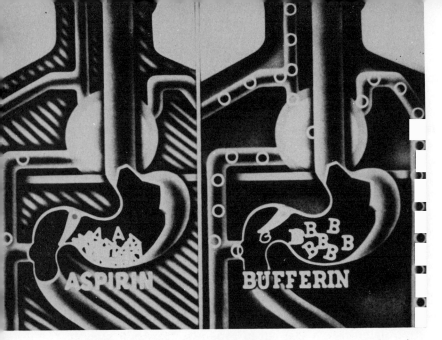

Fig. 29—SIDE-BY-SIDE DEMONSTRATION. Bufferin commercial employs "mechanical man" device to demonstrate speed with which Bufferin ingredients go to work in the blood stream.

| VIDEO | AUDIO |
|---|---|
| PAIN. CYMBALS OPEN AND SHUT AGAIN. | |
| AS CYMBALS MOVE APART AGAIN, MAN'S HEAD FADES OUT AND BUFFERIN BOX COMES ZOOMING UP THROUGH THAT SPACE TO FILL THE SCREEN. | . . . get rid of that headache *fast* . . . with Bufferin. |
| FADE BOX BACK, LEAVING ONLY "BUFFERIN" FROM LOGO ON SCREEN. BELOW THAT, FADE IN SUPER: "TWICE AS FAST AS ASPIRIN." | Because Bufferin acts *twice as fast as* aspirin to relieve the pain of a headache, neuralgia or ordinary aches and pains. |
| DISSOLVE INTO SPLIT SCREEN SHOT OF TWO "MECHANICAL MEN." | Here's why. |

| *VIDEO* | *AUDIO* |
|---|---|
| MOVE IN TO MEDIUM CLOSEUP OF TWO STOMACHS. WE SEE A BUFFERIN TABLET, RIGHT, AND AN ASPIRIN TABLET, LEFT, GO DOWN THE THROAT AND INTO THE STOMACH. | As you see, both Bufferin and aspirin take exactly the same time to get *to* the stomach. But for a pain reliever . . . |
| EACH BREAKS UP INTO TINY "B'S" AND "A'S" RESPECTIVELY. | . . . to do its best and quickest work, it must get out of the stomach, into the bloodstream. |
| STOMACH VALVE OPENS. WE ARE NOW MOVING IN ON THE BUFFERIN STOMACH AND LOSING THE ASPIRIN STOMACH ON THE LEFT. DISSOLVE THROUGH TO BUFFERIN STOMACH. | Now, Bufferin's formula combines aspirin with two special antacid ingredients which get the pain reliever . . . |
| CLOSEUP OF BUFFERIN'S PAIN RELIEVING INGREDIENTS ZOOMING THROUGH THE "PIPES." | . . . into the bloodstream twice as fast as aspirin. |
| DISSOLVE TO MONTAGE. EXTREME CLOSEUP OF BUFFERIN BOTTLE, FROM USER'S ANGLE, AS BOTTLE IS TILTED TO OBTAIN TABLETS. | That's why Bufferin acts twice as fast as aspirin. |
| EXTREME CLOSEUP OF TWO BUFFERIN TABLETS DROPPING INTO LEFT PALM. | What's more, Bufferin doesn't upset your stomach, as aspirin often does. |
| EXTREME CLOSEUP OF MAN AS HE DRINKS. | So get Bufferin today! |
| EXTREME CLOSEUP OF BUFFERIN PACKAGE ON SHELF AS GLASS IS RETURNED. | Bufferin! |

5. *Symbolic Demonstration.* As explained earlier, a commercial can be effective without any demonstration at all. But before the copywriter gives up on the possibility of demonstrating, he should, momentarily at least, channel his thinking into the area of symbols, or analogies.

The symbolic demonstration involves substitution of a symbol for the actual because dwelling on the latter would be too technical, too vague, or in bad taste. To sell pills, one advertiser demonstrated the action of stomach acid by substituting a better-known but less offensive substance. To avoid applying his product directly to the underarm area, a deodorant advertiser specified the same action over the thumb and index finger area. In showing how a tire grips the road, fingers emerged from the tire to emphasize the claim. An electric razor, to dramatize its extreme versatility, shaved a peach, then a brush, on-camera. From this demonstration, in fact, came the theme line, "A peach of a shave!"

"The most effective commercials," asserted one researcher, "stretch the mind a little." The symbolic demonstration does just that.

6. *Humorous Demonstration.* A demonstration is the last place in which one would ordinarily expect to find humor. After all, the demonstration is synonomous with proof, and proof should be neither scoffed at not tampered with.

On the other hand, there is occasionally a situation where a humorous twist is entirely in keeping. One might consider the product whose only demonstration is similar to that being used on television by more than one competitive product. To omit it may be an admission of weakness. To include it may be adding confusion. By doing a parody of the demonstration the copywriter can sometimes add interest and still register his sales points.

One pre-shave lotion commercial featured a comic standing before a blackboard on which appeared a picture of the product and a complicated mathematical formula. In his hands he held a board with three large whiskers. He purposely fumbled his way though the copy. But as he himself apparently began to understand the product's "prop-up" story, he became more and more enthusiastic and actually made the whiskers on the board stand up.

The humorous demonstration must be delicately handled. One of the most hilarious commercials of all time, performed for a canned food product by a famous comedian on his own show, involved a recipe he was trying to make with the assistance of several beautiful girls. Testing of the commercial revealed that the audience loved it, but their response to the sales appeal was nil. The reason—too much silly irrelevancy during the demonstration.

The cheerfully irreverent approach toward a demonstration may not hold promise as the great future formula for selling on television, but now and then it catches competitors off-guard and stimulates talk and sales for the advertised product.

Over the years De Soto has successfully employed practically every conceivable type of demonstration to highlight the various features of the automobile. Atypic of these, however, was the light touch given a heavy subject in the commercial that follows. Regardless of its humorous animated treatment, a serious technical story was effectively told.

ANNOUNCER IN SHOW SET.

ANNOUNCER (On-Camera)

Here's a special guest—the well-known automotive engineer, J. J. Bibberly . . .

DISSOLVE TO ANIMATION:

MEDIUM CLOSEUP OF NICE-LOOKING LITTLE ENGINEER IN FRONT OF BLACKBOARD. HE BOWS SLIGHTLY.

ENGINEER (LIP SYNC)

(CLEARS THROAT) How do you do? I'm here to explain De Soto's new . . .

HE WRITES "TORSION-AIRE" ON BLACKBOARD.

. . . Torsion-Aire Ride. Many people have asked me—

MAN ENTERS.

MAN

*I* didn't.

ENGINEER

Didn't what?

• MAN

*I* didn't ask you.

ENGINEER

Well, you *should* ask, because De Soto's new Torsion-Aire Ride is the *smoothest, softest, steadiest* ride ever invented.

MAN

Oh, come now!

ENGINEER DRAWS IN COMPONENTS OF FRONT SUSPENSION SYSTEM AS HE TALKS.

ENGINEER

It's a new combination of proven suspension systems. On each front wheel, there's a torsion bar—

THE SYSTEM ANIMATES, AND THE WHEEL GOES UP AND DOWN. MAN LEANS AGAINST OUTSIDE FRAME INDIFFERENTLY.

MAN (REPEATING OBEDIENTLY)

Torsion bar.

ENGINEER

Combined with ball-joints—

MAN

Ball-joints.

ENGINEER

*Plus* Oriflow Shock Absorbers.

ENGINEER DRAWS REAR SUSPENSION.

And in back there are big outrigger springs, plus Oriflow Shock Absorbers. The result is —

ENGINEER DRAWS IN FULL FRAME. WHEELS ANIMATE, GOING UP AND DOWN, WHILE FRAME REMAINS LEVEL.

the *smoothest, softest, steadiest* ride ever. And better . . .

ANIMATED FRAME TURNS SHARPLY.

. . . roadability, better cornering.

ANIMATED FRAME COMES TO FAST, SMOOTH STOP.

and better stops—no lurching. And it's *safer,* too, because it's an *all-steel* construction.

MAN

Fiddlesticks! Today *all* cars ride good!

ENGINEER

But some ride gooder!

MAN

Look, Buster . . .

HE POINTS TO VERY CHROMED-UP TWO-DOOR HARD TOP, NOT A DE SOTO.

. . . hop into *my* car and you'll see.

*WIPE TO:*

BROADSIDE OF MAN'S CAR GOING OVER ROUGH ROAD. WHEELS ARE GO-

ING UP AND DOWN AND SO IS THE CAR.

        (SOUND EFFECT: RATTLING AND BANGING)

                *CUT TO:*

TWO-SHOT OF THEM IN FRONT SEAT, BOUNCING UP AND DOWN. MAN IS DRIVING, ENGINEER IS HANGING ONTO HIS HAT.

          MAN

F-feel th-the "F-f-floating on V-v-velvet Ride"?

              *WIPE TO:*

MAN GETTNG INTO DE SOTO FOUR-DOOR HARD TOP. ENGINEER IN PASSENGER'S SEAT.

          MAN

*Now* we'll try the *De Soto.*

              *WIPE TO:*

BROADSIDE OF DE SOTO GOING OVER ROUGH ROAD. WHEELS ARE GOING UP AND DOWN BUT NOT THE CAR.

        (MUSIC: SMOOTH-RUNNING VERSION OF "DE LOVELY." HOLD UNDER:)

              *CUT TO:*

TWO-SHOT OF THEM IN FRONT SEAT.

          ENGINEER

Well, sir, what do you think?

          MAN

There is a big difference! Safety-Flite is amazing!

              *CUT TO:*

CLOSEUP OF ENGINEER.

          ENGINEER

That's what everyone says when they try it.

          MAN

Amazing!

        ENGINEER (TO CAMERA)

I hope you'll try the new De Soto! Safety-Flite Ride makes a big difference!

MAN STICKS HIS HEAD IN.

          MAN

This De Soto is sensational! Drive it, and . . .

MAN HOLDS UP A DOTTED LINE.

. . . when they show you the dotted line—sign on it!

   7. *Technical Demonstration. Business Week* labeled the technical demonstration "technology for the common man."

Whatever else it may be called, the technical approach to a basic sales point can be beneficial provided the advertiser has sufficient commercial time to present his demonstration in a simple, understandable manner. One minute is seldom sufficient.

Ford Motor Company was one of the earlier explorers of this technique. On its program a man of scientific background described and demonstrated the complicated operations of automotive engineering. Indications were that the audience was genuinely interested.

This early series and most commercials since that time which have delved into the technical have actually been of a corporate nature. Such descriptions of technological advances generally represent sound examples to prove the broader over-all concepts and philosophies of the sponsoring company.

And so the futility of confining any demonstration strictly to any one category becomes evident. The Armstrong Excelon Tile service demonstration can also be regarded as "before-and-after." The Wisk "before-and-after" demonstration is also a form of service. The Bufferin side-by-side demonstration is symbolic as well. The De Soto demonstration is both humorous and technical, with a touch of "before-and-after."

But if categorizing succeeds in defining specific areas to be explored in search of hard-selling demonstrations, then the effort is more than justified.

### Safeguards

To derive the most impact from the demonstration he selects for his product, the alert copywriter is sometimes tempted to "lay it on" slightly more than the facts will allow. He would not be human if this were not so, for he is constantly competing with others of equal shrewdness and ability.

However, there are five forces extant to check any excess enthusiasm on his part: (1) the Federal Trade Commission; (2) the NAB Code (see Appendix); (3) the advertiser; (4) the viewer, who may not believe him; and (5) his own conscience. For the most part, point (5) wins out. Copywriters also know that deliberate misrepresentation of a product's performance can result in serious damage at the sales counter. For these reasons, most demonstrations in television commercials are honest in every sense of the word.

The only areas where the copywriter and the producer may resort to legitimate trickery are those where taking certain short cuts make for convenience in staging. Examples: The "dirt" that a vacuum cleaner picks up may be tiny hunks of cork or other material because dirt does not always photograph well. Strawberry jam may be tinted a lighter color lest it show up black on the film. "Cold, frosty" beer may be poured and photographed in a warm state to produce better foam. White icing may be off-white when it is filmed in order to prevent glare. All such alterations help make better-produced commercials, but in no way misrepresent the appearance or performance of the product.

# Making the Words Work

> *Words are also actions,*
> *and actions are a kind of*
> *words.*—Emerson

RECENTLY, in this modern, sophisticated era of television advertising, a well-known announcer brought a massive grumble from several million housewives because a copywriter became careless with one adjective.

As the lead-in situation in a cereal commercial, the announcer apparently tried to establish warmth and rapport with his viewers when he swung a golf club and remarked, "Well, whether you're a hacker like me, or just a plain housewife . . ."

Whether or not housewives are "plain" is not the point. They do not like to be called "plain" and there was probably little of that particular brand of cereal sold that fateful night.

The moral is, one word may not "make" a commercial but it can most certainly "break" it.

Television is primarily a visual medium, to be sure. However, an otherwise sound campaign, fortified with interesting scenes and a fighting theme line, can suffer if the copywriter neglects to give the spoken word its due.

These days too many copywriters devote too little attention to the audio, especially the "straight announcer" copy. By becoming overawed with the power of the pictures they tend to discount the power of the words, a sinfully extravagant habit in a medium as expensive as television. Considering the fact that the advertiser has only 180 seconds of commercial time in a half-hour evening program, he then pays more than *$600 per second* for the privilege of exposing and selling his wares. How, then, can a copywriter dare to take lightly *any* element of a commercial?

The same medium which eats entertainment material alive and requires almost unbelievable stocks of replenishment consumes commercial copy at an equal rate. If the talented performer must constantly change his material to survive the cold, penetrating stares of the vast millions, how then can the copywriter expect to convince this same audience that his product is "amazing" minutes after two or three other products have used the same tired word to describe themselves?

For this one reason alone the copywriter should continually search for fresher words, particularly in the area of verbs and adjectives, each time he composes a commercial message. (Other media were never this unjust!)

## 1. Kill the Cliché

Clever animated commercials and musical jingles automatically stimulate fresh words and sounds, but advertising cannot live on these alone. Most sound tracks are still spoken and will continue to be, thus demanding the full skills of the copywriter. The few "wordless" commercials attempted to date have been little more than interesting novelties.

As a starter, perhaps the most destructive suggestion can be the most constructive; namely, to destroy, to eliminate, to forget forever the following words and phrases, outlawing them from all future television commercials:

> amazing
> yes
> revolutionary
> what's more
> friends
> folks
> here's proof
> hello
> hi
> first thing tomorrow
> that's right

thanks to
you'll love
you've never
why not
remember

With these eliminated, the copywriter is ready for step two.

## 2. Don't Take the Ad Too Literally

Frequently the television copywriter, arriving late on the scene, consults a printed advertisement as his source of material. It is tempting, sometimes mandatory, for him to lift bodily more than the theme line for use in the commercial. As a result, words and phrases written to be *read* are sometimes fed into the unsuspecting mouth of the television announcer without regard to how they will *sound.*

This is neglect of the first order, for words are not generally arranged in the same order for use in the two media. The basic theme line, yes. Text copy, no.

Probably an even greater danger in literally adapting the advertisement to a commercial is the *quantity* of copy involved. Ads generally have room for stacks of words, but all can be arranged and "laid out" in the order of their relative importance. In a commercial every word is equally important at the time it is being spoken. For this reason, when the ad is adapted, only the heart of it should be used. And, except for the basic line, which must remain *stet* in all media, the copy should be rewritten to *sound* convincing.

Simply trying to read ad copy aloud can illustrate the point. The print copywriter is determined to make the best use of the available space. To accomplish this he or she often crams many thoughts or degrees of thought into one sentence. Such construction can be comprehended by a reader but not by a listener. For television consumption it has to be spooned out in smaller servings.

Excerpt from text copy in a printed advertisement:

Tests with more than 3,000 people over a 12-year period proved that those who gargled (name of product) twice daily had fewer, shorter, and milder colds than those who did not.

This one sentence, containing at least ten thoughts, can be read and reread, if necessary, in the ad. In a television commercial this same set of facts will be lost if told in the same concentrated manner. It must, in other words, be spread out and told more slowly, more simply.

An irate viewer wrote to the *New York Times:*

I think it's high time the television advertising community get hold of itself and do what it can now to save its reputation as an acceptable and effective advertising medium.

I'm talking about the commercial treatment of most programs and especially the national spot advertiser. It's no wonder the viewer cringes. He's blasted from outer space; forced to look at a warmed-over magazine or newspaper ad; slapped with a radio announcement with pictures, or dubiously entertained by a cartoon which gets lost in somebody's sales message.

Let's face it. Television is not just another advertising medium to be used as an outlet for conformed print or audio media. TV is a primary medium and, if anything, should conform to it.

Whether the letter was written by an "average viewer" or a television writer tired of being forced to adapt print copy to his own medium, the point was made—overstated slightly, but made.

However, as long as the copywriter is consulting the ad for his copy story, he may just as well look for lines he *can* use as well as for those he *cannot.* The following are excerpts from advertisements that could not be improved on for television:

"This tantalizing dish sets a sunny Mediterranean mood."

"Out of a famous dental clinic comes a totally new type of toothbrush."

"Wow! What an Easter holiday for the kids!"

"Homemade coffee cake—hot and heavenly good!"

But since it is the entity the television copywriter is finally concerned with, his job remains a creative one whether he is working from an ad, or—as is more often the case—from scratch with the basic facts.

### 3. Don't Overwrite

While the words the copywriter uses should be fresh and to the point, he should be especially cautious not to crowd too many into the allotted time. Probably the most common mistake in television commercials today is trying to say too much in the time allotted.

This fault stems from two sources:

1. The copywriter is worried that his pace will drag if he does not provide the announcer with a steady chatter.

2. The advertiser sees no harm in adding one or two more sales points to a scene even though the scene was origanally conceived to illustrate a far more important part of the story.

As far as pace is concerned, the copywriter can relax. Interesting pictures provide pace. A musical background, if the commercial calls for it, provides pace. A deliberate pause in the sound track as the scene completes itself does not have to slow down the commercial whatsoever, The viewer will not fall asleep so long as the commercial interests him.

Adding sales points, thereby filling every possible breath gap, complicates the commercial. It may not only sound hurried, but the total effect will have less impact because the additional minor points confuse the story.

The producer, when asked why the copywriter should not overwrite, will come up with a third reason: the script will need cutting. To him copywriters—even professional copywriters—are notoriously inept when it comes to timing. His advice is: "Time the minute script (fifty-eight seconds of audio) at least seven seconds short. I will guarantee you it will come out comfortably on time."

### 4. Relate Audio to Video

Here is where pictures take precedence over words. A wise rule is to "see" the commercial in the mind before "hearing" it. Analyze each scene for its ability to "stand on its own feet," then supply words only as they are needed to describe the pictures more fully or to forward the thought they express.

For example, when a demonstration is in progress, it should be labeled as such to command still more interest. Since it is probably proving a very basic sales point, the copywriter, to insure complete viewer comprehension, should make certain in this portion of the commercial that every word not needed to explain what the picture is already showing be devoted to *interpreting* the resulting benefit.

The following Coty script illustrates the ideal combination of words and pictures. The audio continually *reacts* to the pictures, *interprets* in a way that makes a sales point of virtually every scene:

| *VIDEO* | *AUDIO* |
|---|---|
| OPEN ON CAN-CAN SKIRTS BEING FLOUNCED FROM SIDE TO SIDE. | (French-type music under:)<br>CAN-CAN GIRLS (On-Camera)<br>Oo la la! |
| PULL BACK AND MATTE ON HAND HOLDING TRAY SO THAT GIRLS ARE DANCING ON TRAY. | It's Paris on a platter! |
| DISSOLVE TO HAZY BALLS OF LIGHT AND MOVE DOWN TO . . . | CAN-CAN GIRLS (O.C.)<br>It's the delicious hint of a French accent . . . |
| . . . MODEL IN AD. | FEMALE MODEL (O.C.)<br>Alo, mon cheri . . . |
| MOVE IN TIGHT ON HER FACE, FOR BEAUTY SHOT, SHOWING GLISTENING LIPS. | ANNOUNCER (V.O.)<br>It's the lipstick color that never was, but always should have been . . . |
| DISSOLVE BACK TO PLATTER OF PARIS, WHICH TILTS UP AND STARTS TO WHIRL, TURNING INTO COLOR WHEEL . . . | "French Spice" . . . not another red . . . but French for Red . . . a scarlet iced and spiced and gone plum wild . . . |
| . . . WHICH DISSOLVES TO LIGHTS AS BEFORE. SUPER: "FRENCH SPICE." | French Spice . . . |
| PAN DOWN TO CAN-CAN GIRLS KICKING. | Red with a *kick* in it . . . |
| DISSOLVE TO PARIS SCENE: SUPER OVER MODEL PUTTING ON LIPSTICK. | . . . the lipstick color that only Coty could fashion for the first truly *new* fashion look in years . . . |

| *VIDEO* | *AUDIO* |
|---|---|
| DISSOLVE TO LONG SHOT, MODEL IN DAYTIME DRESS. SAME BACKGROUND DAYTIME LIGHTING. | . . . to take you in triumph from dazzling days . . . |
| LIGHTS CHANGE TO EVENING. MATCH DISSOLVE TO MODEL IN EVENING DRESS. | . . . through brilliant evenings . . . adding its own French accent to everything you wear. |
| | ANNOUNCER (V.O.) |
| DISSOLVE TO PRINT MODEL. | French Spice . . . subtle seasoning whatever your coloring . . . |
| MATCH DISSOLVE TO SAME GIRL, BLONDE. | . . . whatever you want it to be! |
| CUT TO PRODUCT SHOT AGAINST GLAMOR BACKGROUND. SUPER: "FRENCH SPICE." | Why not season *your* fall fashions with French Spice . . . the Coty color with the taste of adventure . . . the promise of — |
| | ANNOUNCER (O.C.) |
| DISSOLVE TO PRINT MODEL. | —who knows? |
| | COTY GIRL (O.C.) |
| CUT TO COTY GIRL. RUFFLES UNDER HER HAT. | French Spice . . . the new color in Coty's incredibly rich French 24 lipstick and matching super-sheen nail polish. |

## 5. Write As People Talk

Better yet, be selective—write as *certain* people talk.

The reverse of this is related by the copywriter who was riding with the new owner of a certain automobile for which the copywriter created commercials. "On the hope I could get some true-to-life words for my commercial, I asked the owner what he thought of his car. 'Oh, it's really great!' said the owner. 'Finest car I ever owned! Really tops in my book!' Now, suppose I 'picked up' *those* words! People would accuse me of being phony! Don't tell *me* to write the way people talk!"

He had good reason to be skeptical. But people talk in other ways, too. The secret is to wait and listen.

The audio for the following Lucky Strike one-minute television film commercial script sounds like a real person talking. There is nothing trite about it. Dramatic pictures become more dramatic and more relevant with the use of dramatic words—words that could well be heard in intelligent conversation.

| *VIDEO* | *AUDIO* |
|---|---|
| OPEN ON LOW ANGLE SHOT OF AIR HAMMER OPERATOR IN ACTION. | (SOUND: Air hammer in sync, not too loud.) |
| OPERATOR STOPS DRILLING, TAKES A BREATH, LOOKS OFF SCREEN UNAWARE OF CAMERA. | (SOUND: Hammer out. Other construction effects off-camera under:) |
| CUT TO LEVEL MEDIUM CLOSEUP AS HE TAKES OUT A PACK OF LUCKIES. | ANNOUNCER (V.O.)<br>When this man digs into his shirt for a cigarette, he comes up with the genuine article. The name's— |
| TITLE "LUCKY STRIKE" ANIMATES ON IN SYNC. WITH BLASTS OF OFF-SCREEN AIR HAMMER. OPERATOR LIGHTS UP. | (SOUND: Two blasts of air hammer off-screen.)<br><br>—Lucky Strike. |
| CUT TO CLOSER SHOT, LOSING TITLE "LUCKY STRIKE." HE SMOKES UNSELF-CONSCIOUSLY. | A great many men know this cigarette well. They like the taste. It's *honest*— |
| TITLE "HONEST TASTE" CRAWLS UP, FOLLOWED BY LUCKY PACK. | —the honest taste of fine tobacco. |
| CUT TO CLOSEUP OF TRAIN WHEEL, SPARKS FLYING FROM BRAKE SHOES AS TRAIN GRINDS TO A STOP. | (SOUND: Sound of brakes, hissing of steam. Engine yard noises, etc. Not too loud.) |

| *VIDEO* | *AUDIO* |
|---|---|
| PULL BACK TO WIDE SHOT OF BRAKEMAN, AIR HOSE OVER SHOULDER, RIDING FREIGHT CAR WHICH IS ABOUT TO COUPLE WITH ANOTHER. HE IS SMOKING. | You can smoke on the job and *know* you're smoking . . . |
| CUT TO CLOSER SHOT AS TITLE "LUCKY STRIKE" COMES ON AND COUPLES WITH CARS. BRAKEMAN JUMPS TO GROUND AND COUPLES HOSE. | . . . when the one you smoke is—<br>(SOUND: Cars couple)<br>— Lucky Strike. |
| CUT TO CLOSEUP OF BRAKEMAN. HE HAS FINISHED COUPLING AND WALKING IDLY TOWARD CAMERA. HE SMOKES UNSELF-CONSCIOUSLY. | Never was a man who could forget<br>The taste of a genuine cigarette!<br><br>Get the honest taste a man can like— |
| POP ON PACK AT MIDDLE GROUND CAMERA RIGHT, ON BEAT AFTER "FORGET." ZOOM UP ON "TASTE." | The honest taste of a Lucky Strike. |
| CUT ON BEAT TO AIR HAMMER MAN AT SCREEN RIGHT, PACK ON LEFT. | The honest taste of a Lucky Strike.<br>GROUP (Singing)<br>(SOUND: Other yard effects off camera, under:)<br>Fine tobacco and no nonsense. |
| CUT ON BEAT TO TIGHT SHOT OF MAN, LOSING SUPERED PACK. | If you think that *sounds* good; wait'll you *taste* it. |
| ANIMATE ON TITLE: "THE GENU-INE ARTICLE" IN SYNC. | ANNOUNCER (V.O.)<br>Get the genuine article. |
| PAN LEFT LOSING MAN. TITLE | Get the honest taste . . . |

ANIMATES TO LINE WHICH FORMS
PACK AND WORDS "GET THE
HONEST TASTE OF A LUCKY
STRIKE," WRITE ON IN SYNC.

HOLD WORDS. FILL IN PACK IN          . . . of a Lucky Strike.
SYNC.

### 6. Suspect the Obvious

Among the experienced, there are two kinds of copywriters: those
to whom the words come easy and those who have to struggle. The
latter group generally writes the better copy.

It is still possible to be original in copy, but when words flow too
easily on the first draft there is every reason for the copywriter to
wonder whether he is not inadvertently copying phrases from other
commercials. Many copywriters automatically remember good copy
long after they hear it. Consequently in writing their own copy, trying
to separate the new from the familiar is not always easy.

### 7. Find the Right Word

In television—and in all of advertising—finding the fancy words is
not nearly so important as finding the *right* words. Coleridge defines
poetry as the best words in the best order. "TV copy need not be that
perfect, but the right words in the right order should be the standard,"
remarked one creative man.

Lincoln's Gettysburg Address, the Lord's Prayer and many other of
the world's masterpieces are composed primarily of short, simple
words, carefully selected, artfully arranged.

"If the copywriter has it tough, then the musical composer, with only
eight notes to play with, has it tougher," said an unsympathetic advertiser. "I want the words in my commercial to be the everyday variety—
short, crisp, to the point, and arranged in such a way as to sound vibrant
and lively."

### Our Complex Language

Several factors, said one student of words, tend to make us over-
pass language in our time. Among them is the complexity of our vo-

cabulary, with over six hundred thousand words in the largest unabridged dictionary, a million if technical terms were admitted. "The size of the language chills and appals us and makes us pick and choose."

The size of English vocabulary has, in fact, increased almost tenfold in slightly over a century. It has been predicted that the next hundred years will bring the English vocabulary to over two million words!

To the writer, especially the copywriter, probably the most neglected part of speech is the verb. Yet it is the verb that *moves* customers to action. Here is what Charles W. Ferguson, editor, author, and one of the nation's foremost authorities on words, had to say about verbs:

Precisely what any of us would get out of renewed study of the verb in conventional grammar, I do not know. But I do know that if we turned to the verb with an adult attitude, we would enhance our awareness. We might learn the wisdom of eschewing wherever possible any form of the verb "to be." We might learn the power of transitive verbs and the picture value of action verbs. We might note that verbs beat the time and mark the cadence of every effective sentence.

Mr. Ferguson adds:

The hallmark of the true writer is his concern with sound, with the rich diapason of language, the rolling undertone of what he has to say. And by this token and this tocsin, the person who would improve his prose for practical purposes must commence in a most impractical way: he must practice alliteration, cadence, rhyming, and learn to play with words as he would with bells. Only in this way can he hope to get the priceless quality of resonance into what he writes. His style may be clear and his words picturesque, but what he writes will be dead if it does not have sound.

Having pictures to aid him, the television copywriter is not exempt from the challenge of making the most of the words, for words plus pictures can tell far more—sell far more—than words alone. The old Chinese proverb about what one picture is worth is entirely fallacious.

"Advertising," pointed out advertising director Ken Pearson in a *Printers' Ink* piece,

is a craft of symbols, alliterations, rhythms, metaphors, and connotations. The copywriter, account executive, and the client struggle to establish word pictures that shout "desire," then "buy." Ad men are realizing that the real solution to consumer motivation exists right in our own language.

## Grammar

It is a bit difficult to handle words at all without a knowledge of basic grammar. One has only to visit a number of college classes to discover the frightening fact that many of them are overrun by students who were allowed to graduate from high schools with sixth-grade knowledge of the most basic subject on any curriculum.

One college instructor, horrified at the grammatical errors on homework papers in his advertising copy class, improvised a quiz on the simple use of the apostrophe. He wrote one short paragraph on the blackboard and asked each student to copy it, filling in the apostrophes. Although seven were missing, the average number filled in correctly by three copy classes, one year apart, was 3.7!

Ignorance of the proper use of the apostrophe is hardly grounds to condemn a copywriter or the commercial he creates; yet this is only one area of grammar where knowledge is sorely lacking among many otherwise well-educated young men and women. After all, to *express* an idea is fully as important as to *have* an idea. Copywriters without a firm background in the rules of grammar can find themselves at a disadvantage.

On the other hand, those who do not consider "grammar" a dirty word are in a position to make best use of the language in a field where the skillful turning of a phrase can make the difference in extra sales.

## Words Complete the Picture

Important as they are to the total commercial, words, regardless of their brilliance, should never call attention to themselves. The copywriter's goal in making the most of the words is to complete a strong over-all selling impression.

This is why the audio portions of many effective television scripts are not in themselves obvious examples of ingenious writing. The words can seldom, in fact, be isolated and judged on their own merits. A far more vital consideration in the selection and arrangement of words is the role they must play in the commercial entity.

As a guide to the relative importance of words and pictures, the copywriter is well advised to visualize the picture sequence first and then ask himself, "What words are needed to drive the story home?" rather than writing the audio portion first and then asking, "What pictures do I need to support these words?"

## chapter twelve

# Jingles

CONSIDERING all the products they have helped to sell, jingles deserve a higher-sounding name. The *Oxford Universal Dictionary* traces "jingle" back to 1599 and defines it as "a noise such as is made by small bells or loose pieces of metal when struck." By 1645, a kinder meaning: "Affected repetition of the same or similar sounds; a catching array of words, whether in prose or verse." But then it spoils everything by adding: "Chiefly contemptuous."

Herbert Hoover once denounced jingles. A radio station in Detroit once banned them from the air "in the public interest."

As a word, "jingle" has been abused for centuries. As a technique in advertising it has become a basic selling force that is known to have a positive effect on the movement of goods.

A properly conceived and executed jingle is capable of setting into motion an exciting chain of events. Once he hears it, the television viewer may soon start humming it to himself. After he hears it again, he is able to recall some of the message. When he shops, the sight of a label may trigger the music and words, including the basic theme line of the advertising. In other words, he has carried the message directly to the point of sale, and is often prompted by this reminder to reach for a particular brand of merchandise.

It is virtually impossible to underrate the selling power of the jingle. Precisely what transpires—the exact nature of the motivating elements —is difficult to determine through research. Yet the television viewer is definitely affected by jingles. One expert asserts, "All advertising except the singing commercial must sell to the conscious mind. The singing commercial creates an unconscious habit pattern and sells that way."

## Public Acceptance

Jack O'Brian, in his TV column in the *New York Journal American,* was referring to "rock 'n' roll" music when he wrote: "Few records on today's jukeboxes can truly be called good music. Most are just novelties. But commercials are beginning to evidence taste, musicianship, and even wit, all pressed into a minute; sometimes less. The reasons include better creativity."

The fact is, most jingles showed evidence of taste and musicianship years earlier. "In the eighteen years since Pepsi-Cola hit the spot with a jazzy version of the English ballad 'John Peel,' " reported *Time,* "the singing commercial has become as entrenched in U.S. culture as the madrigal in the Italian Renaissance." Even during early radio the jingle, while still a novelty, established itself as a musical form most of the public not only tolerated but actually enjoyed.

## When to Use a Jingle

There is hardly a product that cannot benefit from a well-written jingle. For regardless of the strength or weakness of the copy claims, a jingle sets the product still farther apart from its competition by giving it a unique personality that cannot be copied.

"But," observes the advertiser, "television is *loaded* with jingles. How do I know that mine will be noticed?"

The answer is, "That depends on your jingle and its frequency of use on the air. The fact that jingles are prevalent on television should not be a cause for worry but rather evidence of the jingle's ability to sell."

After all, music provides an inexhaustible source of catchy melodies. All the advertisers in the next thousand years will not even begin to tap it. Said Joseph Hornsby, one of television's most versatile jingle writers, "Beethoven wasn't discouraged by Mozart. Carmichael wasn't discouraged by Porter. Why should Smith's Beans be discouraged by Brown's Floor Wax?"

A jingle, then, is appropriate at any time for any product except:

1. Where its use would be obviously in bad taste.
2. Where the mood of the commercial may be of an especially serious nature throughout.

3. Where the amount of straight copy does not allow room.

4. Where other tricky audio effects dominate the audio.

There are times when the advertiser wants no jingle under any conditions. If he does decide on a jingle, however, he should remember that on-the-air repetition is supremely important. While it may be effective from its very first use, a jingle improves with age. The more it appears, the deeper it penetrates.

## What a Jingle Offers

Besides giving a product a distinct personality, a jingle is useful for the following reasons as well:

1. It registers the name of the product strongly in the mind of the viewer.

2. It plays up the basic theme line of the product.

3. It allows for constant repetition of the name, theme line, and other sales points which might become irritative if repeated as often by the spoken word.

4. It peps up and accentuates animated sequences in the video portion of the commercial.

5. It adds brightness and pace to many live-action scenes.

6. It gives the advertiser a proven technique already accepted by the public.

7. It becomes a property not only for television, but for radio, sales conventions, special trade promotions, and many other uses.

8. It is flexible. It can be created in both long and short versions, sung solo or by a group, played in various tempos by various combinations of instruments, even translated to foreign languages, without losing its basic identity.

## Where Jingles Originate

Because of the universal success of jingles in advertising, the average large agency employs one or more jingle writers on its permanent television and radio copy staff. These specialists create both the words, or lyrics, and the music. Most copywriters, too, write lyrics. If an existing melody is to be used, the copywriter and jingle writer will then, of course, both concentrate on lyrics only.

Many agencies and advertisers depend on a second source; namely, the independent contractor, who assumes responsibility for both creation and production of jingles. Within this area come scores of organizations ranging from those employing composers and arrangers down to one-man operations. Most have built their reputations solely on their work with advertisers. But also among them can be found song writer Frank Loesser of "Guys and Dolls" fame, conductor Raymond Scott, and many others renowned in the popular music field.

Jingles emanate from other sources as well. In a moment of inspiration more than one advertiser has created his own. This is not to imply that jingle writing is easy. Quite the contrary. It is a highly developed craft. And song writing experience by itself is generally not enough. The jingle writer must make every second count. He must understand advertising. He must be able to emphasize both lyrically and musically the vital elements of the advertiser's sales message.

## Qualities of a Good Jingle

A jingle is never an end in itself. Rather than call attention to itself, it should support and strengthen the video. These are the "musts" for an effective jingle:

1. The music must be simple. The viewer should be able to hum or whistle it—better yet, sing it—with very little "coaching."

2. The melody must be as different as possible from others on the air.

3. The melody must be pleasant to the ear. Regardless of style, it must not sound strident.

4. The jingle must never exceed fifty-eight seconds, but the shorter the better. Indeed the average of all jingles, by rough estimates, is eighteen seconds. Even these should be adaptable for use in shorter commercials.

5. The lyrics must be simple, direct, specific.

6. The lyrics must mention the name of the product more than once.

7. The lyrics must recite the basic theme line of the product and, if practicable, repeat it.

8. In recording the jingle, special attention must be given to diction. A group of singers is more prone to "muddy up" the lyrics than a solo voice. But the group may provide the desired sound and can easily achieve word clarity with skillful direction.

9. An attempt must be made to give the jingle a "twist," an identify-

ing mark over and above the melody itself. A sound effect, a pause in the singing, an unusual musical arrangement, or other such idea can give the jingle a unique sound.

## Where to Begin

"Which comes first—the words or the music?" The words—if the music is to be an original melody, as is the case with most jingles. Words come into being in various ways. One way is this: The television copywriter lists on paper the two or three most important selling lines the jingle should include. He then attempts to set up a mental rhythm, which may be suggested by the basic theme line, the name of the product, or one of its ingredients.

The next step is to apply this rhythm to all the material at hand. If a phrase other than the basic theme does not conform to the rhythm, the copywriter adds or substracts a word or two until it does. Up to now, chances are, he has had no specific melody in mind. The result is a rough set of lyrics which he then passes along to the music composer.

The composer takes liberties with all the words except the product name and the basic theme line. The rhythm usually suggests various melodies. He narrows them down to one and continues to "polish" the lyrics to fit. In the final stages, the melody itself may be altered until both music and lyrics merge as a smooth-sounding jingle. This process may take from a few minutes to a few days, depending upon the circumstances.

In the following lyrics, the MR-8 ingredient all but dictated a definite jazz rhythm. Being also a vital part of the copy story, the repetition of "MR-8" made both good jingle sense and good advertising sense.

> Zerex protects with MR-8!
> Zerex protects with MR-8!
> What makes Zerex Anti-Freeze so great?
> MR-8! MR-8!
> Zerex by Du Pont with MR-8
> Is anti-rust, anti-acid—won't evaporate!
> And what makes Zerex Anti-Freeze so great?
> MR-8! MR-8!

The "twist" in the lyrics and musical arrangement came on, of all things, the product name. A slide effect was applied to the "Z" in the word "Zerex." The vocal arrangement called for "Zzzzzzzzerexx" at the beginning of the jingle.

Campbell's Soup has long advertised the idea of soup every day. Hence the line, "Have you had your soup today?"

The following jingle contains this idea and others. The "twist" here is the repetition of the words "have you."

> Have you—have you—had your soup today?
> Campbell's of course! Campbell's, of course!
> Have you—have you—had your soup today?
> Campbell's tastes good! Mm-mm good!
> Have Campbell's every day—
> You get vitamins that way!
> Proteins and minerals, too!
> For breakfast or for lunch—
> For dinner or for brunch—
> Once a day, every day, have soup! Campbell's!
> Have you—have you—had your soup today?
> Campbell's, of course! Campbell's, of course!
> Once a day, every day, you should have a bowl of Campbell's soup!
> Have some Campbell's right now!

Rhyming of lines is not essential. Many jingles, in fact, have no rhyme at all.

## The Melody

Not all jingles are based on original music. The jingle writer has three sources from which to choose: (1) originals; (2) songs in the public domain; (3) popular songs, including "standards" and top hit tunes.

1. Original Tunes. There is no rule on when to tailor-make a tune to fit a product and when not to. The advertiser, in seeking the melody for his jingle, appraises the jingle talent and facilities available, considers the musical policies of his competitors, and weighs the following advantages and disadvantages.

*Advantages*

*a)* With an original tune, the advertiser publicly endows his product with a musical trademark which no other advertiser can duplicate.

*b)* By owning the song outright, the advertiser is not faced with periodic royalty payments to a publisher for its use.

*c)* An original song is carefully fashioned to make the most of the lyrics; and the lyrics, after all, represent the basic copy story.

*d)* An original tune is not likely to distract from the words, as might be the case when a familiar popular tune is used. In the latter case the viewer may sometimes be trying to recall the original lyrics rather than listening to the commercial words.

*Disadvantages*

*a)* An original may take slightly more time than an established tune to register in the mind of the public.

*b)* Since not all jingles are automatically successful, a very slight element of risk is involved in using a melody that has not already proven itself.

*c)* Any original involves risk of infringement on a presently copyrighted melody. To be on the safe side, the advertiser should insist on a thorough investigation and some sort of written clearance before the original is used.

2. Public Domain Tunes. A song may be copyrighted for a period of twenty-eight years. The copyright is renewable once. Consequently any song that is known to be older than fifty-six years is in the public domain and may be used without charge by any advertiser. The works of Stephen Foster and certain Gilbert and Sullivan songs are among countless possibilities within this category.

*Advantages*

*a)* The public domain song is free to the advertiser.

*b)* The melody is generally well established and needs less exposure to start the television viewer humming it.

*c)* By selecting a little-known "P.D." melody, the advertiser can achieve an almost positive uniqueness of sound.

*Disadvantages*

*a)* Again, if the melody is well known, it may distract by reminding viewers of the original lyrics rather than attracting attention to the advertiser's message.

*b)* The better public domain tunes are the obvious choices of many advertisers. "Annie Laurie," for instance, was once reported to represent seven products simultaneously in one southwestern city!

Furthermore a national advertiser spending millions of dollars on television may become extremely embarrassed upon discovering that the melody in "his" jingle happens also to belong to an automobile dealer in one community, a laundry in another, and a chain of shoe stores in another.

*c)* The writer is bound to be less flexible when he must style his copy to fit a tune rather than *vice versa.*

3. Popular Tunes. The popular song, on which copyrights are still in effect, may or may not be available for advertising purposes, depending upon the wishes of the authorized owner. If the song is available, a contract or other legal document is drawn up between the advertiser and the publisher, stating terms of payment, extent of use, and other pertinent facts.

The contract may, for example, allow the advertiser, for a stated price, to use the melody with his commercial lyrics for a period of three years on network television, spot television, network radio, and spot radio. It may also allow him to reprint the lyrics for promotional purposes and produce giveaway recordings. The advertiser is well advised to look beyond his immediate needs for the song to satisfy possible future uses.

*Advantages*

*a)* The "standard" and the current hit tunes ring a bell instantly in the consumer's mind. He is ready at the outset to snap his fingers to the melody.

*b)* Association with a newer song may indirectly dignify an advertiser in the public's mind.

*c)* Having received the rights to a top song, the advertiser can sometimes further exploit his musical property by engaging the singing star who helped popularize the song to sing the commercial version.

*d)* As in the case of the public domain tune, the more popular song sometimes "hits home" with certain products. Example: Cole Porter's "It's D'Lovely" provided De Soto with a strong musical campaign.

*Disadvantages*

*a)* Purchasing the rights to a popular song can be costly to the advertiser.

*b)* Again, the lyrics must conform to an already existent melody.

*c)* The popular song, even more than the public domain song, tends to remind the public of the original lyrics and can cause confusion when new commercial lyrics are substituted.

Luckily for the advertiser, however, the reverse is occasionally true. A recent Hollywood musical was to feature an elaborate production number of a favorite standard song, used in more recent years in the jingle of a national advertiser. At the preview the producer was horrified to hear the audience singing aloud the *commercial* lyrics as the star on the screen struggled with the song's original lyrics! Needless to say, this scene was deleted before the picture was released.

### The "Tag" Jingle

Some jingles are complete in six or seven seconds. Others are so constructed that a short entity of this length can be extracted for use in ten-second I. D. spots and in twenty-second chainbreaks. Another handy use for the short jingle is to "tag," or end, a longer commercial, since this short version invariably includes "name and claim"—the name of the product and the basic theme line.

A famous example of the short length is the six-second jingle for Pepsodent tooth paste:

> You'll wonder where the yellow went
> When you brush your teeth with Pepsodent!

For years Schaefer beer ran a campaign of I.D.s, featuring part of its basic theme in lettering on the screen in conjunction with live-action shots of various musical instruments. To the melody from each instrument, "For real enjoyment" appeared, then animated into a live glass of Schaefer beer as a voice sang: "Get Schaefer! It's real beer!"

### Jingle Recording

Creativity by no means ends once the lyrics and music are written. At the recording studio is where mediocre jingles can become good ones; good jingles, great ones.

On behalf of its client, the advertising agency calls on an outside contractor to supply singers and musicians, vocal and instrumental arrangements, and a conductor for the session. The agency producer and jingle writer supervise the recording.

Assuming for this discussion that the jingle involves both musicians and a group of singers, the producer may follow one of two procedures: (1) record instrumental and vocal simultaneously, or (2) make a "basic track" of the instrumental accompaniment first, then record the singers over the music track. While either way is satisfactory, there is a trend toward the latter method, which modern audio tape facilities now make possible.

Recording the accompaniment first enables the producer to devote full attention to each component of the jingle. It also helps the studio engineer to achieve a better level, or balance, between instruments and voices.

In this instance the music track is fed back either on a speaker with volume held low or on earphones to the singers as they add their voices to make the production complete. The combined version is then recorded on a second tape machine, with the musical track always intact on the first machine so that the singers can record as many "takes" on top of it as they wish.

Once the instruments and voices are properly combined, it is possible, if the producer so desires, to record the singers again, thereby doubling the number of voices heard in the jingle. The combined tape is placed on the first machine, fed back to the singers, and on cue they perform once again. Accompaniment and the double rendition of the singers is combined on the second machine.

"Multiple-track recording" offers infinite possibilities. For example, to the musical basic may be added voices singing in harmony. Added to this may be a solo voice. Then, on a fourth track may come a sound effect or other "gimmick." The producer is thus able to control each step and create the precise sound he is seeking in building his jingle.

Recording on tape has many other advantages, too, over the old-fashioned method of direct cutting of acetates. Tape can be played back immediately after each "take." Tape can be edited while the recording session is in progress. The announcer's spoken copy can even be recorded at an earlier or later session and combined with the jingle to comprise the complete commercial.

Modern studio acoustics, echo chambers, filter effects, improved microphones and highly-skilled technicians, too, are at the disposal of the advertiser. With such facilities it is no wonder that the composer and the producer remain creative during the recording session and generally come away with an even better sound than they had planned on paper.

## Singers

So popular is the jingle as a device for implanting the advertiser's sales message in the mind of the consumer that scores of vocal groups spend their full time—others a good portion of their time—in this type of commercial singing.

The Mellowlarks, Ginger Johnson, Bob Swanson, Lanny and Ginger Grey, Jimmy Carroll, the Satisfiers, Chuck Goldstein, the Ray Charles Singers, Honeydreamers, Blenders, Song Spinners, Skylarks, Phil Davis, Mac Perrin, George Nelson, Bernie Saber and Bob Sande and Larry Greene are only a few of the individuals, groups, and organizations who devote their anonymous skills to the cause of selling by music. Most can do the complete job for the advertiser, including creation of the jingle. When working with the larger agencies for the larger advertisers, only their singing and arranging talents are required since many of the top jingles on the air today are created by the agencies.

At the recording session, the singers' appraisal of their own work is most important. Each time a "take" is made, the singers listen critically along with the producer, and they themselves are often the best judges of the quality of the recording. If the producer is dissatisfied with the general style of singing or the particular arrangement, however, that is another matter. A major change is made, usually on the spot, and the session continues.

It is often said that the entertainment world knows nothing about advertising. Yet singers who make their livings in jingles soon learn that their efforts are not judged by aesthetic values so much as by cash registers. When they sing, their job is to sell rather than to impress the public with their abilities. The fanciest arrangement in the world is worthless if the lyrics are not easy to understand the first time the consumer hears the jingle.

## Emotional Appeal

All jingles have a "hard-sell" intent. Most have logical, reason-why lyrics. A few slant their lyrics to appeal more to the emotions. Many have time only to remind. But all aim to hurry the sale.

Regardless of the lyrics, there is no doubt that music does something to the emotions. Observed advertising specialist Joe Connor in *Advertising Agency Magazine:*

Jingles are often considered silly or nauseous by many sophisticates, but the fact is, the average listener likes them. Most people are emotional, and being emotional they aren't governed by facts. They are controlled by associations and suggestions, as any girl knows who wants to be kissed. She doesn't argue logically—she suggests, and gets action.

Television and radio jingles fit this suggestive, exciting emotional pattern. The jingle is a play on emotions, not an appeal to logic. It is dramatic and exciting— not an earthquake—but still much more stimulating than just a spoken message. And the jingle works by suggestion, association, repetition—not by proof.

The Gayla soap jingle is an example of the emotional appeal extended to the lyrics as well:

> I feel so gay! I feel so gay!
> Just had a Gayla bath!
> Just had a Gayla bath!
> Gee! It feels so good
> To take a Gayla bath!
> Ev'ry time you use it
> It beauty-treats your skin—
> America's first clear soap with Lanolin!
> For face and hands hooray!
> It's G-A-Y-L-A!
> Get that gay Gayla feeling today!

## Future of Jingles

"Products may change, campaigns may change, but jingles go on forever."

The abundance of singing commercials on the air today is not the reason many advertisers decide against them. Whenever a jingle seems appropriate, it is incorporated into the "act" without hesitation.

It seems unlikely that the high number of jingles in television commercials will appreciably increase in the coming years. The only area they have not noticeably penetrated is corporate, or institutional, advertising. One can imagine many valid reasons for not considering them in this regard.

On the other hand, by calling them "songs" instead of jingles, just as corporate commercials are often referred to as "messages," the musical touch, handled in good taste and with proper restraint, may well find its way into this broader area. Many subjects almost too delicate for words alone can be helped along by a touch of song.

Other than that, there is one type of jingle that has not yet reached maturity; namely, the one with novelty lyrics, an ideal companion to animation. Most of the humor today is accompanied by spoken words rather than song. By including humor in the jingle as well as in the accompanying animation, many commercials may score even higher.

## chapter thirteen

# Humor in Television Advertising

A man learns more quickly
and remembers more easily
that which he laughs at.
—Q. H. Flaccus, poet, wit,
and "Publicity Director of
the Roman Empire."

HUMOR is one of the most interesting, yet least understood, types of television advertising. For any advertiser determined to have his commercials noticed, talked about, and even praised, humor, well handled, is a sure-fire formula. An amusing commercial is a relief to the viewer. It entertains him. It makes the selling message easier to take. It elicits his favorable comment. Precisely to what extent it sells him varies with each product.

"But there is nothing funny about our sales story," says one advertiser. "If we don't play it straight, how can we expect the customer to take us seriously?"

"Aha!" says another. "Here's my chance to move in with an 'off-beat' approach while my competitor is beating the customer over the head!"

## Humor in Early Advertising

Wit in advertising antedates commercial television by many years. Will Rogers poked fun in all directions in writing advertisements for

173

Bull Durham. The famous old Chic Sale laxative series would be daring even today.

In 1927 one observer wrote:

Advertising has taken itself too seriously. Manufacturers seem to think their baked beans, non-metallic garters, windshields and folding umbrellas are as much a life-and-death matter to the public as to them. The light touch, the sense of proportion, have been missing. After all, fun is part of existence and has its place in any kind of literature, even the commercial kind, so why not crack a joke occasionally in paid space?

At about the same time Clinton M. Odell of the Burma-Vita Company, confronted with the problem of advertising Burma-Shave, had already spent a considerable sum in campaigns of one kind or another without notable success when he decided to test a new idea—the placing of a series of road signs at short intervals, each carrying a few words of a sequence to give automobile drivers and passengers a smile along with a light selling message.

"Experts" of the day predicted the signs would be a waste of money. Advertising, they reasoned, must prove the superiority of a shaving cream with statistics, testimonials or the old "smiling face" at the top of the column.

But Mr. Odell bought up some old lumber, cut it to size and planted the road signs anyway—six in a series. One read:

> Does your husband
> Misbehave?
> Grunt and grumble
> Rant and rave?
> Shoot the brute some
> Burma-Shave.

Success was instantaneous.

Standard Oil, Flit, Socony, Venus Pencil, 3-in-1 Oil, and Dole Pineapple were also among the early users of humor. Proponents of the new fun approach were calling for more. "Advertising does not have to be cloaked in sackcloth and ashes," cried one. "The most ennuied yawns in this world are elicited from serious advertising," claimed another. A third even tried to list those advertisers who could *not* successfully use humor in their advertising. All he could think of were undertakers, charitable organizations, insurance companies, and churches. "And," he added, "maybe some of these *could* use it."

Yet proportionately few advertisers have capitalized on the risibility of the buying public down through the years.

## Enter Television

The most talked-about commercial of early television was the weekly Sid Stone pitchman act for Texaco on the Milton Berle program. While this series appealed to many as extremely funny, it could hardly be called the forerunner of the humorous commercial as we know it today. Almost the first three-quarters of Stone's act consisted of an irrelevant routine of fun for fun's sake and bore no relationship whatsoever to the product being advertised. Today's humorous commercials are a more harmonious blend of mirth and selling from start to finish.

True to tradition, the light approach to TV commercials remains, and will probably always remain, the exception rather than the rule. Surprising it is, however, that more advertisers do not investigate this route, considering the marked success certain products can attribute to it.

It is also interesting to note that, of the minority of advertisers who have chosen the comical mood for their television campaigns, many have stayed with it and applied it to their print media as well.

Most humorous campaigns in television employ cartoon animation as the main visual technique. The Chinese baby trying desperately to eat Jell-O with chop-sticks, the motorist so in love with the Chevron Supreme gasoline pump that he rips it out and takes it home in his car, the father resorting to every trick in the book to persuade his child to eat Maypo—these are but three of the delightful "gems" executed in animation.

It is a bit more difficult to make humor "come off" in live-action commercials. Where real people are involved, the whimsy is more forced and often more short-lived. This is not to imply that an effective commercial cannot be built on live-action comedy, but more seem to fail by use of this technique than by use of animation.

## Humor As an Art

Humor is not alone style, not mere juggling with the incongruous and the ridiculous. Humor is an art, and when combined with salesmanship it becomes a form of persuasion that stands out in advertising. A truly humorous commercial, executed in good taste and including just the right amount of sell, requires skill to create.

Wrote George Herbert centuries ago:

> All things are big with jest: nothing that's plain
> But may be witty, if thou hast the vein.

Not every television copywriter "hast the vein." Humor, it has been said, lies more in the power to see realities behind outward appearances than it does in the power of expression. "The humorist needs intuition more than intellect." The copywriter needs *both,* plus a knowledge of the principles of selling, plus the power of expression. The television audience, it should be remembered, is exposed to comedy shows regularly and anything less than a professional job is not likely to impress.

A humorous commercial consists of more than funny little characters rushing around madly. It must begin where all good advertising begins—with a selling idea. Conceiving such ideas and applying them to everyday products take some doing.

Examination of the video as well as the audio columns of the following one-minute film commercial script clearly reveals a most serious, hard-selling undertone packaged into a most pleasantly amusing presentation.

| *VIDEO* | *AUDIO* |
| --- | --- |
| OPEN ON LIVING ROOM SCENE WITH NEWSPAPER ON FLOOR, EMPTY EASY CHAIR STATIONED IN FRONT OF A TV SET. ON TV SCREEN: "CHEVRON SUPREME." | WESTBROOK VAN VOORHIS (V.O.)<br><br>When new Chevron Supreme gasoline . . . |
| WORDS ON TV SCREEN ROCKET OUT OF THE SET INTO THE LIVING ROOM. START SLOW PAN RIGHT. | (SOUND: Exploding rocket)<br>. . . burst on the scene, the American motorist . . . |
| CONTINUE PAN RIGHT TO PICK UP CHEVRON MALE CHARACTER WALKING INTO KITCHEN, OPENING REFRIGERATOR DOOR AND DRAGGING OUT A QUART OF MILK. CHARACTER YAWNS. | (SOUND: Click of refrigerator door being opened)<br><br>(SOUND: Loud yawn)<br><br>. . . greeted it with rare enthusiasm and exuberance. |

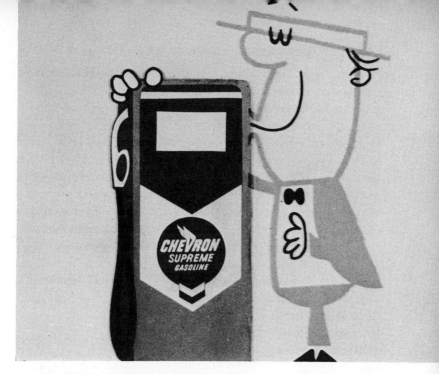

Fig. 30—SO IN LOVE with the Chevron Supreme Gasoline pump was this animated motorist that he ripped it out, tossed it in the back seat of his car, and drove it home with him, but not without serious reasons.

| *VIDEO* | *AUDIO* |
|---|---|
| HE POURS HIMSELF A GLASS OF MILK, TAKES A BIG GULP. | He digested each amazing fact... |
| HE PUTS DOWN GLASS ON TABLE, GETS INTO HIS SUIT COAT, PUTS HIS HAT ON, AND WALKS OUT OF THE KITCHEN. | (SOUND: Walking) |
| CUT TO CHEVRON CHARACTER AS HE EMERGES FROM HIS HOUSE, VAULTS A KID'S WAGON IN HIS PROGRESS TOWARD HIS CAR—A FUTURISTIC-STYLED AUTOMOBILE. OVERHEAD FLIES AN AIRPLANE TRAILING A BANNER THAT READS: "NEW CHEVRON SUPREME." | (SOUND: Put-put-put-put of old-time biplane)<br><br>... gave his undivided attention to each communiqué. |

| *VIDEO* | *AUDIO* |
|---|---|
| HE SWINGS OPEN DOOR OF THE CAR, HOPS INTO THE DRIVER'S SEAT, AND HEADS HIS CAR INTO TRAFFIC. | He learned that . . . |
| DRIVING ALONG, CHEVRON CHARACTER PASSES BILLBOARD WITH WORDS: "CHEVRON SUPREME GASOLINE." | (SOUND: Whoosh of speeding cars) <br> . . . new Chevron Supreme is a super-premium fuel . . . |
| STILL OBLIVIOUS, HE SWINGS HIS CAR IN A NEW DIRECTION PRECISELY AT THE POINT A ROAD SIGN ANNOUNCES "CHEVRON SUPREME AHEAD." | . . . that will deliver all the mileage . . . |
| HE CONTINUES TO DRIVE ALONG, UNAWARE OF FLASHING SIGN THAT TELLS THERE IS A CALSO STATION AHEAD. | (SOUND: Traffic noises) |
| HE PASSES ANOTHER CHEVRON SIGN THAT INDICATES HE IS HEADED AWAY FROM THE CALSO STATION. AT THIS POINT, HIS CAR RUNS OUT OF GAS. | (SOUND: Sputtering noises of car running out of fuel) <br> . . . all the better performance built into his car. |
| CUT TO CHEVRON CHARACTER RUNNING UP TO A CHEVRON SUPREME PUMP. HE CARRIES AN EMPTY BUCKET IN HIS HAND. BEHIND HIM ARE SIGNS: "CALSO STATION" AND "CHEVRON SUPREME GASOLINE." | (SOUND: Patter of running feet) <br> He was drawn irresistibly to the Calso station. |
| AS HE STANDS NEXT TO THE CHEVRON PUMP, IT SUDDENLY DAWNS | Without hesitation he said . . . |

| *VIDEO* | *AUDIO* |
|---|---|
| ON HIM THAT THIS IS THE GREAT NEW GASOLINE HE HAS BEEN HEARING SO MUCH ABOUT. HE FLIPS. | CHEVRON CHARACTER<br>Fill-'er-up! |
| PUMP ANIMATES INTO LABORATORY RETORTS AND BEAKERS. HE HOLDS UP HIS BUCKET AS ONE OF THE BEAKERS POURS OUT GASOLINE. | (SOUND: Gas pouring into bucket and pump ringing out gallons)<br>VAN VOORHIS (V.O.)<br>And from that moment on . . . |
| HE PUTS HIS ARM AROUND THE CHEVRON PUMP AND HUGS IT FONDLY. | . . . an indivisible bond was formed between the American motorist . . . |
| BEAKERS AND RETORTS REANIMATE INTO PUMP. CALSO CHARACTER, SMILING MADLY, LIFTS UP THE CHEVRON PUMP AND RUNS WITH IT TO HIS CAR. | . . . and this great super-premium gasoline. |
| HE PUTS THE PUMP IN THE BACK SEAT AND THEN HOPS IN THE FRONT. | Try Chevron Supreme . . . |
| HE STARTS HIS CAR AND HEADS DOWN THE HIGHWAY, PASSING FLASHING SIGNS THAT READ "NEW CHEVRON SUPREME GASOLINE" AND "SUPER OCTANE FUEL." | . . . a super-octane fuel for . . . |
| CUT TO ANOTHER SET OF CALSO-CHEVRON SUPREME SIGNS AND BILLBOARDS. FRONT OF CHEVRON CHARACTER'S CAR COMES INTO FRAME FROM LEFT. | . . . today's horsepower! |

| VIDEO | AUDIO |
|---|---|
| CUT TO CLOSEUP OF HIM DRIVING ALONG. HE LOOKS TOWARD THE CAMERA AND SPEAKS. | CHEVRON CHARACTER<br>You know, this stuff is great! They oughta advertise it! |
| CUT TO CLOSEUP OF CALSO LOGO ("CALSO STATION") AND WORDS: "CHEVRON SUPREME GASOLINE." | |

### Sell—"Soft" or "Hard"

Probably the most overworked phrases in the business of television advertising are "hard sell" and "soft sell." The former is used to refer to the straight, factual, reason-why approach; the latter, to encompass the lighter styles, including humorous commercials.

Charles H. Brower laid both expressions to rest when he observed, "There is no such thing as 'hard sell' or 'soft sell.' There is only 'smart sell' and 'stupid sell.' "

His point was that any effective commercial or advertisement results from serious "hard.sell," regardless of the approach. Good-humored warmth simply breaks down the barriers between advertiser and consumer and builds up a state of positive friendliness and trust—even gratitude and generosity.

Who could ever call the following Jell-O commercial anything less than "hard sell"? The situation, funny as it is, is based entirely on the product and its various flavors.

| VIDEO | AUDIO |
|---|---|
| ANIMATION:    JELL-O-PACKAGE. POP ON CHINESE CHARACTERS. RAISE CURTAIN ON . . . | (SOUND: Gong) |
| . . . CLOSEUP OF CHINESE BABY IN HIS HIGH CHAIR WAITING EXPECTANTLY. | (VOICE OVER): Beg to plesent ancient Chinese pantomime, "Just for fun of it, Jell-O tonight." |
| PULL BACK TO SEE BABY IN BAMBOO HIGH CHAIR. | Beg to plesent small, Chinese-type baby waiting for dessert. |

Fig. 31 — "BEG TO PLESENT small, Chinese-type baby waiting for dessert." Humorous approach to Jell-O commercial sells hard on flavor.

| *VIDEO* | *AUDIO* |
|---|---|
| CHINESE MOTHER HOBBLES IN, BEARING SHIMMERING MOLD OF JELL-O FOR BABY. | Chinese mother bling baby Jell-O—famous Western delicasy. |
| THE BABY STRUGGLES IN VAIN WITH JELL-O AND CHOPSTICKS. THE JELL-O SLIPS THROUGH, BOUNCES, JUMPS, AND AVOIDS HIM. | Poor Chinese baby—he unable to tell if this Jell-O is stlawbelly, lasbelly, chelly, olange, lemon, lime, apple, black lasbelly, black chelly, or glape! (Jell-O come in all ten flavors.) |
| THE BABY CRIES OUT IN FRUSTRATION. | (Sympathetically) Poor Chinese baby! |
| CHINESE MOTHER BRINGS THE BABY A SPOON. HE LOOKS PUZZLED, BUT HE STOPS CRYING. | But—Chinese mother bling baby gleat Western invention, spoon! |

| VIDEO | AUDIO |
|---|---|
| HIS MOTHER TAKES A SPOONFUL AS HE WATCHES WITH GREAT IN- TEREST. | Spoon was invented for eating Jell-O. |
| SHE HANDS HIM THE SPOON, AND HE TRIES IT TENTATIVELY. | Baby finds this Jell-O glape Jell-O. Is deep, dark and deli- cious new flavor. |
| ONE TASTE, HE BEAMS ALL OVER AND REALLY DIGS IN. | Chinese baby velly happy. So end ancient Chinese pantomime . . . |
| DOLLY BACK ON BABY HAPPILY EATING JELL-O. | . . . "Just for Fun of It, Jell-O Tonight." Is plenty good com- mercial, no? |
| WIPE ON JELL-O PACKAGE FULL SCREEN. | MUSIC: J-E-L-L-O! |

## When to Use Humor

There can be no general rule for selecting or rejecting humor for any specific commercial since much depends upon current conditions and the cleverness of the proposed concept. These are the exceptional situations where humor rates studied consideration:

1. For products whose television commercials enjoy sufficient frequency to register a new lighthearted image on a broad scale.

2. For products whose primary appeal is *taste*.

3. For products which have lacked new features over a number of years.

4. For products needing a sharp change-of-pace in their advertising.

5. For products lacking significant exclusive features or other marked advantages over competing products.

6. For products which suggest fun and pleasantry in their usage.

7. For products which do not rely for their selling on detailed live-action demonstrations.

## Implanting the Image

Once he decides on a humorous campaign in television, the advertiser should also decide to give it a fair trial before attempting to judge

Fig. 32—HUMOROUS APPROACH to bug killer required careful art styling. Bugs could be neither too cute (so that killing them would appear inhuman) nor too realistic (viewers might object).

its merits. If the approach is new to him, he is then actually changing the image of his product in the public eye. He is giving his product an entirely new personality, which will assuredly score strong first impressions—and perhaps early sales results—but which cannot be appraised until the wearing qualities of the campaign have been more accurately determined.

Fortunately most humorous commercials wear well on the viewer. While new ones should be added at intervals to keep the campaign fresh, the mileage on each commercial, provided it is skillfully conceived, is probably greater than that of any other type.

How long should the advertiser who puts a smile in his advertising wait around for something to happen? One may feel a sales stimulus in a matter of days. Another may wait months or more. Strictly an arbitrary suggestion would be to keep faith for at least six months. One brand of beer reportedly waited much longer before the public stopped laughing long enough to buy the product.

While the advertiser should most certainly give such a campaign every chance to work, he should not be tricked into interpreting public praise for his advertising as a completely reliable sign that good things are about to happen saleswise. Favorable comment is all some humorous television campaigns ever attain, and this can hardly be considered the ultimate reward.

### When Not to Use Humor

"Humor in television advertising," stated TV copywriter William Robinson, "can boomerang. It may help you gain and hold attention. It may create a likable, low-pressure atmosphere around your product. But, if not delicately handled, it can alienate the very people you are trying to sell."

There are products—there are situations—where too light a touch can be dangerous. Again, one set of rules cannot apply in all cases, but an advertiser weighing the idea of humorous commercials can profit by keeping in mind the following list of "don'ts."

1.  Have fun with the product, but don't make fun of it.

2.  Don't satirize too strongly the people who use the product and believe in it, nor the people who will try the product for the first time.

3.  Don't be funny in situations that normally are not funny, such as those dealing with health or safety.

4.  Don't be funny just for the sake of being funny. Direct all whimsy to important copy points.

5.  Don't be subtly humorous lest the viewer miss the point and react negatively.

6.  Don't try to be humorous and extremely serious within the same commercial. Commercials are too short for abrupt changes of mood.

7.  Don't resort to humor when your product has vast sales advantages which can be convincingly demonstrated by live-action. Here the light approach may weaken believability.

*Printer's Ink* quoted Stan Freberg, radio and TV satirist who now freelances for agencies and advertisers, as follows:

> Humor is a fragile thing, which in the hands of a novice is like a gun in the hands of a child. You just don't start off whimsically, then clear your throat and say, "But seriously, folks." That's when the consumer's mind goes out to lunch. The woman of the house is badgered by so many bad, loud, irritating commercials on both radio and television, it's a little hard to get the message through the scar tissue.

## Touches of Humor

Humor does not have to be the basis of a campaign to be useful in television commercials. If the change of mood which follows it is not too pronounced, a humorous situation is often appropriate at the beginning of a commercial as a bid for extra attention.

Starting off with a relevant and amusing bit of animation can set up, and even exaggerate, a problem to be solved by a straight, down-to-earth, live-action sequence.

Some serious commercials, too, are strengthened by signing off with a smile. The closing scene may be an animated expression of the basic theme line executed in a manner which the viewer is likely to remember.

## Humor in Perspective

Humorous commercials are fun to create. They are fun to watch. Yet they are in the minority on television and will remain so because more advertisers are convinced that the superior features of their products should be spelled out more directly.

An advertiser doubtless derives some value from having viewers talk favorably about his advertising. And a humorous campaign stands a better-than-average chance of delivering this value. Furthermore, the light approach has proven its ability to sell merchandise.

However, the same positive effect can be achieved by methods other than humor. The use of a jingle, gay background music to soften the mood, a smile in the voice of the announcer, the re-enactment of happy situations—all these help the advertiser attain what he believes to be the right mood for selling his product. Beyond this, he considers his product newsworthy and generally elects to use his few commercial seconds informing, demonstrating, and directly asking for the order.

Yet, lest he fear that by adopting the humorous approach he is moving contrary to public emotions, may he find comfort in these premises:

1. Most people have a sense of humor.
2. A shopping expedition is essentially a pleasant experience.

Any television commercial which begins with this in mind is treading on safe ground.

## chapter fourteen

# Talent in Television Commercials

OF all the steps in the commercial-making operation of television, one of the most painstaking should be the selection of talent—announcers, actors, celebrities, singers, dancers, and models. At least one of these is a part of every commercial except in those rare, freakish cases calling for only an instrumental music sound track or no sound track at all.

Very few products or services are sufficiently unique or appealing to "sell themselves" to the divergent television audience. Most have to be *sold,* and it takes a voice and often a face to help communicate the selling message. More accurately, it takes a *person,* a *salesman,* who knows that to sell a product he must first sell himself—and he must do so in a matter of seconds.

If a company exercises care and patience in picking and training its salesmen for stores and for calling on customers in the field, then surely it should fuss even more over the person who will represent it before millions of customers and potential customers on every network telecast. The person chosen to represent the advertiser becomes a corporate personality who, over the course of a single season, has a thousand—perhaps a million—times more contact with the consumer than the president of the company, chairman of the board, sales manager, or any individual salesman. As the announcer, he is *it* at the moment of telecast. The same applies to national spot advertisers and local advertisers whose messages also are aimed at vast numbers of people.

From results gained in testing several different announcers, each delivering the same commercial, research reveals that the ability of the individual announcer has a direct bearing on the effectiveness of the commercial. This is especially true when the announcer appears on the screen. Actors and models, too, have an effect on how well the commercial performs.

So it is understandable that the advertiser, the producer, and casting director often devote many hours to searching out the best available talent.

### The Commercial Announcer

Contrary to the opinion of many outside the business, announcing on-camera for a television commercial requires an uncommon amount of skill. When the announcer "steps into the living room," he steps in not to visit nor to entertain, but to sell. By nature most people do not enjoy being sold to. So the television announcer, regardless of how well his copy is written, must break through this sales resistance, hold the attention of his viewers, and then put over a strong sales story, usually in sixty fleeting seconds, or less.

There is probably much truth in the saying about first impressions counting the most. Wrote Christopher Marlowe in the sixteenth century:

> Let it suffice,
> What we behold is censured by our eyes.
> Where both deliberate, the love is slight;
> Who ever loved that loved not at first sight?

By appearance as well as by action the announcer must appeal instantly. If he pleases, he attracts. If he annoys, he repels. It is impossible for him to leave *no* impression when he stands before the cruel camera. A smile, a wrinkling of the forehead, a sparkle in the eyes, a twitch of the head—even these seemingly minor traits may telegraph his entire personality before the business of selling begins. And during the commercial the announcer must present the copy points and prove his own sincerity at one and the same time.

Being an intimate medium, television breeds familiarity. Besides making the right first impression, the announcer must "wear" well as a trusted friend.

Poise and confidence, qualities announcers worked hard to acquire during the early days of television, are taken for granted now. Today the struggle of most professional announcers is to avoid *too much* poise and overconfidence because these may suddenly become faults and label them as "phony."

Announcing off-screen, or "voice-over," for the television commercial is quite a different story. Here, as in radio, the voice is the thing, and its powers to attract or distract are far less pronounced.

PERSONAL QUALITIES. Networks, advertising agencies, and talent services have compiled many lists of requirements for the commercial announcer. A study of these, supported by interviews with many of the top announcers, reveals the following to be of prime importance:

*A clear voice.* While a deep tonal quality may be desirable, it has become almost too commonplace on both television and radio over the past few years. True, the high-pitched voice may grate on the nerves of viewers. But the area in between provides opportunity for an entirely new range of sounds. The trend, in fact, seems now to be toward this middle ground, where the whole personality has more room for free expression. But whatever the voice, it must speak the words distinctly, convey the message unobtrusively. It should never call attention to itself. And for network performance, a voice devoid of local or regional dialect is generally desirable.

*A pleasant personality.* Seldom does any announcer appear unfriendly. However, he may go wrong by trying too hard to be friendly. Instead of being himself and trusting the camera to notice, he may inadvertently force himself artificially to appear as a "nice guy." Unfortunately, when this happens, the audience senses it at once. A pleasant personality projects best when the announcer assumes a humble, sensible attitude toward his message.

*Intelligence.* As far as is known, no announcer has ever been asked to show his college diploma. Yet here, as in any vocation, formal education is a useful thing. The intelligent announcer concerns himself more with *what* he is saying than *how* he is saying it. Intelligence has a way of showing through, making the sales story more convincing to the television audience.

*Flexibility.* Granting that the announcer should "be himself" when he sells on television, he must also be sufficiently flexible to respond to professional direction. This does not mean he will be asked to strain out of character. But within the realm of his natural delivery he should be able to slant his emphasis in any of a number of directions. Another reason for flexibility: the announcer may sell one product tonight and another type of product tomorrow night. As products differ, so do the advertising approaches that sell them and so do the people who write the scripts and produce and direct the commercials. The announcer must adjust to these differences and still come out looking and sounding like himself.

*Sincerity.* This without doubt is one of the most overworked words in the advertising business. But sincerity must register or the cause is lost. The television camera has the insidious power of "looking through" the announcer and publicly baring his soul. If sincerity is not there to begin with, then no amount of acting can provide it. Sincerity is easy to come by, however, when the announcer honestly believes that what he is selling is the best there is.

*Stamina.* The busy announcer is under constant time pressure. If he is on the staff of a station or network, he is ruled by the clock. He may do many commercials in the course of a day in addition to announcing station breaks, time signals, news, weather reports, panel shows—whatever the schedule demands. If he is freelance, he must rush from one program or shooting session to another and be on time. His hours are irregular, his meals the same. He must rehearse under hot lights. If he is announcing for film, he must often do many "takes" of the same scene. And through it all he must maintain a neat appearance, a bright-eyed look, and plenty of enthusiasm.

There is no denying that good contacts and just plain luck are helpful to an announcer, too. But once he gets the job, only talent and know-how can hold it for him. Stated talent representative, Charles B. Tranum, "The best television selling style must include a *knowledge* of the product, a good *feeling* for the product, and *enthusiasm* for the product."

PICKING THE RIGHT ANNOUNCER. Concerned at one time by the quality of announcing on network television, I devoted one of a series of articles in *Sponsor* to the subject of talent. In it I offered advertisers eight suggestions for selecting announcers. They still apply.

1. Look for a type who is personally likable, even when he is not performing. Pick him as if you were picking a son-in-law—and this time you have something to say about it.

2. Beware of the "smoothie." He is "conning" only himself.

3. Be sure the candidate has sufficient experience to insure you against a nervous "freeze-up."

4. Match his age bracket to the age appeal of your product.

5. Look for a type who can memorize speedily and whose eyesight is adequate to enable him to read a cue card when one is needed.

6. Self-confidence is second in importance only to humility. No announcer should talk down to a camera lest it up-end him.

7. Encourage suggestions on the part of the announcer as regards the commercial copy, but not to the extent that a serious issue may delay the rehearsal.

8. Be sure the announcer is thoroughly familiar with your product. By exposing him to the full story you will find it easy to test his enthusiasm for what he is selling.

Many a commercial, mediocre from the standpoint of copy and production, is saved by the right salesman. The wrong salesman has an equal chance of neutralizing outstanding copy and production.

HELPING THE ANNOUNCER GIVE HIS BEST. "The announcer," one saying goes, "is as perishable as a head of lettuce. After being picked, he must be properly handled."

The idea could have been stated in a kinder manner, but the thought is there. Announcers are individuals and should be treated as such. Furthermore every announcer is different in temperament, rhythm of speaking, and pace of performance. This is as it should be, for this difference in personality among announcers is reflected in a difference in personality among commercials.

It is a mistake ever to consider the announcer as an "end man" to whom the commercial is "thrown" after all the thinking has been done. This applies particularly to the announcer who has a more or less permanent association with the product or service. He should be let in on the story, given the background, made to feel a part of the team. While the strategy for selling the brand may be out of his province, the announcer should be taken into confidence whenever conditions permit.

"On the air," says one announcer, "you say things in an entirely different manner when you're personally posted about the product. It comes through!"

Even a detail like his script being delivered to him well ahead of time can help the announcer by allowing him to study the commercial message and appreciate its full meaning before facing the camera.

ANNOUNCER LOYALTY. Most times the advertiser has complete control over who will deliver his commercials. It goes without saying he is careful to select an announcer who is not announcing for, and has not recently announced for, a competitive product.

Complications sometimes arise in the varied television activities of multi-product companies. For instance, should the announcer who sells toothpaste on television for Company "A" be allowed to appear in a detergent commercial for Company "B" even though Company "B" manufactures and advertises a toothpaste competitive with that of Company "A"? Chances are, both companies would feel he should not because by representing a product he is representing a company and may be in a position to learn some basic sales secrets of that company.

It sometimes happens that, upon being dropped by one advertiser, the announcer soon ties up with a competitor. In such an event the announcer cannot be blamed for a breach of trust since he makes his living by selling on television. If his performance is voice-over, or off-camera, the public is not likely to notice it anyway.

Does the announcer who delivers commercials for more than one noncompeting advertiser lose effectiveness by spreading his reputation too thin? Or, as one wit put it, "Do too many broths spoil the cook?"

There is no flat answer, but a Schwerin Research Corporation analysis indicated that such "multi-product presenters" generally make out creditably. "There was no indication that personalities suffer from taking on more than one brand," stated the report. "On the contrary, they generally have a better than average record. Of all the cases studied, half were above par in effectiveness, a fourth were average and only a fourth were below par."

"However," Schwerin points out, "it should not be concluded that buying the services of a spokesman who is already working for a couple of other brands is a sure-fire method of achieving advertising success. The presenter's personality must strike viewers as suited to your product, and your story has to be one he can logically deliver."

FEMALE ANNOUNCERS. Up to now the use of the masculine pronoun in referring to announcers has been simply for convenience in writing. Certainly the same qualities discussed apply to female announcers as well.

Saleswomen are not so numerous as are the opposite sex on television, principally because most advertisers prefer to have their commercials delivered by men. Research in this area is inconclusive, but indications are that in general men prefer to be sold to by men; and women prefer salesmen for certain kinds of products and saleswomen for others. There is no definite rule.

In longer commercials the feminine voice is generally considered to be more effective when a male voice is used to balance it off. Sixty seconds or more of selling copy can put a strain on a woman's voice, which by nature is less flexible than a man's in changes of mood and emphasis. Betty Furness, Barbara Britton, Ruth Jackson, Julia Meade, Sheila Jackson, and Jean Sullivan are six of but a handful of women announcers who have proved they can go it alone, and even they at times are joined by men.

In spite of the slight limitations of the feminine voice, however, many television commercials would be less effective without it. Used wisely, it provides so often the spice of authenticity that prompts many a customer to say, "This product is for *me!*"

### Actors and Actresses

Actors and actresses of varying degrees of prominence participate in actual selling on television in two ways: (1) as announcers, either on-camera or voice-over, and (2) in acting roles to dramatize the benefits of the products.

Since the announcer, to be compelling, should be his humble self, the person with theatrical experience sometimes has the advantage. Not that acting is a prerequisite for announcing—far from it—but being oneself during a performance generally takes superior acting.

Many radio announcers never made the grade in television for this reason. Those who did had much to learn. For the actor to step into the on-camera announcer's role is less of a transition although he, too, has much to learn; namely, how to sell.

The acting profession has become a large and valuable source of announcing talent. Even when actors and actresses are not seen on the screen, they offer a wide choice of interesting voices to help make one advertiser's campaign stand out from another's.

When an actor or actress is cast on-camera to dramatize an important feature of the product, the copy itself may spell success or doom. It must be plausible, literally true to life. The late advertising executive Joseph Katz, in an article in *Advertising Age,* illustrated the folly of forcing "advertisingese" into the mouth of actors who are supposed to sound natural. He wrote:

> An advertising agency decides on a theme for a cigarette advertiser's campaign. The theme, for example, is "Milder than mild." The newspaper ads say "Milder than mild." And then comes the TV commercial.
>
> HE: (accepting a cigarette) Thanks! Just my brand!
>
> SHE: (practically swooning with ecstacy) Why do you like it?
>
> HE: (likewise swooning) Because I like a mild cigarette—and this one is "Milder than mild!"
>
> *"You're not kidding anybody."*

Mr. Katz's article was aptly titled, "Ah, Come On, Fellows—People Don't Talk That Way!"

The stilted use of actors can, of course, be avoided by copy that either leaves the actors to pantomime while the announcer talks or gives them something sensible to say. The basic theme has many opportunities to register elsewhere within the commercial.

## Celebrities

A few years ago, at the time television was blooming into maturity, *Time* Magazine predicted: "Old-style commercial announcers, many of whom have spent twenty years selling a multitude of products over the air, may be on their way out. Elbowing them toward the discard is a new breed—most of them entertainers by profession—who have tied their commercial destinies to specific sponsors."

This, of course, has proved to be a faulty forecast as far as announcers are concerned. But it served to call attention to a new kind of salesman and saleswoman whose influence on the buying public is not to be denied. For example, over the years Betty Furness has become so famous selling appliances on television that many forget her main forte is acting. Singers Vaughn Monroe and Dorothy Collins, Douglas Fairbanks, Jr., Adolph Menjou, Jon Hall, Monte Wooley,

Fig. 33—STAR OF THE SHOW often introduces, and sometimes participates in, commercial messages. Ronald Reagan, above, host and super-
visor of General Electric Theater, travels thousands of miles each year to
talk with employees and civic groups in General Electric plant communities.

Joe E. Brown, Mickey Rooney, William Bendix, Phil Silvers—these
and countless others have on occasion stepped before the camera to
demonstrate the reasons why viewers should buy certain brands of
products.

The reasoning behind this is obvious: Despite a certain amount of
public skepticism on the subject, the testimonial is a proven technique of advertising. This is so, providing that the proper personality
is selected for the proper product and the commercial is constructed
in a believable fashion. Celebrities have large followings. They may
or may not be able to control the taste preferences of their fans; but
their very association with the product can well raise its position in
public esteem.

In a class of their own for their personal approach to selling in
radio, and now in television, are Arthur Godfrey, Garry Moore, and
Art Linkletter. Mr. Godfrey for years has been responsible for the
movement of probably more products than any other single personality in the history of television. Once the advertiser informs him of
the principal sales features of his product, Godfrey will generally fol-

low them—and in his own words. Seldom will he ever look at a prepared script. It is difficult to recall any performer ever granted such liberty in a medium as expensive and exacting as television.

Godfrey, Moore, Linkletter, and certain others insist on becoming thoroughly familiar with the products they are advertising. These are not mere men who know how to put words together and where to give them emphasis. They honestly believe what they are saying. They are genuinely proud of what they are selling. The fact that they are being generously compensated for their efforts is simply a worthy tribute to the enthusiasm they manifest in the act of selling.

### "Star of the Show"

On a network program headed by a star performer, research reveals that the star's participation in the commercial, or even his introduction to the commercial, can be a valuable plus for the advertiser. Such headliners as Jack Benny, Steve Allen, Groucho Marx, Ronald Reagan, Ed Sullivan, and Dinah Shore are among those who take special pains to integrate commercials with their own personal touches. They, too, are not averse to delivering complete commercials.

This participation invariably strengthens the sponsor's identification with the program and lends an added hand to the selling of the sponsor's products.

### Singers

Most singing for television commercials, especially group singing, is performed off-screen, where the singers themselves are not seen. Thus, by recording the jingle portion of the commercial prior to shooting, the producer has full control over the quality.

Where singers appear on-screen—and here only one or two are generally involved—problems arise. Most singers are not natural-born actors. Their movements can be awkward. The copywriter, who specifies the action in his original script, and the commercial director are responsible for seeing to it that on-camera singers move and act in a normal, relevant manner.

As in the Hollywood feature film, where a singer appears before the camera in a film commercial, his voice has probably been pre-recorded. As the camera rolls, the singer hears his voice played back on tape and he "mouths" the lyrics for the camera. This way he can concentrate on his actions and not worry about singing the right notes. Better sound quality results, but if the "mouthing" bit is not accurately matched to the sound, the trick then becomes apparent to the viewing audience and detracts from the effectiveness of the message.

## Models

The modeling profession has undergone revolutionary changes since the arrival of commercial television. Prior to 1950 nearly all advertising models earned their way by posing for printed advertisements at from $10 to $25 an hour. Today, although posing for still photographs brings the better models $50 to $65 an hour and more, most have a greater desire to appear in television commercials, where compensation can be far more lucrative.

On-camera models, actors, announcers, and all talent except "extras" in film commercials not only receive a minimum basic fee of $80 at the time the film is shot, but collect considerable repayments from the re-use of the films on the air. One commercial repeated once on a network program, by union scale, means an additional $55 to on-camera performers. One commercial repeated continuously over the course of a year can net the model as much as $3,000!

No longer, then, do many models rely on their faces and figures alone to win their fortunes. Model agencies encourage their models to learn acting and develop any other individual skills they may have that will better qualify them for the highly competitive roles in commercials. Some agencies even offer courses in acting, singing, and dancing. They also look for specialized experience such as sports in order to supply models for commercials featuring swimming, horseback riding, tennis, or golf situations.

Probably the greatest change that has come over the model since television can be seen in a smartly-cast commercial for a household product. The model or actress who demonstrates the product cannot appear as if she just stepped off the cover of *Vogue* if the commercial is to be believable. More and more the fashion type is yielding to the "all-American girl."

## Children

Many a commercial is brighter and more effective when children are a part of it. Casting the right children to the right commercials, however, is always a challenge.

In the early days of television the casting director would give first consideration to child models, chiefly because of their handsome faces. But the tendency now is more toward the hiring of child actors for two reasons:

1. Commercials featuring children almost without exception involve active situations requiring the children to move about in a natural manner.

2. Child actors are more likely to look and act like everyday children than are the more mature-looking child models.

Consequently the pattern here has followed closely that of the adult models, with more and more children who once were models exclusively now studying dramatics to make them more eligible for work in commercials. Children, incidentally, receive the same fees as adults.

Working with children puts a strain on the best director. Because of their close and constant contacts with adults, the children tend to act like adults. It is the director's job—and no easy one—to keep them acting like children.

### Role of the Advertising Agency

The larger advertising agencies are responsible for the casting of all talent in television commercials for their clients. This function is a complex one for these reasons:

1. Commercials as a whole call for many different types of talent.

2. The various categories of available talent overlap in many areas. Many models act, actors announce, announcers sing, singers act—the possibilities are endless.

3. Many different types of talent agents are involved, including the model agency, the talent agency, the theatrical agency, and the personal agent.

Agencies go about talent selection in one of two ways:

*By holding regular auditions and keeping records of talent* in their own files and calling the agents for specific people as they are needed for specific commercials.

*By holding auditions as each commercial goes into production.* For example, if the role is that of a young housewife, the advertising agency issues what is unflatteringly known among talent agents as a "cattle call"; that is, a call for several actresses of a particular type from whom one will be picked for the role.

Batten, Barton, Durstine & Osborn is one of the few advertising agencies that keeps a complete, up-to-date file supplemented by tape recordings of talent of all sorts, maintained through regular and special auditions on its own closed circuit television system.

When a commercial is ready for casting, the agency copywriter, producer, and casting director, Nancy Marquand—and often a representative of the client—will consult on the exact type of talent needed. Upon agreement, a call then goes out for specific people to fill specific roles. In cases where consultation does not clearly define the type needed, more than one announcer or actor or actress will be brought in to re-audition before a larger group, which then makes the selection.

## Talent Unions

Talent for television aired nationally is affiliated with unions. Advertisers must pay a minimum union scale for their services.[1] In certain areas of the country, local advertisers, too, are affected.

Among the unions having jurisdiction are the following: (1) the *Screen Actors' Guild* (SAG), over "players" in filmed commercials and in videotaped commercials produced in areas outside broadcasting studios; (2) the *Screen Extras Guild* (SEG), over "extras" in filmed commercials—talent appearing in the video portion of filmed commercials but whose faces cannot be seen or whose role is secondary and not directly concerned with the advertised product; (3) the *American Federation of Television and Radio Artists* (AFTRA), over talent appearing in live commercials and in videotaped commercials produced in broadcasting studios; (4) the *Radio and Television Directors Guild* (RTDG), in general over directors and assistant directors in live commercials and in videotaped commercials produced in broadcasting studios; (5) the *Screen Directors' Guild of America* (SDGA), over directors and assistant directors in film commercials produced in the Hollywood area; (6) the *Screen Directors' International Guild,* over directors and assistant directors in film commercials produced in the New York area; (7) the *American Federation of Musicians* (AFM), over instrumental talent.[2]

Since both SAG and AFTRA talent receive payment for participat-

---

[1] The advent of videotape, contemporaneous with the publishing of this book, brings almost weekly changes in the jurisdictional positions of certain unions, final settlement to be resolved by the National Labor Relations Board.

[2] At time of this writing, the Musicians' Guild of America was making a strong bid for jurisdiction over all west coast musicians.

ing in the commercial and repayment as the commercial is reused, certain provisions of both contracts are discussed here.

*SAG.* The Producer-Screen Actors' Guild contract[3] covers minimum compensation plus use and re-use payments for all acting, announcing, singing, and other talent in commercials made as motion pictures, whether produced by means of film or videotape outside the broadcasting studio, except those classed as "extras." Though the contract is between SAG and the motion picture producer, the advertiser is directly concerned since it is he who is ultimately billed for the production expenses, including the cost of talent.

Whether the commercial is to be used as a spot or on a program, the "player" (the term used to describe the announcer, actor, actress, and all SAG talent) appearing on-camera receives minimum compensation of $80 for an eight-hour day, which also constitutes payment for the first commercial made for one designated advertiser. If the player participates in more than one commercial in the same day, he then receives upon completion of his services, an additional minimum fee of $80 for each commercial in excess of one.

Off-camera players are employed on the basis of recording sessions. Announcers and all players, including solo singers not performing with a group, receive a minimum of $55 for a two-hour recording session. Group singers (two to four voices) receive $35 each for a four-hour recording session. Group singers (over four voices) receive $30 each for a four-hour session. As in the case of the on-camera talent, this minimum compensation applies as payment for one commercial. If more than one commercial is completed at the same session, the players then receive the equivalent of a session fee for each commercial in excess of one.

To this point, then, all players have received their "minimum compensation," which allows the advertiser to put the commercial on the air—but not for long before talent repayments are in order. Since nearly all film commercials are repeated many times before they are discarded, the advertiser takes careful note of the provisions which follow.

Compensation for *spots* is divided into classes, depending upon the number of cities in which the commercial is telecast. Class C covers

[3] 1958 contract, effective until June 1, 1960. A copy of the current Producer-Screen Actors' Guild commercials contract may be obtained by sending one dollar to Screen Actors' Guild, Publications Dept., 7750 Sunset Blvd., Hollywood 46, Calif.

1 through 5 cities; class B, 6 through 20 cities; class A, 21 through 60; class AA, 61 through 125; class AAA, over 125. New York counts as 11 cities; Los Angeles and Chicago, each as 7 cities. Any two constitute class A; all three, class AA.

The following payment chart applies to all players except group singers off-camera in television film commercials used as *spots:*

| Class | On-Camera Rate for each 13 weeks use | Off-Camera Rate for each 13 weeks use |
|---|---|---|
| C | $80 | $55 first 13 weeks |
| | $130—26 weeks guaranteed and paid for prior to first use | $45 each 13 weeks thereafter |
| B | $125 | $72.50 |
| A | $170 | $105 |
| AA | $220 | $150 |
| AAA | $260 | $170 |

In other words, if an actor appears on-camera in three commercials for one advertiser, and these commercials are used, for example, in the number of cities constituting class AA, he receives $240 (three times $80) as his minimum compensation included in the total of $660 (three times $220) for the first thirteen weeks plus an additional $660 every thirteen weeks the three commercials are continued.

Group singers off-camera in spot commercials receive a top of $67.50 each in class AAA for two to four voices every thirteen weeks, and $50 each for over four voices.

For film commercials to be used on programs, the SAG contract again bases its rate for players on number of cities. Class C comprises 1 through 5 cities; class B, 6 through 20; class A, over 20 cities. New York, Los Angeles and Chicago carry the same weights as in spots.

All players except group singers off-camera are paid for filmed program commercials as follows:

| Class | On-Camera Rate | Off-Camera Rate |
|---|---|---|
| C (each 13 weeks) | $120 | $80 |
| B (each 13 weeks) | $170 | $125 |
| A   *First Use:* | $80 | $55 |
| *Each Re-use:* | $55 | $42.50 |

Class C rates provide for a slight discount if the player is guaranteed twenty-six weeks and paid prior to the first use of the commercial. With Class A rates, where the player is paid for each exposure of the commercial, discounts are provided for advance guarantee of eight uses in thirteen weeks and thirteen uses in thirteen weeks. Where the latter use occurs without previous guarantee, further uses beyond thirteen in a thirteen-week period are at the rate of 17½ per cent of the applicable individual re-use fee.

Payments for group singers off-camera in filmed program commercials range roughly from one-quarter to one-half of the above rates per voice.

The SAG contract also specifies rates for program openings and closings, off-camera signatures, and dealer commercials, and contains many other provisions, which the advertiser should read and study carefully before authorizing production of film commercials.

The present SAG contract is a modification and revision of the original document signed in 1952 between producers and the guild. Before 1952, any actor, announcer, model, singer or other talent was paid only once, and the advertiser was free to use the film commercial as many times as he pleased.

Today, of course, talent continues to receive repayments as long as the film commercial is used. The result, since the advent of SAG in the TV commercial field, has been an over-all simplification of commercials by many advertisers seeking to save money on talent costs. Where once four people may have been pictured enjoying the product, the advertiser may now settle for one.

Commented one trade columnist, "No one would seriously quarrel with the principle of the SAG stand for commercial talent, but some very obvious inequities remain unsolved. One major television client is spending a half million a year on re-use payments alone. Another major advertiser pays more than $100,000 each year to a single unidentified voice (the announcer is never shown on-camera)—and his total labors never exceed a week's work." These are extreme examples, to be sure, but they demonstrate that familiarity with the broad SAG provisions and the AFTRA rates which follow is essential to the advertiser active in the medium.

*AFTRA.* Until 1958, when videotape became a major factor, the American Federation of Television and Radio Artists had no sliding scale rate structure for talent repayments, or "residuals."

Although AFTRA also has jurisdiction over performers in live television commercials, its Videotape Commercial Code,[4] covering performers in taped commercials produced in broadcasting studios, deserves highlighting here.

*Program Use (Entire Country).* Commercial performers within a program sponsored by an advertiser (as against those in participating commercials) except group singers off-camera and "extras" are paid in the following manner:

| On-Camera | Off-Camera |
|---|---|
| $93 (includes 5-hour taping session and first use) | $67 |
| $85 (covers second use of same commercial) | $60 |
| $70 (third use) | $50 |
| $57 (for each use from 4 through 13) | $45 |
| $20 (for each use from 14 through 20) | $10 |
| $10 (for each use over 20) | $8 |

When the performer is guaranteed eight uses of the commercial in thirteen weeks, the advertiser receives a 10 per cent discount; for thirteen uses in thirteen weeks, 20 per cent.

Off-camera group singers individually receive the following:

| 3 or 4 Singers | 5 or More Singers |
|---|---|
| $47 (includes 3-hour recording session and first use) | $40 |
| $40 (covers second use of same commercial) | $35 |
| $35 (third use) | $30 |
| $30 (for each use from 4 through 13) | $25 |
| $8 (for each use over 13) | $8 |

The same discounts as above apply.

*Program Use (Local).* When the advertiser sponsors a program on one or more individual stations, performers are paid the following rates for unlimited use of the same commercial for each period of thirteen weeks:

| No. of Cities | On-Camera Performers | Off-Camera Performers | Off-Camera Group Singers 3–4 | 5 or more |
|---|---|---|---|---|
| 6 through 20 | $200 | $150 | $57.50 | $50 |
| 1 through 5 | $145 | $95 | $50 | $40 |

In the event the list of cities includes New York, Chicago or Los Angeles, the 6-through-20 rate automatically applies.

---

[4] A copy of the Code may be obtained by sending 75¢ to AFTRA, 15 West 44th Street, New York 36, N.Y. (At time of writing, code still subject to confirmation by both parties.)

*Spot Use.* For unlimited use of the same commercial for each period of thirteen weeks:

| No. of Cities | On-Camera Performers | Off-Camera Performers | Off-Camera Group Singers 3–4 | 5 or more |
|---|---|---|---|---|
| Over 125 | $312 | $205 | $75 | $60 |
| 21–125 | $225 | $150 | $60 | $50 |
| 6–20 | $150 | $90 | $45 | $38 |
| 1–5 | $93 | $67 | $30 | $25 |

New York, Chicago, and Los Angeles each count as eleven cities when used in addition to other cities. Discount provisions cover certain categories when the performer receives a twenty-six-week payment in advance.

Payments to talent appearing in dealer spots are on the basis of six months or one year. On-camera performers receive $450 for six months, $825 for twelve; off-camera performers, $310, $525; off-camera group singers (3–4), $145, $360; off-camera group singers (5 or more), $125, $210.

"Extras" receive $35 when the commercial (either program or spot) is produced, plus a final $35 if the commercial is used beyond thirteen weeks. An advance payment of $60 to an "extra" frees the advertiser from further payments to that person for the duration of the life of the commercial.

# Selling the Corporate Concept

GOOD products, good services, and good product advertising all build a company's reputation with the public. But these alone can never convey to the American people, who are a lot of other things besides consumers, those basic ideals which enable any company to outlive many product lives.

In short, the whole of a corporation is more than the sum of its parts. The broad objective of any large or growing business is to gain and maintain public confidence not only in its products but in its policies, its practices, and its contributions to everyday life.

To achieve this many companies set aside specific budgets for "corporate advertising," a term which also includes, for purposes of this chapter, "public relations advertising" and "institutional advertising."

Since 1908, when the American Telephone & Telegraph Company launched the first large-scale endeavor to build favorable public sentiment, American business has recognized the many benefits—in certain cases, the necessity—of this form of advertising.

Several years ago, in recommending the need for such advertising, Bruce Barton said to the chairman of the board of one of the country's largest corporations: "You will always have public relations advertising. The Attorney General of the United States will do it for you; labor unions will do it for you; the FTC will do it for you; editors and reporters will do it for you. The only question is, how much money are you willing to spend for some public relations advertising you yourself can control?"

Most of America's largest business firms—each with its own set of specific objectives, of which favorable public attitude is paramount—have chosen television as a major medium in which to present their corporate philosophies. Among them are Du Pont, United States Steel, and General Electric. Indeed, corporate advertisers on television read like a "Who's Who" of American business: American Telephone & Telegraph, American Can, Chrysler Corporation, Westinghouse, General Motors, Kaiser Aluminum & Chemical, Firestone, Prudential, American Gas Association, Union Carbide, and many more.

## Why Television?

Television is the ideal medium for corporate advertising because it enables a company to reach masses of people and to tell its story in the most forceful manner. With sight, sound, and motion—and film facilities to reproduce whatever the advertiser requires to register favorable impressions—television brings the message to life before the viewer.

Research has proved time after time that its very association with a high quality television program immediately raises a company's rating in the eyes of the general public.

Most corporations, in fact, beam their messages to various "publics." These may include consumers, stockholders, employees, distributors, competitors, suppliers, bankers, communities in which they operate, and the government. One company has found that every two of its television programs reach 75 per cent of its employees, a feat it had not been able to equal through other advertising media.

While many companies still rely on magazines, newspapers, and radio as vehicles for their corporate campaigns, television seems to be making the deepest impressions for those who use it.

## Uses of Television

Corporate advertisers can select from a variety of formats on television. Some sponsor full-hour programs every other week or once a month. Some sponsor weekly half-hours. Still others buy "specials," or "spectaculars."

Some devote their full commercial time on every program to their corporate messages, and sell their products on different programs entirely. Others alternate their programs between product advertising and corporate advertising. Still others cover product and corporate within the same show on the same evening. One format seems to work as well as another.

## Corporate Objectives

Except for the basic desire to be looked upon with favor by the general public, no two companies have precisely the same set of objectives. Listed here is a composite of the corporate objectives of several large companies using the television medium today:

1. The company is a good citizen.
2. The company is a good neighbor.
3. The company is a good place to work.
4. The company is owned by thousands of stockholders.
5. The company helps hold the line against inflation.
6. The company is vital to our national defense.
7. The company is a good example of free enterprise.
8. The company works with and helps small business.
9. The company faces competition, providing people a wider choice of better products.
10. The company pioneers in research for new products to meet human needs.
11. The company creates new jobs and business opportunities.
12. The company provides basic materials and/or products of high value.
13. The company fulfills its responsibilities to customers, stockholders, employees, suppliers, and the general public.
14. The company's large size enables it to engage in important research and development of new products for tomorrow.
15. The company's large size enables it to sell products at reasonable prices through mass production.
16. The company is diversified. It makes many products of high quality for many uses.
17. The company is efficient, well managed.

Curiously, sales stimulation is never included in the expressed objectives of pure corporate advertising. It is the job of such advertising to convey ideas, change people's minds, or create opinions where none existed before, all with the purpose of helping to create and maintain a favorable climate in which the company may do business. For proper climate is essential to any company expecting to continue its growth through the sale of goods or services.

## The "Bigness" Factor

Some companies feel that the greatest single factor in opposition to favorable climate is public prejudice against "bigness" in business. With this feeling go the implications of "control," "monopoly," and economic influence over people.

There is nothing new in this prejudice. It has ebbed and flowed for three-quarters of a century, and today it is at one of its low points. The Opinion Research Corporation reported, "The overwhelming majority of American adults today accept—and endorse—the viewpoint that big business is a good thing for the country. Those who approve outnumber those who disapprove by a proportion of ten to one." It adds, "The findings also establish that three times as many people worry about the power of big labor unions as worry about the power of big business."

Even though the general public accepts the bigness of business as non-objectionable, it is interesting to note how exposure of one corporate TV commercial changed the thinking of one audience in a theater test.

Before the commercial was shown, more than three-quarters of the audience signified approval of big business; after seeing the commercial, 90 per cent. But what is even more significant are the "before" and "after" reasons given for their opinions.

These were the results:

THE IDEA OF "BIGNESS"

| *Before Seeing Commercial:* | *After Seeing Commercial:* |
|---|---|
| Favorable 76% | Favorable 90% |

| *Reasons for Favoring "Bigness":* | *Reasons for Favoring "Bigness":* |
|---|---|
| Success | Mass Production |
| Money | Low Cost |
| Expansion | Low Prices |
| Control | Research |

It is obvious here that not only were some opinions changed from unfavorable or indifferent to favorable; but, of the majority who were favorable to begin with, new reasons—sounder reasons, as far as this particular company is concerned—became the basis for their opinions.

The single word impressions, incidentally, were gained from an "association word test," which is only one phase of an over-all research project, in which respondents are given a list of many words and asked to check which ones they associate with a given company or product.

In the test just mentioned, those who favored big business associated more stereotyped reasons before exposure to the commercial than after.

Few corporations encounter the bigness issue directly in their television messages, but the trend in this direction is growing stronger. Most of the accomplishments the larger corporate advertisers dramatize, and the philosophies they expound, relate closely to the concept that big business is good for the country.

### Typical Subjects

Once a company sets its corporate objectives for television exposure, the next task is to select subject matter which will both effectively illustrate the objectives and be interesting to the audience. More than one TV research group, in fact, declares that the impact of the corporate commercial message upon the public is directly related to the interest value of the subject matter itself.

Nearly every large corporation is a virtually endless source of subject matter which lends itself to dramatic treatment in corporate commercials. For example, one company may document its activities in solar energy to support its objective of showing its leadership in research. On the other hand, it may dramatize its manufacture of a basic material to illustrate how it works with other businesses, large and small.

Television has had strong positive effects on the very nature of corporate advertising. The strongest reason advanced for this, besides the dynamics of the medium, is the imaginative choice of subject matter on the part of the sponsoring companies to drive home their objectives. Many companies who would have hesitated to do so a few years ago now talk freely about future plans and future products, knowing of the rewards that accrue from increased viewer interest in management's intentions.

To list here innumerable subjects covered by various companies may not mean a great deal especially when they are not tied to the specific objectives they are intended to represent. However, as an illustration of their built-in interest value, a typical few should be mentioned:

> Atomic electricity
> Creative saving plan
> Life after retirement
> Opportunities through education
> Steel in modern architecture
> Color conditioning
> Solar energy
> Dyes
> Modern school lighting
> The company's annual report

## Measuring Effectiveness

It is important, when a company undertakes to spend large sums of money to further its corporate cause, that accurate records be kept of its progress. Measurement of good will and its many facets is not so complicated as it may sound.

Until recently the most useful measurement these companies relied on were periodic impression surveys of television viewers versus non-television viewers. Respondents in the latter category were those in non-television areas of the United States, but these are fast becoming extinct.

A more current method is to poll those in television areas who are regular viewers of the advertiser's program and compare their attitudes and reactions with irregular viewers and non-viewers of the program. Naturally, while these polls are national in scope, they represent the feelings of a small portion of the show's total audience. But by scientific sampling and proper interviewing, as is carried on by several professional survey companies, the advertiser can learn a great deal about the effect of his television messages on the general public.

A second measurement of the effectiveness of corporate television messages is an adaptation and expansion of certain existing techniques of commercial research.

1. *Viewer vs. Non-Viewer Surveys.* One company, which features its corporate slogan in all of its product advertising as well as its institutional advertising in all media, found that twice as many viewers of its television program recognized the slogan as did those who did not watch the program regularly.

The same method of measurement can also indicate to what extent an advertiser is registering his corporate concepts in his commercial messages. One study compared the responses of viewers and non-viewers in regard to the company's various efforts in such areas as defense, developing new products, creating new jobs, aiding small business, providing a good place to work, furthering the education of employees, and conducting research. In every area viewers responded more favorably toward the company than non-viewers, for these areas were among those covered within the corporate television messages.

Successful at these objectives, some companies have taken a further step in their commercials by discussing profits, depreciation costs, and other timely, more provocative subjects in an attempt to inform the public of, and seek its understanding attitude toward, the day-to-day problems of conducting a large business.

Still another significant study compared the public awareness of two large companies, only one of which employed television as the carrier of its corporate message. When asked for either a favorable opinion or no opinion of each, the company on television outscored the second company more than three to one on "favorable opinion." Yet in the category of "no opinion," the non-TV company scored highest by a ratio of two to one.

Survey after survey reveals that the public not only has a higher regard for companies advertising on television, but knows more about them. Conversely, misinformation about these companies—plus the "don't knows" and "no opinions"—are considerably reduced.

Sometimes regular and irregular viewers of a corporate program are even asked to what degree they think the sponsoring company is interested in the general welfare of the public. As an indication of the good-will value of one specific series of programs, the following results were obtained:

|                      | Irregular Viewers | Regular Viewers |
|----------------------|:-----------------:|:---------------:|
| Very interested      | 66%               | 86%             |
| Fairly interested    | 23%               | 14%             |
| Not at all interested| 11%               | 0%              |

2. *Commercial Research Methods.* Corporate TV advertisers can gain more specific indications of the effectiveness of their individual commercials by adapting certain of the present accepted commercial research procedures described in detail in the following chapter.

The basis of this research as applied to corporate advertising is *recall* by respondents of the facts and ideas expressed in the commercials. Since every corporate message has, or should have, one or more clear-cut objectives, it is vital to find out whether these objectives are being successfully conveyed to the audience.

Attitudes, too, can be learned by this type of research. Attitudes are closely akin to public opinion. And the molding of favorable public opinion, after all, is an important target of most corporate advertisers.

Both areas—recall and attitude studies—have revealed elements of useful information. However, a more interesting area, and perhaps someday a more productive one, is depth research, where the mind of the viewer, with all of its fears, prejudices, and basic beliefs, is made more accessible in order that the advertiser may find valid guidance to the most intelligent approach.

## Corporate-Product Relationship

Corporate advertising reaches beyond the shorter-term goals of product advertising. Nevertheless emphasis on one invariably has an effect on the other.

In one survey the question was asked of retailers: "Which manufacturers are best advertising this product (and here a particular type was identified) in a way that helps you sell this product to customers?" The company rating highest in the field was a TV advertiser. Half the retailers named television as the most effective of all media.

However, the story has a peculiar twist. This company *was* advertising on television, but not the product the retailers were asked about! In other words, the TV effort, which combined commercials on others of the company's products with a corporate commercial, produced a "rub-off" effect, apparently to the point of putting extra dollars into the retailers' pockets.

If one is to define corporate advertising as merely non-product or institutional or public relations advertising, he is ignoring a large and important factor; namely, that product advertising helps to attain a number of corporate objectives. For example, a great many people may think favorably of a company because of the performance of one or more of its products.

It is not necessary therefore to devote all of the allotted commercial time on a given program—three minutes of a half-hour or six minutes of an hour—to corporate objectives only. Many companies effectively mix product and corporate commercials within the same program and thereby enjoy an interrelated two-way benefit as a result.

### Creating the Corporate Message

There is no formula for creating the ideal corporate message for television. Advertisers differ in their make-up and in their objectives. Their programs differ, their production budgets differ. Besides, they each prefer their messages to be as distinctive and unique as possible.

The first step for the copywriter is to study carefully the objectives of the particular advertiser. A series of commercials means a series of objectives, all pointing toward the goal of a more favorable public opinion toward the company.

Step two is to pair each objective with a specific "story" or "for instance." If an objective, for example, is to prove that the company is a leader in the research of new products for the betterment of all, the copywriter will seek interesting facts about one or more of the specific new products and the story behind them. With this proof he can then dramatize the story to prove the objective in a manner that is interesting to the audience and forceful in its moral.

*Techniques.* The writer generally has a choice of several effective techniques as he settles down to the job of actually creating the corporate TV message.

More than one company centers live-action film messages around a "company spokesman," an announcer who appears on-camera frequently as he narrates the copy, demonstrates the proof, and puts the corporate point across in a warm, friendly way. He substitutes his own personality, to a degree, for the personality of the corporation and aims to break down the cold, impersonal image many people still hold for large corporations, It is a fact that a spokesman who wins the confidence of the audience wins friends for the company, provided that the story he tells, and the principles and philosophies he represents, make sense to the viewer.

Many companies have no spokesman on-camera, but do develop a "corporate voice," which lends a consistent sound to the various messages. Obviously, however, a voice is more subordinate to the subject matter than is a spokesman on-camera. While being less personal in its approach, this plan directs more attention to the pictures themselves and has proved no less effective than the spokesman method.

Film is generally preferred over live presentation because film allows the writer to cover a much broader area. For example, manufacturing shots, research laboratories, testing of new products and the like are difficult to illustrate within the confines of a live studio. Film can also be edited and the commercial can be approved in advance, before it goes on the air.

Animation is beginning to make a narrow inroad into corporate commercials. It is interesting to consider for three reasons: (1) It tends to simplify the story. (2) It allows for a lighter approach and can make a heavy subject more acceptable to the viewer. (3) It permits exaggeration without offending.

Animation, however, should be handled with care. If it is too amusing, it may destroy the point the advertiser is trying to make. Animation nearly always commands more than average attention. It behooves the copywriter to use it only where he firmly believes live-action would be inadequate.

It is not necessary, of course, to carry the animated technique entirely through the commercial. It may, for example, add interest to the opening sequence. It is especially effective when used diagrammatically to explain the functioning of a complex part of the story.

Actually the copywriter may call upon any recognized technique that will help him tell his story in a clear, interesting manner. It is desirable, however, to give the series of messages a "family look," characteristic of the particular advertiser.

*Copy.* Corporate commercials are generally longer than the customary one-minute program commercials. But this does not give the copywriter proportionately more freedom because there are more facts to be told. He must make every scene and every word count.

Since copy is a product of creativity, the best to be offered here is a set of principles which the copywriter may consider at the outset:

1. Be dignified but never stuffy. Corporations are human, practical citizens.
2. At the very first scene select a situation which will interest the viewer or a premise with which he will agree.
3. Try to cover only one major objective in one commercial. Direct all examples toward it.
4. Keep the viewer's self-interest in mind. In other words, try to talk about the company in ways that relate to him.
5. Don't be too selfish. It is unlikely that any one company has yet changed the course of world events. Boast modestly and the viewer will be more likely to play along.
6. Tell the story simply.
7. Avoid too much generalizing. Concentrate on specifics.

### Financing the Corporate Effort

Providing that sound thought and judgment are applied to the strategy of the specific messages, corporate advertising on television is not considered to be a risky, speculative venture. While the objectives are more long-range than those of product advertising, corporate efforts have been known to "pay off" promptly and tangibly.

When a company is faced with the decision of whether or not to proceed with such a plan, the major problem to be solved is a financial one: How much can the company afford to allot to this type of advertising on a continuing basis in addition to its normal competitive product advertising? And where will the money come from?

A large company finances its TV corporate program in one of three general ways: (1) It sets aside an additional amount of money over and above the normal product budget. (2) It assesses proportionally the existing advertising budget of each product. (3) A combination of the two. The second and third methods are the most common.

While each company actually creates its own formula for raising the corporate money, the plan is likely to resemble one of the three above.

It is perfectly understandable for a product manager to have mixed emotions when his product budget is lowered to help finance a corporate budget. True, his interest lies solidly in the future of his company and its long-range objectives. But his immediate job is to fight competition on every front, and he enlists every available dollar to accomplish the job. When some of his ammunition is diverted to other uses, he must then revise his strategy for advertising the particular product or products with which he is concerned.

On the other hand, many corporate commercials, while proving a broad company objective, do a yeoman's selling job on certain of the company's products, which are used as subject matter. More than one corporate commercial has, in fact, resulted in sales the next morning.

*Example.* The following script example and the two additional examples in the Appendix demonstrate the variations possible in objective, subject matter, and technique in the handling of corporate advertising in television.

# DU PONT

FADE UP ON:

1. CLOSEUP OF CHEMICAL APPARATUS SHOT.
         (MUSIC: Up to theme, holding up for:)
2. SUPER DU PONT OVAL AND START TO TILT UP WITH OVAL SUPERED OVER APPARATUS AND MOVING WITH CAMERA. OVAL CASTS A SMALL SPOTLIGHT AS IT MOVES.
         (MUSIC: Continues)
3. PAN RIGHT TO FLORENCE FLASK AND HOLD. INSIDE OF FLASK IS PROCESSED A DRAMATIC SHOT OF THE SUN . . . SAME AS SECOND SHOT OF SHOW OPENING. DISSOLVE OFF DU PONT OVAL.
         (MUSIC: Segue to more dramatic strains)

DISSOLVE TO:

4. EXTREME CLOSEUP OF YOUNG LADY USING PHONE.
                    REPORTER (Voice over)
     This telephone is *powered* with energy from the sun!

CUT TO:

5. MAN IN FARM CLOTHES DRINKING GLASS OF WATER.
     This water has been *purified* by the sun!

CUT TO:

6. YOUNG GIRL EATING HAMBURGER.
     This food has been *cooked* by the sun!

CUT TO:

7. EXTERIOR SOLAR HOUSE.

. . . and someday you may live in a house like this . . . heated by the sun.

CUT TO:

8. CLOSE ON HEAT TRAPS.

The devices on the roof are heat traps . . . built with various Du Pont experimental plastic films.

DISSOLVE TO:

9. ANIMATION SHOWING AIR BEING CIRCULATED THROUGH HOUSE.

The sun hits these traps and heats the air inside. The warm air is then circulated by fans through the entire house.

CUT TO:

10. SHOW STORAGE BINS UNDERNEATH HOUSE.

The hot air not used during the day is drawn into this storage bin for later use.

DISSOLVE TO:

11. CLOSEUP OF BOARD ABOUT TWO FEET SQUARE AND SLANTED AT ABOUT A 45-DEGREE ANGLE TOWARD SUN. THE BOARD IS MOUNTED ON TOP OF A TELEPHONE POLE. ON THE BOARD IS A SERIES OF ONE-INCH SILICON DISCS WITH WIRES LEADING DOWN TO A STORAGE BATTERY ABOUT 6 INCHES SQUARE.

Telephones in some rural areas already have been powered by the sun's energy . . .

CUT TO:

12. CLOSEUP OF SILICON BOARD.

. . . which is converted directly into electrical energy by tiny discs made of a Du Pont product called Silicon. At night, or when it's cloudy, the sun's energy, which has been stored in this battery, still works to power telephone lines.

WIPE TO:

13. EXTERIOR OF SOLAR STILL AT DU PONT EXPERIMENTAL STATION.

Du Pont scientists are also seeking economical ways of using the sun to turn salt water into pure drinking water.

CUT TO:

14. CLOSEUP OF MAN TAPPING AS WATER FORMS.

Here you see water that has already been purified.

CUT TO:

15. LONG SHOT OF SOLAR STILL.

These solar stills are models of units that may some day make it possible to purify large amounts of salty water. Here's how they work:

DISSOLVE TO:

16. ANIMATION OF CONDENSATION ACTION.

The heat from the sun causes the salt water to evaporate. Pure water then condenses inside the dome made of an experimental Du Pont film and is collected in basins on either side.

WIPE TO:

17. LONG-SHOT OF DESERT LAND.

Think of the *other* benefits of purifying water. Arid lands in this country and throughout the world could change . . .

DISSOLVE TO:

18. SIMILAR LONG-SHOT OF FERTILE LAND.

. . . into fertile lands if vast sources of impure water could be purified cheaply.

DISSOLVE TO:

19. EXTERIOR DAYTIME SHOT OF FAMILY ON PICNIC. FATHER IS SETTING UP PORTABLE COOKING UNIT.

There's a lot new under the sun. Here's an outdoor cooking device, lined with a metallized Du Pont plastic film that concentrates the sun's heat. Although still experimental, it promises to be fine for picnics—

CUT TO:

20. CLOSEUP OF MEAT COOKING ON GRILL.

. . . and, more important, a low-cost way of cooking in countries where fuel is scarce.

DISSOLVE TO:

21. LONG-SHOT OF FAMILY PICNIC. SUNLIGHT IS STREAMING THROUGH TREES.

These are some of the ways Du Pont scientists are working to harness the greatest source of energy within the reach of man—the sun.

DISSOLVE TO:

22. EXTERIOR OF DU PONT EXPERIMENTAL STATION.

Scientists at this Du Pont Experimental Station in Wilmington, Delaware, work with universities, with government agencies and with other research-minded businesses. In this way Du Pont applies its knowledge and its large scientific resources to a brighter future for us all . . .

DISSOLVE TO:

23. CHEMICAL APPARATUS SHOT. DISSOLVE ON DU PONT OVAL MOVING ALONG APPARATUS.

(MUSIC: Builds Under)

. . . to bring you . . .

24. "BETTER THINGS FOR BETTER LIVING . . . THROUGH CHEMISTRY" LETTERING MOVES UP AND HOLDS.

. . . Better things for better living . . . through chemistry.

25. DU PONT OVAL ENLARGES AS ALL BACKGROUND DISSOLVES OUT.

(MUSIC: Up to end)

## chapter sixteen

# How to Use Television Commercial Research

SINCE the advertiser invests in television in order to sell products, services, or corporate ideas, it is only natural that he is keenly interested in the relative effectiveness of his individual commercials. If he is disappointed with his sales picture, among other things he will ask himself, "How can I make my commercials work harder?" Or even if he is happily riding the crest of a high sales curve, he still has every right to wonder, "How do I know my commercials are doing the best possible job?"

Over and above these factors there is the cost of television advertising to consider. Whether the advertiser is paying a hundred or a hundred thousand dollars to sponsor one program, he deserves every possible assurance that he is using his few minutes of commercial time to the very best advantage. The spot advertiser may be buying high frequency but he, too, wants to be sure his commercials are making the most of the investment. Either way, the advertiser looks to television research to give him indications of strength or weakness and any interpretive hints on how to improve his technique of selling.

## Status of TV Research

Today television commercial research is indeed revealing quantities of useful information. But let it be stated at the outset that few of the revelations are of a cut-and-dried nature. Through various techniques which have been developed it is possible to study (1) various components within a commercial and (2) the total effect of the commercial itself. Yet findings within the former area are much more specific than within the latter.

For example, national advertisers can seldom measure the *sales* effectiveness of a given commercial, principally because that commercial is but one of a myriad of forces at work selling the product. These are but a few:

1. In addition to his television campaign the advertiser may concurrently be running advertisements in other media such as newspapers and magazines.

2. The sales and merchandising activities of competition fluctuate from day to day.

3. Competitive advertising may change during the course of the testing period.

4. The salesman in the store does a better job on some days than on others.

5. Even the weather has an effect on the availability of customers over a given period of time.

There are many more. Thus separating the commercial from this family of influences is next to impossible where the larger advertiser is concerned. The problem is almost nonexistent, of course, for the local advertiser since he often can feel the results of a commercial in a matter of hours.

### Development of Research

From the beginning, research has contributed to better advertising. It never has, and never will, provide the creative man with a magic formula for writing the perfect commercial or advertisement, but it has given him valued assistance from the days when the printed word was the only form of advertising down through the discovery of radio and today in the age of television.

For each new form of communication the researcher has had to vary his techniques and develop entirely new ones. With television, which is said to command more attention and more concentration on the part of the public than any other medium, research is now facing its greatest challenge. For here is advertising not only for the eye, not only for the ear, but for both—plus motion. Here is a medium which actually reached maturity faster than did the tradesmen who began as a part of it. Yet through these few hectic years the advertiser's and the copywriter's persistent search for improvement has accelerated noticeably the breadth of television research.

Most advertising agencies employ at least one television research specialist. The larger agencies maintain an entire department for this one activity. Independent research organizations have sprung up throughout the country. A few have attained big business proportions. Many have established standard systems of testing commercials and still more will tailor a technique to meet the problem at hand. Methods vary, opinions differ, but all have the identical goal—to determine as accurately as they can what effect, if any, commercials and portions of commercials have on the minds of the viewers.

## Methods of Measurement

Reducing current practice to its simplest terms, television research explores for its findings in these two general areas: Recall and Impact.

1. *Recall.* While few methods put full faith in Recall alone, it is the original, and still most widely employed, single measurement. Basically it consists of asking a group of respondents, either in their homes or congregated in one room, various elements they individually remember about a television commercial they saw earlier.

Here, as will all types of research, it is obviously impossible to interrogate every one of the thousands or millions of viewers who saw the commercial on the air, so a sampling of at least one hundred, and preferably three or four hundred, is considered representative of the entire audience. Samples have been known to go as high as twelve thousand, but this number is impractical from a cost standpoint for most advertisers. It is essential in every case that great care be exercised in selecting the viewers who will take part in the test to insure that they are typical of the total audience of viewers in age, sex, income, marital status, and in other relevant categories.

Recall of sales points can be measured in many ways, the following three being the most common:

*a)* In home—within 24 hours[1]

Trained interviewers visit a number of homes the day after a given program appears on the air.

First, respondents are asked which programs they viewed the previous evening.

[1] *Gallup and Robinson method.*

Second, they are asked to recall which company sponsored a particular program.

Third, they are asked to recall all of the products advertised on the program.

Fourth, respondents are asked to prove they saw the commercials for each product they mentioned advertised on the program. When they supply sufficient details about the commercials to indicate clearly they have seen them, verbatim testimony is reported.

Finally, respondents are asked:

1.  What reasons did the commercial give for buying the product?
2.  Did the commercial make a strong case for buying the product?
3.  Did the commercial make people want to do anything about it?

*b)* By telephone—minutes after the program[2]

Interviews are made by telephone for exactly one hour immediately following the program. Again the viewer is questioned after watching the commercial under normal conditions and without prior knowledge that he or she will be questioned, but this time while the memory is still fresh. This may sharpen the Recall rating but the advertiser understandably hopes the sales arguments he puts forth in his commercial will be remembered for longer than a few minutes.

This system evaluates the commercial by these standards:

1.  By reaching people. (How many program viewers are paying attention to each commercial?)
2.  By informing people. (Are sales points getting across to commercial viewers?)
3.  By influencing people. (How do commercial viewers feel about the product? What do the sales points mean to them?)

Both the "in home" and "by telephone" types of Recall research offer the advertiser flexibility in questioning. That is, besides the basic questions peculiar to the system, additional ones may be added to help supply the advertiser with certain supplemental information he may want.

Both methods also attempt to go beyond pure Recall by asking viewers their feelings about the product after they have seen the commercial. This type of questioning should not be confused with "impact" or "depth" or "motivational" research since a viewer's candid answer does not necessarily reflect to what extent the commercial *really* in-

[2] *Daniel Starch and Staff and Qualitative Research Methods.*

Fig. 34—TELEVISION RESEARCH SESSION under controlled theater conditions. Audience reacts to programs and commercials and indicates preferences for certain advertised products before and after exposure to commercials. *(Schwerin Research Corp.)*

fluenced him to purchase the product. In other words, he is merely expressing a feeling, an opinion.

  *c)* "Theater Audience" [3]

A third Recall measurement for testing television commercials operates under more artificial conditions but exercises better control over the types of respondents. The research group conducting the project contacts its audience by telephone or mail, inviting a representative cross section of viewers to attend a testing session at a given hour in a large room or theater. Those participating may receive gifts.

The session begins with a short orientation by the test director. Respondents are then shown a film or kinescope of a television program, with commercials in their normal positions. In this manner both the program and the commercials can be tested simultaneously. Since program research is discussed in detail in another chapter, emphasis here is on commercials only.

Immediately after viewing the program, members of the audience are asked to write down on a blank sheet of paper the name of the

[3] *One phase of the Schwerin Research Corporation method.*

product or products advertised and everything they remember having seen or heard in the commercials. This may be followed by a discussion period, during which comments of the audience are transcribed as supplemental data.

In all of the Recall techniques the results are tabulated and cross-tabulated to determine a score, or rating, for the commercial. These, in turn, can be compared against benchmarks established from previous testing of hundreds of similar commercials.

It should also be mentioned that while footnotes have identified the three basic Recall systems as those followed by specific research organizations, they actually are representations of techniques practiced generally by a large number of such research companies.

## Reliability of the Recall Method

Recall is only one phase of television commercial research. It is easy to conduct, easy to understand, but not a basic end in itself. The copywriter sincerely hopes the viewer *will* remember the various sales points from the commercial. Yet the over-all motivational effect on the viewer is much more meaningful to him, and hence to the advertiser. There is no way of knowing whether remembrance of copy points on the part of the viewer has anything whatever to do with his resultant desire to buy the particular brand of product. In other words, may he not sometimes be more influenced by the commercial whose components he does not remember so well? Or, to phrase it another way, is the commercial which sells hardest *at the moment it is being seen* necessarily the commercial whose various copy points are best retained in the mind? There is no definite answer.

Schwerin Research officials look upon Recall simply as one possible aid. But to employ remembrance alone as a clue to effectiveness, they say, "is to be guilty of 'inapplicability of measure.'" They cite this case history as typical of many to strengthen their theory:

The study in question was of commercials for two toothpastes. Brand A obtained a marked increase by our Competitive Preference measure (where the respondent's preference for the product before his exposure to the commercial is compared with his preference for the same product after he has viewed the commercial), being in fact one of the best toothpaste commercials we have tested. Brand B had no significant increase.

The ineffective commercial, however, achieved by far the greater total playback of copy points. It stressed five main ideas and put all of them across. The only hitch was that the commercial for Brand A, though it had fewer ideas, happened to include the one that influenced the audience—involving demonstrated proof of the benefits of brushing your teeth with this toothpaste.

We see here a reason why total remembrance is no tipoff on effectiveness: You can get a large number of ideas well recalled, and none of them may be important to the consumer.

This suggests another reason why Recall alone is an incomplete measure of effectiveness. With Recall there is generally no before-questioning. That is, respondents are questioned *after* they have seen a commercial. There is no way of knowing what they may have known about the product before they were exposed to the stimulus of the commercial. No response or interpretation that plays back from the commercial can be fully significant, say many experts, unless some comparison with what the respondent knew about the product before exposure to the commercial is available.

Certainly Recall has been useful to the copywriter by helping him prove to the advertiser a basic principle he learns from the start; namely, "Don't cram the commercial with copy points. Instead treat one or two, demonstrate them, pound them home. Be convincing with a few rather than confusing with many."

Recall, in short, is one obvious measurement. It is interesting. It is helpful if properly used. It is dangerously misleading if followed too literally in television commercial research.

2. *Impact.* While Recall is a precise, almost mechanical, measurement of remembrance, Impact encompasses a far broader, more intangible area. Here the researcher studies the *effect* of the *total* commercial on the viewer's mind—the motivational forces resulting from seeing the commercial, which lead the viewer closer to or farther from actual purchase of the product.

Attempting to measure television's power to motivate is indeed an ambitious undertaking. Two hundred respondents may view the same commercial under so-called controlled conditions. They may even be scientifically picked as average and typical of the larger television audience.

But at this point the control factor ends. Every one of the two hundred has a mind different from the next one. His ability to absorb information, his resistance to the selling "pitch," his way of living, his very values are peculiar to him alone. The "thousand-and-one problems" he has on his mind when he views the commercial are not the same "thousand-and-one problems" besetting his neighbor. Yet research would try to average this individual in with one hundred and ninety-nine others, determine the degree of influence the commercial attained, and then project this result to apply to the entire television audience.

In spite of these variables, however, the copywriter is interested in any indications that will help him better understand how the viewer goes about making up his mind on a specific purchase. This knowledge helps him so design his commercial as to move the viewer to positive action.

Schwerin's Competitive Preference test represents one way of measuring total Impact. In the same session where Recall of sales points is tested, the following procedure is also followed:

Before screening the program with the commercials, the audience is asked to fill out a questionnaire. On it is a list of leading brands within one product category. Respondents are asked to indicate which one they wish to receive if they are the winners in a drawing. The drawing is held immediately, with the brands they selected to be sent to their homes, a year's supply being awarded in the case of the lowest cost items.

The audience then sees the program, including the commercials, at least one of which advertises a brand which appeared on the list given respondents earlier.

After the program, the audience is informed there will be a second drawing. Each person is handed a list identical to the one he earlier checked and he is asked again to pick the brand he would most like to win. The percentage difference shown for the advertised product between the before- and after-exposure constitutes the "increment," or Competitive Preference score for the commercial. By comparing this score with the average scores of similar products already tested, the advertiser gets a definite impression as to the pulling power of his commercial.

As noted earlier, the particular commercial which scores highest in Competitive Preference may not necessarily be the commercial that scores highest in Recall. In other words, there seems to be no visible correlation between the extent of remembrance and the expressed intent to buy.

## The Truisms of Television Research

Research groups, after testing hundreds of commercials, can draw certain conclusions. Many come under the heading of truisms, which are a guide to the more inexperienced advertiser and copywriter. Among them are:

Keep the commercial simple.

When possible, demonstrate the product's most appealing feature.

Be sure the audio is relevant to the corresponding pictures.

Enable the viewer to identify himself in the commercial.

## The Likability Factor

An advertiser by nature enjoys hearing his commercials praised. A copywriter is flattered beyond words when his friends compliment him on a particularly clever job. But when this happens, it is wise to beware. There is no reliable evidence in all of television research to prove that likability is in any way related to sellability.

Many research techniques today include a question regarding the respondent's feeling toward the commercial itself. "Did you like the commercial?" Or, "How would you say this commercial compares with others you have seen?" Or, "What did you like most—or least— about the commercial?"

In the first place, say those experts opposed to such questioning, the average viewer is in no position to judge a commercial *per se*. If he volunteers a liking for the commercial, chances are he is reflecting the entertainment reward he derived from it. In the second place, most viewers seem to prefer watching animated commercials because they generally lean partly on entertainment to help them sell. Naturally, the easier the commercial is to watch, the more the public likes it.

While a commercial should never be purposely irritating, it nevertheless should leave a serious message. If entertainment fits the mood, fine.

One researcher sums up the likability factor with this story: "The doctor administered an injection, then asked the patient how he liked it. 'I hated it,' replied the patient. 'Well, it helped you more than you realize,' the doctor reassured him. The same goes for commercials. A viewer is no more qualified to judge a commercial than a patient is to judge the medication his doctor prescribes."

Secondly, calling too much attention to itself may conceivably weaken the commercial's power to sell the product or service. Some research shows that viewers are so fascinated by the technique of the commercial that the message has no effect on them.

Actually the tendency today is for research to inquire less and less into what consumers think of commercials as such.

### The Believability Factor

The advertiser intends and expects his television commercial to be believed. For if the viewer disbelieves, the cause is lost.

Perhaps in the future, if and when true depth research emerges as a trusted evaluator, some light will be shed in this vital area. But up to now research groups have handled the problem in a rather blunt manner. Included in the questions to the viewer may be one of these: "Did you find the commercial believable?" "Would you say this one is more believable or less believable than other commercials you have seen?" Confronted with such a query the viewer may well become suspicious and start doubting what he has already accepted.

As long as the copywriter remembers that honesty and common sense are basic to all commercials, he can then police himself to be believable by not resorting to faked demonstrations, phony claims, or unnecessary superlatives. If he is fortunate enough to be creating a commercial for a product that is really revolutionary, he still has a problem. Most of the adjectives he would ordinarily use have already been worked to death by products of lesser merit. He must be resourceful indeed to make viewers believe the truth!

### The Psychological Factor

A few years ago a struggling young agency copywriter wrote the following memorandum to the television research department:

"What we're really trying to find out is what goes on in people's minds. Why don't we hire a psychologist, rent a couch, and invite a few television viewers to lie down?"

That may not have been the event that triggered the trend, but since then agencies have added staff psychologists to contribute ideas on research. They are not literally following the copywriter's suggestion as to technique, but they do initiate important projects which are beginning to pay off for the advertiser.

One activity, which does not attempt to rate a television commercial but rather reveals to the creative people interesting insights into viewer reaction, is the Focus Group Interview. This new procedure calls several viewers together to view a commercial and then simply encourages them to express their thoughts orally in the hour that follows. The group is usually confined to eight or nine. Comments are recorded on tape. The psychologist then spends hours analyzing and interpreting their comments for the benefit of those responsible for the commercial. A series of such intimate discussions may even bring forth a flow of consistent information that could alter the copywriter's entire viewpoint.

Another psychological technique is based on the theoretical finding that the consumer is motivated toward or away from purchase of a product by the patterns of responses between him and the commercial —a two-way continuous interchange between stimulus and response.

While this area of research is a complex one, it is another attempt to find out why consumers behave as they do. Possibilities for future experiments along this line are infinite.

## The Wearability Factor

The advertiser, hoping to amortize the production costs of his film commercials, poses one of television's trickiest questions: How many times can a film commercial be repeated before its effect on the viewer begins to wear off?

Research has little to offer except opinion in this direction. Contacting the same audience for repeated tests or showings of the same commercial and keeping tab on how many times each respondent may have seen it on the air present an almost impossible task. For one thing, no advertiser is willing to pay the prohibitive price of calling the same audience back numerous times for theater audience sessions. And interviewing respondents in their homes offers no accurate base for measurement either.

A few tests have been conducted on a given audience when the commercial was new and on a "matched" group some months later, after the commercial had been on the air. Comparison of these results showed a relative effectiveness difference, but the findings were still general and inconclusive.

From the little evidence available, it is probably true that more advertisers underestimate than overestimate the number of times commercials can be profitably repeated.

At the same time it must be realized that some product types, some campaigns, some techniques have greater staying powers than others.

Of course, the life expectancy of a film commercial does not depend entirely upon the commercial itself. When a program commercial is repeated, a good proportion of the audience is seeing it for the first time. When it is repeated again, there are still many first viewers.

### Pre-Testing of TV Commercials

The advertiser asks: "Before I pay to put this commercial on the air, what assurance can you give me that it will move merchandise?"

The researcher replies: "We cannot predict how many products it will sell, but we can give you indications of the strength of your commercial by present research standards."

The advertiser asks: "Before I pay to put this commercial on film, what assurance can you give me that it will measure up to a sound commercial?"

The researcher replies: "We can't honestly give you any assurance unless you produce the commercial. However, simple live-action commercials may lend themselves to low-cost 16-millimeter treatments. These we can test."

The advertiser asks: "Can't you test my commercial at an earlier stage?"

The researcher replies: "We are now experimenting in the testing of storyboards, but we cannot yet promise definite answers by this method."

If storyboard testing ever proves to be a valid measurement of the over-all commercial, it will become an extremely popular form of pre-testing among advertisers. Studies now under way are following this pattern:

The artwork frames of the storyboard are put on slides and projected on a screen before the testing audience. The sound track is either recorded and played to the audience or read aloud by the test director. While the respondents see no motion and must bridge the gap in their minds from the pictures they are seeing one at a time to the finished production, they are able to express certain feelings, which can be measured to some extent by application of the Recall method, the Competitive Preference method, or both.

In a few such tests to date, ironic complications have arisen. So fascinated are some test audiences with this crude fashion of presentation of the commercial message they seem to pay more attention rather than less, with the result that some storyboards are scoring as high in Impact as the filmed versions of the same commercials! This, of course, does not happen with every commercial but just enough to add confusion to the study.

The testing of a storyboard is especially helpful in revealing audience playback of certain copy points within the commercial. In other words, at this stage it bears some resemblance to a form of TV copy testing.

Storyboard testing also will not definitely show the superiority of one production technique over another. However, when two such techniques are directly opposite, there may be a notable difference in recall. The point to be remembered here is that the absence of production values in the case of a storyboard leaves a certain vacuum for which the viewer is unable to compensate. Obviously a storyboard of simple live-action is able to convey better to an audience the final idea of the commercial than is a static storyboard of animation.

*Examples of Storyboard Testing.* Here are three different approaches to actual experimentation that have been carried on in storyboard testing:

1. Three versions of a corporate commercial were tested—the finished film, the script, and the storyboard. It was found that in terms of recall and comprehension the results from the storyboard were similar to those obtained using the film. The script version, read to the audience, was far less comprehensible and left little for the audience to remember.

2. A food product, a newcomer to TV advertising, tested two storyboards, each containing a different basic theme, to determine which left more of an impression. But here, as in the corporate test, Recall was the only criterion of judgment. A test of Impact would be the next logical step.

3. Four commercial storyboards on the same product, each with a

different copy approach, were tested in order to find out, in relation to the objectives of the campaign, which scored highest in remembrance of sales points as well as in audience preference for the product before and after viewing.

To derive the most benefit from storyboard testing as it now stands, the advertiser should compare commercials with the least number of variables. Keeping most scenes constant and changing only the theme line, or keeping both constant and changing only the demonstration portion, would reveal the simplest and most reliable difference between the two. As yet, storyboard testing is no substitute for research of the finished commercial. Even the latter has a long way to go.

*Limitations.* On the surface, pre-testing of the finished television commercial, as contrasted with the storyboard, comes closer to the answer. Here, some argue, is just another safeguard for the advertiser before he invests large sums in production and air time.

Yet, while many advertisers *do* pre-test many of their film commercials, more *do not* for the following reasons:

1. Pre-testing costs money because it involves the responses of many people.

2. What happens to the fully-produced, paid-for commercial that does not come up to standards in the pre-test? Is the research reliable enough to justify the scrapping of a commercial which cost several thousand dollars to produce?

3. Pre-testing cannot guarantee infallible predictions.

4. Pre-testing measures but one impression of the commercial and cannot predict what effect repeated showings of the commercial will have on the home audience.

5. Pre-testing may be unnecessary if the lessons learned from post-testing are properly applied to new ideas.

## Copy Testing

The most basic part of any television commercial—or radio commercial or advertisement, for that matter—is the theme line of the particular advertiser. This represents the one idea above all others the advertiser wants consumers to remember. On his theme line is built his entire advertising campaign.

The basic theme and the copy plan which develops it can be tested before the television commercial is ever written. There are many valid methods of copy testing, and this phase of basic research should be step one wherever possible, in order to establish a firm footing for the prime selling idea before the techniques of each medium take over.

Among other things, copy research tests various possible themes, and often brings to light the strongest appeal for the product to adopt.

Market research, too, is a source of countless useful facts which enable the advertiser to undertake a more intelligent commercial. Any source of broad, reliable information beforehand obviously relieves the burden on research applied to a specific medium such as television.

## New Areas for Television Research

With all of its progress to date in trying to help the advertiser eliminate part of the guesswork in his commercials, television research is still a new science with a world of mysteries before it. Just now it is breaking into entirely new areas, finding at least partial answers to:

1. Is the same television commercial equally effective as a spot announcement and on a program?

2. What effect does the content of a program have on a commercial within it?

3. Does one type of program provide a better selling climate for a particular type of product than another?

4. Are there such things as compatible and incompatible products advertised within the same program?

5. What does a famous personality really add to the value of the commercial?

6. To what extent should a program commercial relate to the mood of the program?

7. What does the use of color add to the effectiveness of a commercial?

Certain facts which already are coming to light may eventually prompt the advertiser to take another look at his commercial format.

## Climate Testing

Although the program's effect on the impact of commercials was covered briefly in the chapter devoted to program ratings, this new research development rates more detailed consideration in the area of commercial testing.

Advertisers, their agencies, and research organizations have suspected for a long time that the effect of a commercial upon an audience is directly related to the program itself and to the climate it provides for selling the product.

As he considers sponsoring a particular program the advertiser should be concerned with far more than ratings. It does not necessarily follow that the greater the audience, the more sales the commercial can deliver. As one agency expert observed, "Is there any sound commercial sense in 'reaching' thirty million people at a very high cost when you can only sell a million and a half of them—and when, at a much lower cost, you can reach nine million people and sell four million of them?"

"Climate" is the key word, one which will become more and more of a programing factor for the advertiser in the years to come. Does the program provide the right kind of climate within which the commercial can do its best job of selling?

Considerable research is now being conducted in this area. By one method the identical commercial is placed in two contrasting shows and tested against controlled "matched" groups of respondents. The variation in findings sometimes borders on the incredible. Under one set of circumstances the audience is receptive and willing to switch to the brand advertised. Under another the same commercial fails to make a significant impression.

Even when the commercial performs evenly in two given programs, it is well for the advertiser to take another look. One package product commercial convinced 8 per cent of the audience to change to the advertised brand in each of two programs. However, in Show A, the figure was almost 11 per cent among respondents in the sixteen-to-thirty-five age group and only 5½ per cent in the over-thirty-five group. In Show B, by contrast, the same commercial "sold" less than 3 per cent of the younger age group and more than 12 per cent of the over-thirty-five. The advertiser naturally weighed these results against the age-appeal of his product.

Climate testing is still a new phase of television research. While results are extremely interesting and revealing, they are not yet conclusive enough to offer the advertiser a "yes" or "no" answer as he picks between one show and another. It is, of course, entirely possible to obtain the perfect match—high rating and favorable climate—in one program. It is possible in some instances for the program promising the higher rating to become the proper vehicle if special creative attention is applied to tie the commercial closer to the mood of the show.

## Costs of Television Research

Authentic research necessarily means either gathering large numbers of people together, calling them on the telephone, or visiting them in their homes. For research must be based on an adequate sample in order to be considered valid. In order to achieve this, many man-hours are involved both in the testing process and the tabulation and interpretation of the results.

For these reasons most television research is fairly expensive. To test one television commercial may cost the advertiser several hundred dollars. A regular schedule of such testing runs into several thousand dollars per year.

Perhaps the best way to save money on television research is to use it sparingly. Instead of following the pattern of a few literal-minded advertisers who test practically every commercial created for them, a better rule is to test at intervals according to a set plan, applying any new knowledge gained along the way.

## An Appraisal of Television Research

"I don't believe that the response of a couple of hundred people can tell me whether a commercial is good, bad, or indifferent."

That, frankly, is the other side of the coin, expressed frequently in the trade. The person who utters such a remark is not attacking the smallness of the sample so much as he is the finality so many advertisers attach to the research findings. Research is a handy source to quote in a creative argument because research represents evidence, inconclusive though it might be. Indeed some advertisers have developed a sort of naïve worship for any generalities that might be drawn from research results.

Professional research people are the first to caution against careless interpretations of their findings. They are the first to admit that research is not the magic cure-all for weak advertising nor the substitute for a great creative idea.

A few years ago copywriters especially were critical of television research. Some referred to it as "scientific hindsight." But today, after living with and learning about research, the copywriter's attitude has mellowed—and not because he has to live with it whether he likes it or not. He knows research cannot provide him with the "big idea." He knows research cannot write his next commercial for him. He knows that research personnel, while trained to be deep-thinking analysts, are striving for common sense conclusions on his behalf. Copywriters are taking more than an active interest in television research by posing questions to be answered. After all, it is much more practical for the copywriter, who lives with the problems, to supply the questions than for the researcher to do so.

There is a delicate line between the proper use and flagrant abuse of television research. On the one hand research is dynamic as it develops and accumulates facts and thus becomes more and more valuable to the advertiser. On the other hand the well-intentioned practice of scoring commercials for so-called effectiveness has probably steered more than one advertiser off a sound course and into an area of serious trouble.

Many a copywriter, familiar with the ways of research, is slanting his approach today in the safe direction that will assure him a high research score rather than down the more daring path where mightier conquests so often await.

To make the best use of research it is up to the advertiser to treat it sensibly. When the score is high, may he not order his copywriter to "follow it out the window." When it is low, may he not become panicky. The secret is to encourage sensible analysis, learn what can be learned, then continue to search for more and more *new ideas*.

## chapter seventeen

# Growth and Effect of Television

THE rapid growth of television and its social and political aspects, while not akin to advertising per se, are significant to those who are a part of it. For the advertiser, network and station personnel, agency specialists, and those who perform before the camera have special reason to appreciate the aims, principles, and broad meanings of the medium in which they work.

Television, after all, has become an intimate part of the American home. Determining and guiding its future is better accomplished through understanding the over-all picture of the present and the dramatic events of the past.

## Rise of Television

Experiments for sending visual images by electrical impulses are said to date back over a hundred years. In 1884 a German patent was issued for a system of conveying motion over wires with electricity. In 1923 the iconoscope tube was patented. Two years later a British experimenter transmitted what many consider to be the first television image in motion.

In 1928 the first "visual broadcast stations" were licensed in the United States.

Yet, four years later, the *Encyclopaedia Britannica* stated, "The radio broadcasting of television for entertainment purposes is still in an experimental stage, with no clear answer as yet whether television may ultimately be expected to compare in value with sound broadcasting."

In December, 1938, a report issued by *Business Week* was titled "1939—Television Year." The National Broadcasting Company, in April of the same year, began the first television broadcasting by covering the opening ceremonies of the New York World's Fair.

By 1946 there were about a dozen television stations and only a few thousand receiving sets in the United States. While television technically could have been considered to be almost a century old at this point, only then was it about to become a commercial advertising medium.

By 1950 television was in high gear, having already reached 10 per cent penetration of U.S. homes. As the following chart[1] shows, the 10 per cent more than doubled in the year that followed:

| Year | Total Homes | TV Homes | Penetration |
|------|-------------|----------|-------------|
| 1950 | 43,600,000 | 4,200,000 | 10% |
| 1951 | 44,410,000 | 11,025,000 | 25% |
| 1952 | 45,400,000 | 15,800,000 | 35% |
| 1953 | 46,139,000 | 21,628,000 | 47% |
| 1954 | 46,800,000 | 27,600,000 | 59% |
| 1955 | 47,621,000 | 31,000,000 | 65% |
| 1956 | 48,800,000 | 35,500,000 | 73% |
| 1957 | 49,525,000 | 39,300,000 | 79% |
| 1958 | 50,500,000 | 42,500,000 | 84% |

In 1948 the Federal Communications Commission held up new station permits in order to allow time to work out the problem of allocating sufficient channel assignments to make television a truly national medium. During the "freeze period," in effect until July, 1952, only 108 stations were on the air. Yet the sale of sets continued, and television reached a higher and higher percentage of homes. Once the "freeze" was lifted, new stations were built at a rapid rate. More than 500 are now on the air.

Until 1953 all existing television stations were what have come to be called VHF, or Very High Frequency, in contrast to another category of stations which broadcast a signal known as UHF, or Ultra

[1] Source: A. C. Nielsen.

High Frequency. VHF consists of those channels numbered from 2 to 13. The need for UHF, which represents channels above 13, became apparent when the demand for channel allocations exceeded the supply. Where there are only twelve channels in the VHF band, there are sixty-eight in the UHF band. Problems naturally arise where both VHF and UHF stations operate in the same geographical areas since sets receiving the former must be converted in order to receive the latter signal as well. In many sections, some UHF stations have been forced out of business because of this complication.

## The "Progress" of Color Television

Spectacular as it is, color television has been disappointingly slow in arriving. These are considered the major factors that have held it back:

1. The high cost of the set to the consumer.
2. The lack of sufficient color programing by networks to justify the consumer's spending the extra hundreds of dollars for a color receiver.
3. The lack of production of color sets except by one or two manufacturers.
4. The ability to view the same program in black and white and still enjoy the entertainment.
5. The comparatively poor reproduction of a black-and-white picture on a color set.

Such technical limitations, however, will be overcome in time. Color, after all, is the only remaining advantage certain other media have over television.

## Television's Effect on Other Media

With the rise of television as a major tool of advertising in the past few years, other media were destined to suffer.

Again taking the top twenty advertisers, while network television has grown significantly since 1950, network radio has suffered. However, when non-network radio advertising, or spot radio, is included, the picture is not nearly so dark. Radio stations themselves are faring generally well, with most of their revenue coming from the sale of national and local spot announcements on and between music and news programs, which predominate.

Magazines and newspapers have suffered only slightly in percentage since 1950. On a revenue basis, however, both magazines and newspapers have risen considerably since the inception of television.

The slow growth of leisure time on the part of the average American has resulted in a proportionately constant growth of opportunity for all mass media. But of even more significance is the fact that much of the money allocated by advertisers for television has come from the additional sales it has helped to create.

C. Wrede Petersmeyer, president of the Corinthian Broadcasting Corporation, expresses this thought strongly:

> The living sight-sound-and-motion TV commercial . . . has set off a chain reaction to buying, production and employment never before dreamed of. The advent of TV has brought about a vastly significant and revolutionary change in the line of mass communication between 130 million Americans and American industry . . . A strong case can be made that TV has been *the* key factor in the increase in Total Sales to Consumers in the past eight years of more than 100 billion dollars annually . . .
>
> Between 1949 and 1957 Total Sales to Consumers in the United States rose from 180.6 billion to 280 billion dollars. Is it mere coincidence that *during this same period* homes owning TV sets increased from less than one million to more than forty-one million? Between 1949 and 1957 the Index of Industrial Production rose forty-four per cent. Is it mere coincidence that *during this same period* advertisers increased their expenditures on the TV medium from 57.8 million dollars to 1.3 billion to showcase their goods and services?

### Television As a Social Force

There is much disagreement among sociologists as to whether television is a favorable or unfavorable influence on family members. On the one hand are statements like these:

"Marriage after marriage is preserved by keeping it drugged on television."

"Children and adolescents frequently revert to thumb-sucking while watching."

"Television smothers contact, really inhibiting inter-personal change."

Television has been blamed for stomach trouble, eyestrain, illiteracy, juvenile delinquency, marital problems—even the common cold.

On the other hand, states William Y. Elliott in *Television's Impact on*

*American Culture,* television can be a growth-promoting experience, an enriching force of the most tremendous power.

"Horizons have been greatly expanded: millions of people have seen the ballet, have traveled to distant lands, have explored some of the country's best museums; experiences they could never have in their own lifetimes. Television has taken its viewers into the United Nations, into the meetings of Congressional investigating committees. It has led a mass audience into intimate, active participation in the political heart of the country in a way never dreamed possible.

"The range here is without bounds. Television can produce a people wider in knowledge, more alert and aware of the world, prepared to be much more actively interested in the life of their times. Television can be the great destroyer of provincialism. Television can produce a nation of people who really live in the world, not in just their own hamlets. It is here that the great opportunity of educational television lies."

## Television in Education

Noncommercial stations now on the air number in the mid-twenties. Actually the FCC has reserved 258 channels for educational television, two-thirds of them UHF, which means that in many cases they may be difficult to receive.

As of recently, about a dozen educational television stations around the nation were carrying programs designed for children to watch while in school. Fifty colleges and universities have offered more than two hundred courses for academic credit. The Joint Council on Educational Television and the Committee on Television of the American Council on Education found by survey that seventy schools, colleges, and universities were operating closed circuit television installation.

Although an educational station can operate for a whole year on less money than an advertiser may spend on one ninety-minute "special," the financial positions of most of the present educational stations is precarious. It is unlikely that the number of such outlets will grow very rapidly.

In a broader form it can be argued that today's commercial television offers educational opportunities. In addition to the special events that are telecast as a public service, dramatic stories range from fairy tales to Shakespeare. Even some quiz shows appeal to the intellect. One

Fig. 35—POLITICAL CONVENTION coverage by television networks reaches elaborate proportions. Drawing above depicts NBC's complex communications center. (1) Main TV studio for convention news commentary; (2) master control; (3) central news desk; (4) newsprinter room; (5) radio studios; (6) side arena TV cameras; (7) central TV camera platform; (8) press gallery; (9) radio booths. (NBC-TV)

noted television columnist opined, "As far as plays go, I feel strongly that television has had more worthwhile dramatic material on it than Broadway has."

Ironically, when commercial television goes "all out" to create and produce a purely educational-type show, not enough people bother to watch to make the future of the program secure. Yet stations, networks, and advertisers are doing an industrious job, within the bounds of good business judgment, of keeping the standards of programing high.

## Television and Politics

From time immemorial a political campaign has involved four things: a candidate, an organization, money, and communication. The first three have remained unchanged over the years. But communication *has* changed in a big way.

At first, political communication meant tacking up a few posters and speaking to a small crowd in an auditorium or from the observation platform of the campaign train. But today we are living in a world of mass communication—television and radio. Both major political parties make extensive use of these media—especially television—during the period preceding elections. In fact, about 90 per cent of the money spent in mass communication media during the 1956 campaign was spent in television.

While many experts criticize the concentrating of the television effort at the close of the campaign as against more continuity of action between campaigns, there are two reasons why the former practice is preferred: (1) No party has unlimited funds, and it has happened that a party has enthusiastically spent so much money at the start that there was not enough left to keep it going at the end; and (2) studies over the past fifteen years show that, while the majority of the voters have made up their minds before the campaign even begins, about 25 per cent make their decisions in the last two weeks of the campaign.

Because of the television camera's unchallenged ability to X-ray the inner personality of the subject, some say the medium may eventually improve the quality of the candidates who dare to stand before it. Be that as it may, there is no doubt that television has stimulated a renewed interest in political issues among many millions of once-indifferent Americans.

The role of the advertising agency in political campaigns remains a source of wonder, and sometimes criticism, on the part of those unfamiliar with the operation.

Until recent years political parties have been slow to take advantage of the advertising and public relations techniques which have been developed for industry. These techniques are merely ways of telling as

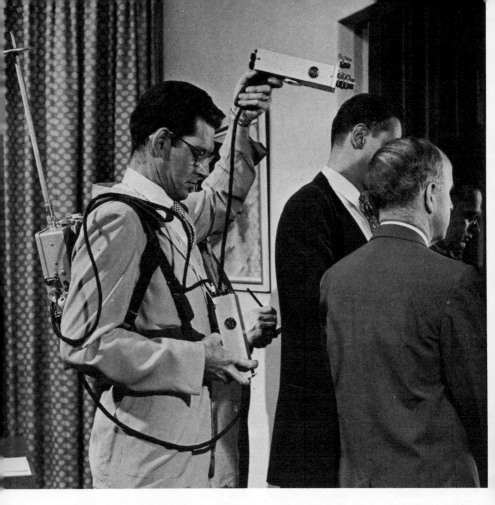

Fig. 36 — SMOKE-FILLED ROOMS, too, are within range of portable vidicon camera, sometimes called the "creepie-peepie." Unencumbered by cables, cameraman watches picture on small view-finder on his chest, wears transmitter on his back. *(NBC-TV)*

many people as possible (within a given budget) as convincingly as possible about the benefits of a product. It has therefore become the feeling of political leaders that it is the duty of people in public life, too, to take advantage of every means possible to put over their ideas as effectively as possible.

The advertising agency can, and has, helped political candidates and men in office to reach more people more effectively. To accomplish this, the advertising agency is organized to conduct research to determine the values of certain appeals; to suggest ideas of approach and technique; to buy time periods on stations and networks on behalf of the party, and to supervise production of television programs and spot announcements in order that lighting and other technical details are at their best.

By calling upon the agency, a party is simply calling upon a specialist. Because of the agency's ability to perform these useful functions, a party now calls upon its talents, usually at campaign time, as a matter of course.

# APPENDIX

# APPENDIX I

## Television Code of the National Association of Broadcasters[1]

### PRESENTATION OF ADVERTISING

1. Ever mindful of the role of television as a guest in the home, a television broadcaster should exercise unceasing care to supervise the form in which advertising material is presented over his facilities. Since television is a developing medium, involving methods and techniques distinct from those of radio, it may be desirable from time to time to review and revise the presently suggested practices:

   a) Advertising messages should be presented with courtesy and good taste; disturbing or annoying material should be avoided; every effort should be made to keep the advertising message in harmony with the content and general tone of the program in which it appears.

   b) A sponsor's advertising messages should be confined within the framework of the sponsor's program structure. A television broadcaster should avoid the use of commercial announcements which are divorced from the program either by preceding the introduction of the program (as in the case of so-called "cow-catcher" announcements) or by following the apparent sign-off of the program (as in the case of so-called "trailer" announcements). To this end, the program itself should be announced and clearly identified, both audio and video, before the sponsor's advertising material is first used, and should be signed off, both audio and video, after the sponsor's advertising material is last used.

[1] Excerpts, reproduced by special permission.

*c)* Advertising copy should contain no claims intended to disparage competitors, competing products, or other industries, professions, or institutions.

*d)* Since advertising by television is a dynamic technique, a television broadcaster should keep under surveillance new advertising devices so that the spirit and purpose of these standards are fulfilled.

*e)* Television broadcasters should exercise the utmost care and discrimination with regard to advertising material, including content, placement and presentation, near or adjacent to programs designed for children. No considerations of expediency should be permitted to impinge upon the vital responsibility toward children and adolescents, which is inherent in television, and which must be recognized and accepted by all advertisers employing television.

*f)* Television advertisers should be encouraged to devote portions of their allotted advertising messages and program time to the support of worthy causes in the public interest in keeping with the highest ideals of the free competitive system.

*g)* A charge for television time to churches and religious bodies is not recommended.

## ACCEPTABILITY OF ADVERTISERS AND PRODUCTS—GENERAL

1. A commercial television broadcaster makes his facilities available for the advertising of products and services and accepts commercial presentations for such advertising. However, a television broadcaster should, in recognition of his responsibility to the public, refuse the facilities of his station to an advertiser where he has good reason to doubt the integrity of the advertiser, the truth of the advertising representations, or the compliance of the advertiser with the spirit and purpose of all applicable legal requirements. Moreover, in consideration of the laws and customs of the communities served, each television broadcaster should refuse his facilities to the advertisement of products and services, or the use of advertising scripts, which the station has good reason to believe would be objectionable to a substantial and responsible segment of the community. The foregoing

principles should be applied with judgment and flexibility, taking into consideration the characteristics of the medium and the form and content of the particular presentation. In general, because television broadcast is designed for the home and the family, including children, the following principles should govern the business classification listed below:

*a)* The advertising of hard liquor should not be accepted.

*b)* The advertising of beer and wines is acceptable only when presented in the best of good taste and discretion, and is acceptable subject to federal and local laws.

*c)* Advertising by institutions or enterprises which in their offers of instruction imply promises of employment or make exaggerated claims for the opportunities awaiting those who enroll for courses is generally unacceptable.

*d)* The advertising of firearms and fireworks is acceptable only subject to federal and local laws.

*e)* The advertising of fortune-telling, occultism, spiritualism, astrology, phrenology, palm-reading, numerology, mind-reading or character-reading is not acceptable.

*f)* Because all products of a personal nature create special problems, such products, when accepted, should be treated with especial emphasis on ethics and the canons of good taste; however, the advertising of intimately personal products which are generally regarded as unsuitable conversational topics in mixed social groups is not acceptable.

*g)* The advertising of tip sheets, race track publications, or organizations seeking to advertise for the purpose of giving odds or promoting betting or lotteries is unacceptable.

2. Diligence should be exercised to the end that advertising copy accepted for telecasting complies with pertinent federal, state, and local laws.

3. An advertiser who markets more than one product should not be permitted to use advertising copy devoted to an acceptable product for purposes of publicizing the brand name or other identification of a product which is not acceptable.

4. "Bait-switch" advertising, whereby goods or services which the advertiser has no intention of selling are offered merely to lure the customer into purchasing higher-priced substitutes, is not acceptable.

## ADVERTISING OF MEDICAL PRODUCTS

1. The advertising of medical products presents considerations of intimate and far-reaching importance to the consumer, and the following principles and procedures should apply in the advertising thereof:

   *a)* A television broadcaster should not accept advertising material which in his opinion offensively describes or dramatizes distress or morbid situations involving ailments, by spoken word, sound, or visual effects.

   *b)* Because of the personal nature of the advertising of medical products, claims that a product will effect a cure and the indiscriminate use of such words as "safe," "without risk," "harmless," or terms of similar meaning should not be accepted in the advertising of medical products on television stations.

## CONTESTS

1. Contests should offer the opportunity to all contestants to win on the basis of ability and skill, rather than chance.

2. All contest details, including rules, eligibility requirements, opening and termination dates, should be clearly and completely announced and/or shown, or easily accessible to the viewing public, and the winners' names should be released and prizes awarded as soon as possible after the close of the contest.

3. When advertising is accepted which requests contestants to submit items of product identification or other evidence or purchase of product, reasonable facsimiles thereof should be made acceptable.

4. All copy pertaining to any contest (except that which is required by law) associated with the exploitation or sale of the sponsor's product or service, and all references to prizes or gifts offered in such connection should be considered a part of and included in the total time allowances as herein provided. (See Time Standards for Advertising Copy.)

## PREMIUMS AND OFFERS

1. Full details of proposed offers should be required by the television broadcaster for investigation and approved before the first announcement of the offer is made to the public.

2. A final date for the termination of an offer should be announced as far in advance as possible.

3. Before accepting for telecast offers involving a monetary consideration, a television broadcaster should satisfy himself as to the integrity of the advertiser and the advertiser's willingness to honor complaints indicating dissatisfaction with the premium by returning the monetary consideration.

4. There should be no misleading descriptions or visual representations of any premiums or gifts which would distort or enlarge their value in the minds of viewers.

5. Assurances should be obtained from the advertiser that premiums offered are not harmful to person or property.

6. Premiums which appeal to superstition on the basis of "luck-bearing" powers or otherwise should not be approved.

## TIME STANDARDS FOR ADVERTISING COPY

1. In accordance with good telecast advertising practices, the time standards for advertising copy are as follows:

| Length of program (in minutes) | 5 | 10 | 15 | 30 | 45 | 60 | 90 | 120 |
|---|---|---|---|---|---|---|---|---|
| "AA" and "A" Time | 1:00 | 2:00 | 2:30 | 3:00 | 4:30 | 6:00 | 9:00 | 12:00 |
| All Other Time | 1:15 | 2:10 | 3:00 | 4:15 | 5:45 | 7:00 | 10:30 | 14:00 |

Above time standards are for sponsored programs. "Participation" programs, carrying announcements for different individual advertisers, may not exceed one minute of advertising per five minutes of programing. (See paragraph 4)

2. Reasonable and limited indentification of prize and statement of the donor's name within formats wherein the presentation of contest awards or prizes is a necessary and integral part of program content shall not be included as commercial time within the meaning of paragraph 1, above; however, any oral or visual presentation concerning the product or its donor, over and beyond such identification and statement, shall be included as commercial time within the meaning of paragraph 1, above.

3. The time standards set forth above do not affect the established practice of reserving for station use the last 30 seconds of each program for station break and spot announcements.

4. Announcement programs are designed to accommodate a designated number of individual live or recorded announcements, generally one minute in length, which are carried within the body of the program and are available for sale to individual advertisers. Normally not more than 3 one-minute announcements (which should not exceed approximately 125 words if presented live) should be scheduled within a 15-minute period and not more than six such announcements should be scheduled within a 30-minute period in local announcement programs; however, fewer announcements of greater individual length may be scheduled, provided that the aggregate length of the announcements approximates three minutes in a 15-minute program or six minutes in a 30-minute program. In announcement programs other than 15 minutes or 30 minutes in length, the proportion of one minute of announcement within every five minutes of programing is normally applied. The announcements must be presented within the framework of the program period designated for their use and kept in harmony with the content of the program in which they are placed.

5. Programs presenting women's services, features, shopping guides, market information, and similar material, provide a special service to the listening and viewing public in which advertising material is an informative and integral part of the program content. Because of these special characteristics the time standards set forth above may be waived to a reasonable extent.

6. More than two back-to-back announcements plus the conventional sponsored 10 second station ID are not acceptable between programs or within the framework of a single program. Announcements scheduled between programs shall not interrupt a preceding or following program.

7. Any casual reference by talent in a program to another's product or service under any trade name or language sufficiently descriptive to identify it should, except for normal guest identification, be condemned and discouraged.

8. Stationary backdrops or properties in television presentations showing the sponsor's name or product, the name of his product, his trade-mark or slogan may be used only incidentally. They should not obtrude on program interest or entertainment. "On-camera" shots of such materials should be fleeting, not too frequent, and mindful of the need of maintaining a proper program balance.

## DRAMATIZED APPEALS AND ADVERTISING

1. Appeals to help fictitious characters in television programs by purchasing the advertiser's product or service or sending for a premium should not be permitted, and such fictitious characters should not be introduced into the advertising message for such purposes.

2. Dramatized advertising involving statements or purported statements by physicians, dentists, or nurses must be presented by accredited members of such professions.[2]

## SPONSOR IDENTIFICATION

Identification of sponsorship must be made in all sponsored programs in accordance with the requirements of the Communications Act of 1934, as amended, and the Rules and Regulations of the Federal Communications Commission.

# TELEVISION CODE INTERPRETATION #1
## June 7, 1956

*COMBINATION ("PIGGY-BACK") ANNOUNCEMENTS*

The NAB Television Code Review Board has reviewed a number of spot announcements advertising more than one product. The Board has concluded that when unrelated products are advertised as separate and distinct messages within one announcement, they in effect constitute separate announcements. The Board observes that it is an acceptable practice to advertise related (e.g., various frozen food products, or automobiles of one manufacturer) or compatible (e.g., pancakes and syrup, or furniture and carpeting) products within the framework of a single announcement, when integrated to form a single message.

# TELEVISION CODE INTERPRETATION #2
## June 7, 1956
## Revised June 9, 1958

*"PITCH" PROGRAMS*

The "pitchman" technique of advertising on television is inconsistent with good broadcast practice and generally damages the reputation of the industry and the advertising profession.

[2] This amendment to the NAB Television Code approved by the NAB Television Board on June 18, 1958.

Sponsored program-length segments consisting substantially of continuous demonstration or sales presentation, violate not only the time standards established in the Code, but the broad philosophy of improvement implicit in the voluntary Code operation and are not acceptable.

## TELEVISION CODE INTERPRETATION #3
## June 7, 1956

*HOLLYWOOD FILM PROMOTION*

The Television Code Review Board has formally concluded that the presentation of commentary or film excerpts from current theatrical releases in some instances may constitute "advertising copy" under section 1, "Time Standards for Advertising Copy." Specifically, for example, when such presentation, directly or by inference, urges viewers to attend, it shall be counted against the advertising copy time allowance for the program of which it is a part.

## TELEVISION CODE INTERPRETATION #4
## June 7, 1956

*NON-ACCEPTABILITY OF "INTIMATELY PERSONAL PRODUCTS"*

The Television Code Review Board has reviewed several advertisements in view of Paragraph 1 (f) "Acceptability of Advertisers and Products–General" and in particular of the specific language ". . . the advertising of intimately personal products which are generally regarded as unsuitable conversational topics in mixed social groups is not acceptable."

The Board has concluded that products for the treatment of hemorrhoids and for use in connection with feminine hygiene are not acceptable under the above stated language.

(The following amendment to the NAB Television Code was approved June 18, 1958, by the NAB Television Board.)

*Subliminal Perception*

The use of the television medium to transmit information of any kind by the use of the process called "subliminal perception," or by the use of any similar technique whereby an attempt is made to convey information to the viewer by transmitting messages below the threshold of normal awareness, is not permitted.

# APPENDIX II

(Supplement to Chapter 5)

## LOCAL TELEVISION

RESPONSES to the BBDO Station Managers' Survey comprise the only complete and up-to-date picture of U. S. television stations extant. Answers to the detailed questionnaire represent far more than just a sampling of information. A total of 484 stations were queried. An amazing total of 331 responded. The result is an unprecedented fund of information of interest to advertisers, national and local; to the stations themselves; to advertising agencies; and, finally, to students of "the most dynamic local medium of entertainment and mass communications."

This section is devoted to a further detailed extension of the information contained in Chapter 5.

## STUDIO SIZE

| Square Footage of Largest Studio | No. of Stations | Percentage of Stations |
|---|---|---|
| Under 1,000 | 32 | 10% |
| 1,000–1,999 | 106 | 31% |
| 2,000–3,499 | 123 | 37% |
| 3,500–4,999 | 31 | 9% |
| 5,000–6,999 | 11 | 4% |
| 7,000 and over | 3 | 1% |
| No answer | 25 | 8% |
| Total | 331 | 100% |

## STATION STAFF SIZES

| Number of Persons | No. of Stations | Percentage of Stations |
|---|---|---|
| Under 11 | 6 | 2% |
| 11–19 | 17 | 5% |
| 20–29 | 30 | 9% |
| 30–49 | 70 | 21% |
| 50–69 | 84 | 25% |
| 70–99 | 62 | 19% |
| 100–159 | 39 | 12% |
| 160–199 | 8 | 2% |
| 200–and more | 2 | 1% |
| No answer | 13 | 4% |
| Total | 331 | 100% |

# TYPES OF LOCAL BUSINESS ADVERTISING ON TELEVISION

| Type of Concern | Rank by Frequency of Mention | "REGU-LARLY" Percentage of Stations | "OCCA-SIONALLY" Percentage of Stations | "NEVER" Percentage of Stations | No Answer |
|---|---|---|---|---|---|
| Soft Drink Bottlers | (1) | 83% | 12% | 1% | 4% |
| Banks | (2) | 82% | 14% | 1% | 3% |
| Dairies | (3) | 80% | 13% | 2% | 5% |
| Auto Sales, Service | (4) | 79% | 17% | — | 4% |
| Grocery Stores | (5) | 74% | 19% | 3% | 4% |
| Bakeries | (6) | 73% | 18% | 3% | 6% |
| Appliance Stores | (7) | 71% | 25% | 1% | 3% |
| Local Utilities | (8) | 68% | 19% | 7% | 6% |
| Oil Companies | (9) | 64% | 22% | 8% | 6% |
| Home Furnishings | (10) | 61% | 33% | 1% | 5% |
| Local Brewery | (11) | 51% | 7% | 31% | 11% |
| Department Stores | (12) | 51% | 43% | 2% | 4% |
| Jewelry Stores | (13) | 44% | 47% | 3% | 6% |
| Cleaning, Dyeing | (14) | 43% | 43% | 9% | 5% |
| Drug Stores | (15) | 40% | 44% | 9% | 7% |
| Shoe Stores | (16) | 39% | 47% | 8% | 6% |
| Local Manufacturers | (17) | 37% | 40% | 15% | 8% |
| Movie Houses | (18) | 33% | 58% | 5% | 4% |
| Restaurants | (19) | 31% | 54% | 9% | 6% |
| Floor Coverings | (20) | 31% | 55% | 8% | 6% |
| Lumber Yards | (21) | 28% | 49% | 17% | 6% |
| Real Estate | (22) | 26% | 59% | 10% | 5% |
| Hardware Stores | (23) | 21% | 57% | 13% | 9% |
| Meat Markets | (24) | 18% | 27% | 40% | 15% |
| Discount Houses | (25) | 17% | 33% | 41% | 9% |
| Nurseries | (26) | 14% | 53% | 23% | 10% |
| Produce Markets | (27) | 12% | 27% | 43% | 18% |
| Beauty Parlors | (28) | 11% | 46% | 34% | 9% |
| Mail Order Houses | (29) | 10% | 35% | 46% | 9% |
| Coal Companies | (30) | 7% | 25% | 58% | 10% |

Besides the check list, supplied to stations as aided recall, voluntary responses brought additional categories of local business concerns advertising on television. Among them were these:

| | | |
|---|---|---|
| Farm Products, Services | Home Repair | Tire Companies |
| Men's Wear | Amusement Parks | Race Tracks |
| Do-Nut Shops | Construction Firms | Optical Houses |
| Savings & Loan Assns. | Leather Goods | Hotels |
| Insurance Firms | Recreational Areas | Marine Equipment |
| Roofing and Siding | Exterminators | Paint and Glass Stores |
| Ladies' Apparel | Scrap Metal Dealers | Food Plans |
| Bowling Alleys | Sporting Goods | Builders |
| Office Supply Stores | Garages | Motels |
| Political Groups | Resorts | Auto Wrecking |
| Air Conditioner Dealers | Clothing Stores | Van and Storage |
| Local Blue Cross | Toy Stores | Specialty Shops |
| Farm Auction Services | Pump Companies | Prebuilt Homes |
| Dog Tracks | Meat Packing | Photo Supplies |
| Heating, Plumbing | Music Stores | Newspapers |
| Florists | Cosmetic Firms | Irrigation Supplies |

## REASONS GIVEN BY NON-TV ADVERTISERS FOR NOT USING TELEVISION

| Reasons | Percentage of Stations Mentioning[1] |
|---|---|
| High cost (both time and production) | 63% |
| Experience with, confidence in, newspapers | 12% |
| Lack of knowledge, unfamiliarity with medium | 9% |
| Coverage too great to be economical; TV areas much larger than trade area | 8% |
| Lack of confidence in the medium; belief that TV "won't do the job" | 6% |
| Insufficient number of trained personnel on advertiser's staff to plan television campaign | 4% |
| Local branches of national concern would like to use TV, but over-all advertising plan of parent company forbids; advertising budget governed by home office | 2% |
| Difficulty in making effective commercials | 2% |
| Lack of available class "A" or "AA" time periods | 1% |
| Some co-op money does not recognize television | 1% |
| Tried it once, or a few times, but failed to get the immediate results expected | 1% |
| Experience with, confidence in, radio | 1% |
| Found it difficult to measure results (even though there was no apparent desire to measure results of newspaper advertising) | 1% |
| Business is too small | 1% |
| No Answer | 13% |

[1] Total percentage exceeds 100 because certain stations listed more than one reason given by certain non-TV advertisers.

# APPENDIX III

## Further Script Examples of Corporate Television Advertising

(Supplement to Chapter 15)

### UNITED STATES STEEL

| *VIDEO* | *AUDIO* |
|---|---|
| OPEN ON STYLIZED ANIMATED BACKGROUND OF DISTANT STARS AND PLANETS, REPRESENTING OUTER SPACE. | (MUSIC: Futuristic strains throughout) |
| A FUTURISTIC SPACE SHIP ENTERS FRAME AT UPPER RIGHT AND PASSES IN FRONT OF CAMERA TO THE LEFT, LEAVING BEHIND IT LINES REPRESENTING ROCKET TRAILS. A SECOND SPACE SHIP, THIS ONE RESEMBLING A FLYING SAUCER, ENTERS FRAME AT UPPER LEFT, ALSO LEAVING BEHIND IT LINES REPRESENTING ROCKET TRAILS. | (MUSIC: Continues) |
| THE SECOND SPACE SHIP CROSSES THE PATH OF THE FIRST. BOTH FLY OUT OF FRAME. | GEORGE HICKS (Voice Over) The Space Age is *here!* . . . |

| *VIDEO* | *AUDIO* |
|---|---|
| A THIRD SPACE SHIP, TRIANGULAR IN SHAPE, ENTERS FRAME AT LEFT, AND FLIES RAPIDLY TOWARD CAMERA. | . . . with its fantastic speeds . . . |
| CAMERA FOLLOWS SHIP AS IT ZOOMS UPWARD, PASSING A NUMBER OF DIFFERENT PLANETS. | . . . incredible heights, and complex problems that must be solved. |
| CUT TO MEDIUM SHOT OF A MISSILE FLYING HORIZONTALLY, HIGH ABOVE THE SURFACE OF THE EARTH. IT IS GRAYISH, TO INDICATE THAT IT IS MADE OF ORDINARY METAL. | One of the most critical problems . . . |
| AS THE SURFACE OF THE EARTH DROPS OUT OF FRAME, THE NOSE AND TAIL SURFACES OF THE MISSILE BEGIN TO GLOW FROM FRICTIONAL HEAT. | . . . is the terrific heat caused by traveling through the atmosphere at supersonic speeds . . . |
| DISSOLVE TO SAME MISSILE FLYING VERTICALLY AGAINST A BACKGROUND OF DISTANT STARS, WITH LEGEND "700 m.p.h." SUPERED. | . . . and then some. Ordinary metals worked fine . . . |
| MISSILE FORCES ITS WAY THROUGH CIRCLES REPRESENTING SOUND WAVES, AND LEAVES THEM BEHIND AS IT CONTINUES ITS UPWARD FLIGHT. | (SOUND: Bursting noise as missile breaks sound barrier) . . . in breaking the sound barrier . . . |
| SUPER DISSOLVES TO "1200 m.p.h." AS MISSILE CONTINUES TO FLY UPWARD. | . . . and even up to 1200 miles an hour, where the heat, generated by friction . . . |

| VIDEO | AUDIO |
|---|---|
| A THERMOMETER SUPERS OVER THE MISSILE. SUPER DISSOLVES TO "400° F." | . . . raises the temperature to 400 degrees Fahrenheit! |
| ALL SUPERS DISSOLVE OFF. MISSILE CONTINUES TO FLY UPWARD AS A SECOND MISSILE, IDENTICAL IN SHAPE BUT BRIGHTER TO SHOW THAT IT IS MADE OF STAINLESS STEEL, ENTERS FRAME FROM THE BOTTOM AND RISES RAPIDLY TO OVERTAKE FIRST MISSILE. | But it now appears that stainless steel is the only metal . . . |
| NOSE OF FIRST MISSILE CHANGES FROM A SHARP POINT TO A BLUNT ROUND SHAPE TO SHOW HOW ORDINARY METALS MELT AT HIGH SPEEDS BECAUSE OF FRICTIONAL HEAT. | . . . available in quantities that can do the job . . . |
| STAINLESS STEEL MISSILE PASSES BLUNTED MISSILE, WHICH DROPS OUT OF BOTTOM OF FRAME. | . . . *above* 1200 miles per hour. (SOUND: Rocket noise out. MUSIC: Punctuation) |
| DISSOLVE TO MEDIUM SHOT OF THE STAINLESS STEEL MISSILE STANDING UPRIGHT AGAINST A NEUTRAL BACKGROUND. | Another major problem arises from the fact . . . |
| STARTING AT THE TOP, BROAD WHITE LINES ANIMATE DOWNWARD TO OUTLINE THE INDIVIDUAL STEEL SHEETS IN THE MISSILE'S "SKIN." | . . . that the small size of the sheets . . . |
| A FLAT STAINLESS STEEL SHEET APPEARS BEHIND THE MISSILE AT | . . . requires a large number of joints, increasing the difficulties |

| VIDEO | AUDIO |
|---|---|
| THE TOP. THE MISSILE MOVES TO THE RIGHT AS THE SHEET DROPS DOWN BESIDE IT. | of fabrication. The challenge that . . . |
| A DOTTED WHITE LINE ANIMATES UPWARD TO FORM A RECTANGULAR OUTLINE NEARLY THE SAME HEIGHT AS THE MISSILE, AND WIDER THAN THE SHEET. | . . . U. S. Steel faced was to make large, thinner sheets . . . |
| SHEET MOVES TO THE LEFT OF THE DOTTED OUTLINE. | . . . of alloy and stainless steels to reduce the number of joints. |
| DISSOLVE TO PATTERN OF ENGINEERING SYMBOLS—CALIPERS, TRIANGLES, COMPASSES, SLIDE RULES, ETC., MOVING AGAINST A BACKGROUND OF GRAPH PAPER. | This is the kind of problem U. S. Steel engineers welcome . . . |
| OUTLINES OF FOUR SEPARATE STAINLESS STEEL SHEETS, LYING HORIZONTAL TO CAMERA BUT TILTED FOR PERSPECTIVE, POP ON AND MOVE UP AS THE PATTERN OF SYMBOLS DISSOLVES OUT, LEAVING NEUTRAL GRAY BACKGROUND. | . . . and here's their answer— sandwich rolling. |
| THE OUTLINES FILL IN TO FORM SOLID STEEL SHEETS, AND, ONE BY ONE, DROP DOWN INTO A SINGLE PILE. | Standard plates of stainless or alloy steels . . . |
| TWO SOLID BLACK SHEETS OF STEEL, THICKER THAN THE FIRST FOUR, MOVE IN TO COVER THE TOP AND BOTTOM OF THE PILE AND FORM A "SANDWICH." | . . . are *sandwiched* between two heavier plates of ordinary carbon steel. The men in the plants call it a "Dagwood" sandwich. |

| VIDEO | AUDIO |
|---|---|
| LINES REPRESENTING HEAT AP-PEAR AROUND THE SANDWICH. THE SANDWICH TURNS WHITE TO SHOW IT HAS BEEN HEATED. LINES DISAPPEAR. | It is heated . . . |
| HEATED SANDWICH PASSES BE-TWEEN ROLLERS, WHICH SQUEEZE IT TO A LARGER SIZE. | . . . and rolled in existing mills to become thinner . . . |
| SANDWICH REVERSES ITS MOTION AND AGAIN PASSES THROUGH THE ROLLERS, BECOMING STILL LARGER. | . . . longer . . . |
| SANDWICH PASSES THROUGH THE ROLLERS AGAIN BECOMING STILL LARGER. | . . . and wider. |
| SANDWICH CONTINUES MOVING RIGHT. THE TWO OUTER SHEETS TURN BLACK AGAIN AND PEEL OFF TO EXPOSE THE INNER SHEETS OF STAINLESS STEEL. | The carbon steel is removed . . . |
| THE FOUR SHEETS OF STAINLESS STEEL, MUCH LARGER NOW, SEPA-RATE AGAIN, AND TOP SHEET MOVES TO THE ORIGINAL SHEET STANDING BESIDE THE LARGER DOTTED OUTLINE. | . . . and out come uniform stain-less steel sheets . . . |
| THE ROLLED SHEET OF STAINLESS STEEL FITS ITSELF NEATLY INTO THE DOTTED OUTLINE. OUTLINE DISSOLVES OFF, LEAVING THE TWO STEEL SHEETS STANDING SIDE BY SIDE FOR COMPARISON. | . . . thinner, wider, and with a larger area than ever possible before. |

| *VIDEO* | *AUDIO* |
|---|---|
| THE LARGE SHEET OF STAINLESS STEEL CURLS INTO A VERTICAL TUBE. | These larger, thinner sheets ... |
| NOSE CONE AND TAIL FINS DISSOLVE ON THE TUBE TO COMPLETE THE MISSILE AS BEFORE. PULL BACK AS SILHOUETTES OF DIFFERENT AIRPLANES AND MISSILES POP ON BACKGROUND SURROUNDING MISSILE. | ... make possible better space vehicles designed for improved performance and greater ease ... |
| FLAMES SPURT FROM TAIL OF MISSILE AND IT TAKES OFF. | ... of fabrication.<br>(SOUND: Missile takes off.)<br>Of course we're proud ... |
| CUT TO MEDIUM SHOT OF SAME MISSILE IN UPWARD FLIGHT AS IT PASSES STARS AND PLANETS. | ... of this dramatic Space Age achievement—and we were prouder when the Air Force's Air Materiel Command— |
| SUPER CRAWL OVER MISSILE: "WE DID NOT EXPECT DEVELOPMENT OF SANDWICH STEEL FOR FIVE YEARS OR MORE. YOU SHOWED US AMERICAN INDUSTRY AND INITIATIVE IN ACTION. THE BENEFITS OF YOUR ACHIEVEMENT EXTEND EVEN BEYOND AIR FORCE REQUIREMENTS FOR THIS SPACE AGE." | ... told us: "We did not expect development of sandwich steel for five years or more. You showed us American industry and initiative in action. |
| HOLD SUPER. DISSOLVE BACKGROUND TO ORIGINAL ROLLING SEQUENCE. | The benefits of your achievement extend even beyond Air Force requirements for this Space Age." |

| *VIDEO* | *AUDIO* |
|---|---|
| DISSOLVE TO TRAVELING SHOT OF THREE ROCKETS FLYING SIDE BY SIDE. | (SOUND: Rocket roar, up and under)<br><br>Welcome words, indeed, to the scientists and engineers of United States Steel . . . |
| ROCKETS TURN UPWARD AND FAN OUT INTO THREE SEPARATE FLIGHT PATHS. | . . . who continually search for the new way . . . |
| U. S. S. LOGO, IN OUTLINE, APPEARS IN CIRCLE OF FLAMES COMING OUT OF REAR OF ROCKET FLYING AWAY FROM CAMERA. IT MOVES UP TOWARD CAMERA AS ROCKET DISSOLVES OUT, LEAVING BACKGROUND OF DISTANT STARS. | (SOUND: Rocket noise fades out)<br>. . . to make the new and finer . . . |
| LOGO FILLS IN SOLID. | . . . steels to meet tomorrow's challenge.<br>(MUSIC: Up to finish) |

# GENERAL ELECTRIC

REAGAN (On-camera)

Tonight, Don Herbert, our General Electric progress reporter, shows us a very important kind of progress—the change in the ownership of American industry . . . from the few to the many.

OPEN ON:

DON HERBERT AND GARY, A TWELVE-YEAR-OLD BOY, STANDING IN FRONT OF A PAINTED BACKDROP SHOWING AN ORNATE ENTRANCE TO A LARGE FACTORY OF THE GAY NINETIES PERIOD. IT IS OBVIOUSLY A BIG FACTORY, WITH MANY BUILDINGS AND CHIMNEYS VISIBLE IN THE BACKGROUND. THERE IS A SIGN IN THE FOREGROUND IN PERIOD LETTERING THAT READS, "TYPICAL MANUFACTURING COMPANY," AND A PRACTICAL DOOR.

HERBERT (On-camera)

Now, Gary, there's an example of a business that's gone out of style.

GARY (On-camera)

You mean because it's so old and funny-looking, Mr. Herbert?

CAMERA STARTS TO DOLLY IN AS A MAN WALKS OUT OF DOOR IN SET. HE IS DIGNIFIED GENTLEMAN IN HIS 40's, WITH A HANDSOME HANDLE-BAR MUSTACHE, AND IS DRESSED IN THE HEIGHT OF PERIOD FASHION. HIS CLOTHES INDICATE WEALTH—TOP HAT, LONG CUTAWAY COAT, STRIPED TROUSERS, GOLD CHAIN ON HIS VEST, GOLD-HEADED CANE, ETC.

HERBERT (Voice over)

No, because of that genetleman. Know who *he* is?

CUT TO:

CLOSEUP OF OWNER SO WE CAN GET A GOOD LOOK AT HIM AND HIS CLOTHES. HE DOES A BUSINESS OF TAKING OUT HIS WATCH TO SEE WHAT TIME IT IS. THE WATCH HAS AN OLD-FASHIONED CASE WITH A GOLD COVER OVER THE FACE.

GARY (Voice over)

He looks kind of important. Is he . . . the owner?

CUT TO:

HERBERT AND GARY. OWNER WALKS OUT OF FRAME.

HERBERT (On-camera)

He's the owner. And a very important person. You see, in his day, a *few* people owned most of the major businesses in our country. Of course. . . .

PAN WITH PAIR AS THEY START TO WALK TO NEXT FRAME.

. . . we've made important progress since then.

CUT TO:

MEDIUM SHOT OF HERBERT AND GARY AS THEY REACH THE EXTERIOR OF A LARGE MODERN FACTORY. THE SIGN IN THE FOREGROUND READS, IN MODERN LETTERS, "TYPICAL MANUFACTURING COMPANY." THERE IS A PRACTICAL DOOR.

HERBERT (On-camera)

Now, here's a modern business . . .

MAN IN MODERN WORK CLOTHES, CARRYING A LUNCH BOX, STEPS OUT OF DOOR.

Can you guess who that man is?

CUT TO:

CLOSEUP OF WORKER, WHO DUPLICATES ACTIONS OF PREVIOUS MAN, LOOKING AT MODERN WRIST WATCH.

GARY (Voice over)

(SURPRISED) Him? He works there, doesn't he?

CUT TO:

HERBERT AND GARY LOOKING AT WORKER, WHO WALKS OUT OF FRAME.

HERBERT (On-camera)

Yes, but he's also an *owner.*

GARY (On-camera)

No kidding!

HERBERT

Because he's buying stock in the company.

A TYPICAL HOUSEWIFE, CARRYING A BAG OF GROCERIES, WALKS THROUGH THE FRAME AS THOUGH THERE WERE A SIDEWALK IN FRONT OF THE FACTORY.

HERBERT

There goes another owner.

GARY

(AMAZED) A woman!

HERBERT

That's right. A housewife. She owns stock in the company, too.

CUT TO:

CLOSEUP OF GARY, WHO LOOKS PUZZLED.
### GARY
You mean there's more than one owner?

CUT TO:

MEDIUM SHOT OF HERBERT AND GARY.
### HERBERT
*That's* the idea, Gary. Today, American industry is owned
by *many* people, instead of just a few.
HERBERT STARTS TO WALK GARY OVER TO CHART.
Guess how many.

CUT TO:

CLOSEUP OF GARY.
### GARY
A million?

CUT TO:

HERBERT BY CHART. IT IS A FRAME SUSPENDED IN LIMBO THAT ENCLOSES
A SHEET OF PAPER WITH THE HEADING, "AMERICAN SHARE OWNERS,"
AND NINE RECTANGLES ALONG THE BOTTOM LIKE THE FACE OF AN ADD-
ING MACHINE.
### HERBERT
Many more. Look here . . .

CUT TO:

CLOSEUP OF CHART. AS HERBERT TALKS, EIGHT FIGURES OF PEOPLE IN
MODERN DRESS REPRESENTING DIFFERENT PROFESSIONS POP ON IN FORE-
GROUND, AND NUMBERS "8,000,000" APPEAR IN RECTANGLES BELOW.
### HERBERT (Voice over)
American corporations today, are owned by more than *eight
million people.*

CUT TO:

HERBERT, GARY, AND CHART.
### GARY (On-camera)
Eight million! Wow!
### HERBERT (On-camera)
That's not all. Enough others own stock in small, private
concerns . . .

CUT TO:

CLOSEUP OF CHART. TWO ADDITIONAL FIGURES POP ON, AS THOUGH THEY

WERE STANDING BEHIND THE FIRST FIGURES, AND NUMBER BELOW
CHANGES TO "10,000,000."

HERBERT (Voice over)

. . . to bring the total up to *ten million!*

CUT TO:

HERBERT AND CHART.

HERBERT (On-camera)

And most of us own stock indirectly. We put our money in
mutual savings banks, life insurance, mutual funds, and
pension plans. Those institutions, in turn, buy stock with
the money.

CUT TO:

CLOSEUP OF CHART. MORE FIGURES POP ON BEHIND THE PREVIOUS ONES
TO FILL THE CHART COMPLETELY, GIVING THE IMPRESSION OF A NUM-
BERLESS CROWD. NUMBERS BELOW CHANGE TO "100,000,000."

HERBERT (Voice over)

So, actually, American business now belongs to more than
*100 million people!*

CUT TO:

HERBERT, GARY AND CHART.

GARY (On-camera)

That many? Gosh, I thought you had to be *rich* to own
stock!

HERBERT FLIPS CHART, WHICH IS PIVOTED WITHIN FRAME. OTHER SIDE
SHOWS THREE OUTLINE FIGURES, TITLE: "SHARE OWNERS."

HERBERT (On-camera)

Not any more.

CUT TO:

CLOSEUP OF CHART, WHICH ANIMATES. TWO OF THE THREE OUTLINE
FIGURES FILL IN SOLID, AND NUMBERS "7500" APPEAR.

HERBERT (Voice over)

Today, of all the share owners of American business, two-
thirds earn *less* than $7500 a year.

CUT TO:

HERBERT AND GARY BY CHART.

HERBERT (On-camera)

But the *important* thing is that millions of people are becoming owners.

PAN WITH PAIR AS THEY WALK TO A SMALL FRAMED SCREEN HANGING
IN LIMBO. SCREEN HAS ON IT A FROZEN FRAME SHOWING MANY PEOPLE
AT THE GENERAL ELECTRIC SHARE OWNERS' MEETING.

HERBERT

For example, take General Electric. General Electric is
owned by about a half million people.

CUT TO:

CLOSEUP OF GARY, LIMBO BACKGROUND.

GARY

That many own just *one* company?

CUT TO:

HERBERT AND BOY AGAIN.

HERBERT

That's right. Actually General Electric has many more
owners than employees.

CUT TO:

CLOSEUP OF SCREEN, WHICH ANIMATES TO SHOW DIFFERENT SCENES
TAKEN AT THE MEETING.

HERBERT (Voice over)

Here are just a few of General Electric's share owners at a
recent annual meeting in Schenectady, New York. Many of
the share owners are employees of the company; others are
farmers, lawyers, workers, housewives. No one person owns
more than one-tenth of one per cent of General Electric
stock.

*CUT TO:*

CLOSEUP OF HERBERT AND BOY.

HERBERT (On-camera)

So you see, Gary, here in America we've developed a new
way of doing business. In our system, *many* people—not
just a privileged few—own the industries that make America great. That's why we call it "People's Capitalism." General Electric is doing all it can to encourage this system
because it represents real progress toward a better life for
us all.

CAMERA PANS OVER TO SCREEN, WHICH IS BLANK.

HERBERT

And as you know, at General Electric . . .

DISSOLVE TO:

PROGRESS LEGEND APPEARS ON SCREEN.

HERBERT (Voice over)

Progress is our most important product.

# APPENDIX IV

## TOP 150 U. S. TELEVISION MARKETS

### 1,000,000–5,000,000
*TV Homes*

1. New York
2. Los Angeles
3. Chicago
4. Philadelphia
5. Detroit
6. Boston
7. San Francisco
8. Cleveland
9. Pittsburgh

### 545,000–764,000
*TV Homes*

10. St. Louis
11. New Haven-Hartford
12. Cincinnati
13. Minneapolis
14. Washington
15. Baltimore
16. Milwaukee
17. Kansas City
18. Dallas-Fort Worth
19. Johnstown-Altoona
20. Atlanta

### 426,000–532,000
*TV Homes*

21. Indianapolis
22. Providence
23. Kalamazoo-Grand Rapids
24. Charlotte
25. Lancaster[1]
26. Buffalo
27. Houston
28. Seattle-Tacoma
29. Memphis
30. Huntington-Charleston

### 335,000–412,000
*TV Homes*

31. Columbus, Ohio
32. Dayton
33. Louisville
34. Birmingham
35. Syracuse
36. Portland, Ore.
37. Lansing
38. Steubenville-Wheeling

[1] Includes Harrisburg.

39. Greensboro-Winston-Salem
40. New Orleans

*296,000–332,000*
*TV Homes*

41. Schenectady
42. Champaign
43. Asheville
44. Nashville
45. Binghamton
46. Miami
47. Sacramento
48. Omaha
49. Rock Island-Moline-Davenport
50. Raleigh-Durham

*256,000–296,000*
*TV Homes*

51. Green Bay
52. Oklahoma City
53. Toledo
54. Tulsa
55. Rochester, N. Y.
56. Denver
57. Greenville, S. C.
58. Wichita-Hutchinson
59. Cedar Rapids-Waterloo
60. Norfolk

*222,000–256,000*
*TV Homes*

61. Roanoke
62. Tampa-St. Petersburg
63. San Diego

64. Bay City-Saginaw
65. Des Moines-Ames
66. Baton Rouge
67. Wilkes-Barre-Scranton
68. Jacksonville
69. Jackson, Miss.
70. Richmond

*193,000–218,000*
*TV Homes*

71. San Antonio
72. Knoxville
73. Shreveport
74. Fresno
75. Little Rock
76. Sioux City
77. Madison
78. Spokane
79. Terre Haute
80. Bristol-Johnson City

*170,000–193,000*
*TV Homes*

81. Cape Girardeau-Paducah
82. Mobile
83. Portland, Maine
84. Fort Wayne
85. Saint Joseph
86. Evansville-Henderson
87. Salt Lake City
88. Phoenix
89. Sioux Falls
90. Lincoln

*146,000–167,000*
*TV Homes*

91. Greenville-Washington, N. C.
92. Youngstown
93. Montgomery
94. Orlando-Daytona Beach
95. Springfield, Mo.
96. Charleston, S. C.
97. Valley City-Fargo
98. South Bend
99. Florence, S. C.
100. Columbia, S. C.

*130,000–146,000*
*TV Homes*

101. Duluth-Superior
102. Decatur, Ill.
103. Rockford
104. Peoria
105. Bakersfield
106. Mason City
107. Pittsburg, Kansas-Joplin
108. Springfield-Holyoke
109. Austin, Tex.
110. Beaumont-Port Arthur

*115,000–128,000*
*TV Homes*

111. Chattanooga
112. Clarksburg
113. La Crosse
114. Hannibal-Quincy
115. Lubbock
116. Monroe

117. Cadillac-Traverse City
118. Pensacola
119. Columbus, Ga.
120. Wichita Falls

*104,000–115,000*
*TV Homes*

121. Augusta, Ga.
122. Tyler
123. Macon
124. Utica
125. Temple-Waco
126. Topeka
127. Amarillo
128. Salinas[2]
129. Burlington-Plattsburg
130. Ottumwa

*91,000–104,000*
*TV Homes*

131. Austin-Rochester
132. Bangor
133. Bluefield
134. Kearney-Hastings
135. Albuquerque
136. Springfield, Ill.
137. Texarkana
138. Thomasville
139. El Paso
140. Wilmington, N. C.

*77,000–91,000*
*TV Homes*

141. Yakima

[2] Includes San Luis Obispo.

142. Great Bend
143. Savannah
144. Meridian
145. Wausau
146. Jackson, Tenn.

147. Ada
148. Eugene
149. Lake Charles
150. Corpus Christi

## UNDUPLICATED TV COVERAGE OF TOP TV SPOT MARKETS

| Markets | Unduplicated TV Homes | Percentage U.S. TV | Percentage U.S. TV Cumulative |
|---|---|---|---|
| 1–10 | 16,900,000 | 41.0% | 41.0% |
| 11–20 | 5,250,000 | 12.7% | 53.7% |
| 21–30 | 3,820,000 | 9.3% | 63.0% |
| 31–40 | 2,840,000 | 6.9% | 69.9% |
| 41–50 | 2,470,000 | 6.0% | 75.9% |
| 51–60 | 1,990,000 | 4.9% | 80.8% |
| 61–70 | 1,680,000 | 4.1% | 84.9% |
| 71–80 | 1,430,000 | 3.5% | 88.4% |
| 81–90 | 1,140,000 | 2.8% | 91.2% |
| 91–100 | 930,000 | 2.3% | 93.5% |
| 101–110 | 480,000 | 1.1% | 94.6% |
| 111–120 | 490,000 | 1.1% | 95.7% |
| 121–130 | 360,000 | 0.9% | 96.6% |
| 131–140 | 525,000 | 1.3% | 97.9% |
| 141–150 | 285,000 | 0.7% | 98.6% |

# GLOSSARY

ABSTRACT SET. A nonrealistic background in which a minimum of units is employed in order that complete attention can be given the foreground.

AD. Assistant director.

ADAPTATION. A version of a story translated from another medium.

ADJACENCY. The program immediately preceding or following the one in question.

AFM. American Federation of Musicians.

AFTRA. American Federation of Television and Radio Artists.

ANGLE. Direction from which a scene is shot by the camera.

ASCAP. American Society of Composers, Authors, and Publishers.

ASPECT RATIO. The three-to-four unit proportion of picture dimensions in television.

AUDIO. Sound portion of a television program or commercial.

AUDITION. Tryout for talent or an entire program.

BALOP. Balopticon-type projection of artwork.

BASIC SET. A set without props or other objects.

BG. Background, applying either to scenic backdrops or background music, sound effects, or other sounds.

BILLBOARD. Name and talent to appear on program, usually announced at the beginning.

BMI. Broadcast Music, Inc.

BOOM. Device for moving a suspended overhead microphone.

BRIDGE. Transition from one scene to the next.

BUSINESS. Stage action.

CAMERA LENS TURRET. Revolving part of camera on which are fastened the various lenses for quick interchanging.

CANS.   Headphones worn by production crew.

CLIENT.   The relationship of an advertising company to its advertising agency. Most large companies are clients of agencies, who specialize in the creation of advertising.

CLIP.   A short piece of film inserted in a program or commercial.

CLOSED CIRCUIT.   Live television transmitted by cable for private viewing.

CLOSEUP.   A close view of the person or object being televised.

COAXIAL CABLE.   Cable which carries TV signal.

CONTINUITY.   Script for the TV program.

CONTRAST.   The relationship of light to dark tones within the picture.

COW CATCHER.   A brief commercial at the very beginning of a program.

CROSS FADE.   The act of fading out one sound or scene and fading in another.

CU.   Closeup.

CUE CARD.   Announcer's or actor's prompting card, sometimes unflatteringly called an "idiot card."

CUE IN.   Signal for the beginning of action, music, or other element of a program or commercial.

CUT.   End of action.

CUT TO.   To stop the action with one camera and immediately start action with another.

CYC.   Neutral background.

DB.   Delayed broadcast.

DEFINITION.   Degree of focus and contrast in a picture.

DIRECTOR.   The person who conducts the entire TV production.

DISSOLVE.   Simultaneous fading out of one scene and fading in of the next.

DOLLY.   Camera movement toward or away from an object.

DRY RUN.   Rehearsal without cameras.

DS.   Dissolve.

DUBBING.   The combining of several sound tracks for recording on film.

DUPE.   A duplicate negative film print made from a positive.

ECU.   Extreme closeup.

E.T.   Electrical transcription.

FACILITIES.   Physical setup needed to stage a program or commercial.

FCC.   Federal Communications Commission.

FILTER.   Sound device to give voice or sound a quality comparable to that heard on a telephone.

FLAT.   Temporary wall which provides a background in an indoor set.

FLOOR MANAGER.   The person who executes the director's orders on the studio floor.

FM.   Frequency modulation, the method by which television sound signals are transmitted.

FORMAT.   The standard plan of a television show or commercial to give it a consistent framework from week to week.

FRAME.   Composition of a picture for telecast as seen by a fixed camera.

FTC.   Federal Trade Commission.

GHOST.   An extra image in the television picture, sometimes resulting from a signal reflection.

GO TO BLACK.   Completely fade out the final picture until the screen is completely blank.

HITCH HIKE.   A brief commercial at the very end of the program.

I.D.   A ten-second local station-identification announcement in which the advertiser shares his message time with the station's call letters.

IMAGE.   The picture as seen on the television screen.

IMAGE-ORTHICON.   The present supersensitive camera tube, successor to the Iconoscope pickup tube for studio or outdoor use.

IN THE CAN.   Completed program or commercial ready for shipping in metal containers.

IRIS IN.   Gradual appearance of a picture through a steadily enlarging circle until it fills the picture.

IRIS OUT.   The reverse, where the picture disappears through a diminishing circle.

JUICER.   An electrican.

KINESCOPE.   The RCA picture tube in receivers or monitors.

KINESCOPE FILM.   TV recording, photographed from the face of the Kinescope tube.

LAB.   The laboratory where film negatives are developed and positives made.

LAP DISSOLVE.   A slow dissolve, during which the picture fading in and the picture fading out are momentarily visible within the same frame.

LEADER.   Portion of film in advance of picture which enables the operator to thread it through projector.

LEGEND.   Lettering superimposed or matted on the television picture.

LIMBO.   A plain setting foreign to the regular action.

LIP SYNC.   Synchronization of lip movement and voice. In film, the direct recording of sound from the scene being photographed.

LONG SHOT.   A full view of considerable depth, where the principal object would appear distant from the camera.

LOOP.   A portion of film spliced in a loop for continuous projection.

LS.   Long shot.

MCR.   Master control room.

MCU.   Medium closeup.

MONITOR.   A kinescope or viewing screen for control room use in checking the picture going out over the air.

MONTAGE.   A fast series of related pictures which together create a single impression.

MOVIOLA.   A projection apparatus specially designed for film editing.

MS.   Medium shot.

MURAL.   Large photographic enlargement, usually of exterior scene, intended to appear realistic when used as a background.

NAB.   National Association of Broadcasters.

NETWORK.   A lineup of stations carrying the same program simultaneously.

O & O.   A station owned and operated by a network.

PAN.   Continuous movement of a camera to follow the action.

PRE-EMPT.   To remove one program from the air in order that another may be scheduled in its place.

PRE-TEST.   Research evaluation of a program or commercial before it is put into use.

POST-TEST.   Research after the program or commercial has appeared on the air.

PRODUCT IMAGE.   The personality built into a product through advertising.

PROP.   Any portable article placed on the set to dress it or equip it for certain actions.

PULL BACK.   To move the camera away from the subject.

REAR PROJECTION.  A translucent screen background on which is projected from the reverse side either slides or motion picture footage.

RECALL.  One basis for effectiveness measurement of a commercial, in which respondents are asked to report what they remember seeing and hearing in the commercial.

REMOTE.  Telecasting by mobile equipment from outside the studio.

RESPONDENT.  A person interviewed in a research project.

SAG.  Screen Actors' Guild.

SEG.  Screen Extras' Guild.

SEGUE.  The blending of the end of one musical section with the beginning of another.

SET.  The area constructed in the studio on which the program or commercial is performed.

SIGNAL.  Transmission of the picture and sound.

SIMULCAST.  A program on both television and radio simultaneously.

SLIDE.  A still picture or title projected directly into the film studio camera and then telecast.

SOUND TRACK.  The sound portion of a film.

SPOT ANNOUNCEMENT.  Commercials between programs on or participating programs.

STORYBOARD.  Drawings of the various scenes combined with the script.

SUPER.  Images of two cameras combined and shown on the screen simultaneously.

TAG.  The finish of an action routine or musical number.

TAKE.  One shot of a camera.

TD.  Technical director.

TILT.  Vertical movement of the camera.

TRANSMITTER.  The station's structure for sending the signal out on the air.

TRUCK.  Camera movement which parallels the scene.

TWO-SHOT.  A shot wide enough to frame two people.

UHF.  Ultra High Frequency.

VHF.  Very High Frequency.

VIDEO.  The visual portion of a television program or commercial.

VTR.  Videotape recording.

ZOOM.  A lens action which permits a rapid move-in or pull-back from the subject.

# INDEX

ABC Film Syndication, 48
Academy Awards, 18
Actors, actresses, 186, 192–193
Adell Chemical Co., 42
Advertisers, local, 54
  importance of TV to, 4–5
  *see* Stations, local
Advertisers, national, 3
  aims of, 3
  competition of, 4
  importance of TV to, 3–4
  use of local personalities, 64–65
*Advertising Age,* 52, 193
Advertising agency, 6, 9, 10, 12, 14, 26–27, 28, 100, 168, 188, 197–198
*Advertising Agency Magazine,* 171
Advertising, creation of, *see* Creation of TV advertising
Advertising Research Foundation, 37
Affiliation agreement, 6
Allen, Steve, 195
Alternate sponsorship, 17
American Broadcasting Co. (ABC), 48, 49, 55, 107
American Can Co., 205
American Council on Education, 241
American Federation of Musicians (AFM), 198
American Federation of Television and Radio Artists (AFTRA), 198,
  videotape code, 201–203
American Gas Association, 205
American Research Bureau (ARB), 9, 29, 33, 34–35
American Telephone & Telegraph Co., 204, 205
Ampex Corp., 121, 123, 124, 126

Anderson, Mrs. "Teddy," 31
Animation, 85, 87–90, 104
  cautions, 88–89
  costs, 99
  full, 89
  limited, 89
  semi-, 89–90, 100
"Annie Oakley," 48
Announcers, 186–192
Answer print, 104
ARB, *see* American Research Bureau
Arbitron, 34–35
Armstrong Excelon Tile, 134–135, 146
Art director, 76, 98, 116
Associated Artists Programs, 48
Audience, reaching the, 19
  competition, 19
  composition, 9, 20
  cost-per-thousand, 11–12
  late-night viewing, 52
  lead-in, 10
  "mass audience," 3–4
  selling the, 4
  total and average, 32
  unduplicated, 17
Audience participation programs, 16, 19
Auditions, program, 25
Auditions, talent, 197
Availabilities, 10

"Bait-switch" advertising, 251
Balops, 45
Barton, Bruce, 204
Basic themes, 67–69, 75
  building, 68
  requirements, 67
  standards, 68–69

Basic track, 169
Batten, Barton, Durstine & Osborne, Inc., 31, 40, 54, 198, 257
Be-attitudes for the copywriter, 73–74
Bendix, William, 194
Benny, Jack, 95, 195
Berle, Milton, 175
Billboards, see Programs, openings
Bing Crosby Enterprises, 123
Blair-TV, 52
Blenders, 170
Brainstorming, 83
Britton, Barbara, 192
Brower, Charles H., 83, 180
Brown & Williamson Tobacco Co., 42
Brown, Joe E., 194
Budget relief, 17,
Bufferin, 90, 139–141, 146
Bull Durham, 174
Bulova Watch Co., 66
Burma-Shave, 174
Burns and Allen, 48
Business Week, 145, 238

California National Productions, 48
Campaign, 67, 70–71
    product image, 70–71
Campbell's Soup, 79, 90, 165
Carroll, Jimmy, 170
Cartoon animation, see Animation
CBS TV Film Sales, 48
Celebrities, 186, 193–195
Cellomatic, 115
Charles, Ray, 170
Chevron Supreme gasoline, 175, 176–180
Children in TV commercials, 196–197
Chroma key, 113
Chrysler Corp., 205
Class "A," 7, 11, 20, 43, 59, 200, 253
Class "AA," 43, 44, 253
Class "B," 8, 43, 200
Class "C," 7, 8, 200
Class "D," 7
Climate, program, 12, 15, 25–26, 40
    testing, 233–235
"Coincidental" measurement, 34
Coleridge, 157
Colgate-Palmolive Co., 42
Collins, Dorothy, 122–124, 193
Color television, 100, 239
Columbia Broadcasting System (CBS), 48, 49, 55
Commercial cost vs. program cost, 101–102
Commercial time, 20, 253–254
Commercials, 71–72

Commercials (cont.)
    cost vs. program cost, 101–102
    creation of, 73–83
    "cross-plug," 17, 18, 19, 72
    effectiveness, 21, 26
    film, 84–105
    integration of, 108, 109, 110, 127
    lengths, 72–73
    live, 106–119
    time standards, 253–254
    uses, 72
Composite print, see Answer print
Connor, Joe, 171
Contests, 57, 252
Contiguity, 8
Continental Baking Co., 42
Control room, 107
Copy plan, 67, 69–70
    scope, 69
Copy, spot, 44–45
Copy testing, 232–233
Copywriting, see Creation of TV Advertising
Corinthian Broadcasting Corp., 240
Corporate-product relationship, 211–212
Corporate TV advertising, 204–218
    "bigness" factor, 207–208
    creating the message, 212–214
    examples, 215–218, 262–273
    financing the effort, 214–215
    measuring effectiveness, 209–211
    objectives, 206–207
    theme lines, 21
Cost-per-thousand, 11–12
Coty, 152–154
Creation of TV advertising, 66–83
    "be-attitudes" for copywriter, 73–74
    copywriting secret, 76–77
    corporate, 212–214
    creativity, 82– 83
    demonstrations, 129–147
    film commercials, 84–105
    four steps to selling, 67–73
    humor, 142–143, 173–185
    jingles, 160–172
    live commercials, 106–119
    presenting the idea, 80–81
    script forms, 77–78
    script guides, 75–76
    storyboards, 78–80
"Creepie-peepie," 244
Crosby, John, 36
"Cross-plug," 17, 18, 19, 72
Cut, 92, 115

Dailies, see Rushes

Dancers, 186
Daniel Starch and Staff, 222
Davis, Phil, 170
Daytime television, *see* Programs
Demonstration, 84, 88, 109, 119, 129–147
  safeguards, 146–147
  types, 132–146
  when to demonstrate, 131
  where to begin, 131–132
Department stores, 61, 62
Desilu, 48
De Soto, 143–145, 146, 167
Dairy measurement, 33, 36
Diffusion lens, 112
Discounts, 8, 44, 51
Displays, 57
Dissolve, 92, 94, 115
Dole pineapple, 174
Drama programs, 16, 17, 19
Dramatized appeals, 255
Du Pont, 90, 205, 215–218

Eastern Effects, Inc., 93
Educational television, 241–243
Effect wheels, 113
Electronic background insertion, 113
Electronic ripple, 113
Elliott, William Y., 240
Emerson, 148
Encyclopaedia Britannica, 237
Exterior filming, 84

Facilities contract, 11
Fact sheets, 45
Fairbanks, Douglas, Jr., 193
Federal Communications Commission
  (FCC), 238, 241
Federal Trade Commission, 146
Ferguson, Charles W., 158
Film commercials, 71, 84–105
  advantages, 84–85
  animation, 85, 87–90
  as spots, 45
  basic techniques, 85–92
  competitive bids, 100
  conversion table, 105
  copywriter's task, 85
  costs, 98–100
  delivery time, 101
  live action, 87
  opticals, 85, 92–94
  short cuts in cost, 102–103
  sizes, 103
  special effects, 94–96
  stages, 103–104

Film commercials *(cont.)*
  stop motion, 85, 90–92
  which technique to choose, 96–98
Film conversion table, 105
"Film network," 49
Film sizes, 103
Filter lens, 112
Firestone, 205
Five-plan, 44
Flaccus, Q. H., 173
Flip cards, 45
Flip wipe, 94
Flit, 174
Focus group interview, 229
Food products in spot TV, 42
Ford Motor Co., 146
Foreman, Robert L., 77
Freberg, Stan, 184
Front projection, 113
Full program sponsorship, 17
Furness, Betty, 192, 193

Gallup and Robinson, 221
Gayla soap, 171
General Electric, 194, 205, 269–274
General Foods Corp., 42
General Motors, 205
Glossary, 279–283
Godfrey, Arthur, 194, 195
Goldstein, Chuck, 170
Graphics, 45
Greene, Larry, 170
Grey, Lanny and Ginger, 170
Gross-Krasne, 48

Haber, Bernard, 94
Hall, Jon, 193
Hart, Everett, 119
Herbert, George, 176
Hicks, George, 262
"Highway Patrol," 48
Honeydreamers, 170
Hoover, Herbert, 160
"Hopalong Cassidy," 48
Hornsby, Joseph, 161
Humor in TV advertising, 142–143, 173–185
  as an art, 175–176
  early, 173–175
  in perspective, 185
  touches of, 184–185
  when not to use, 184
  when to use, 182

I. D. announcement, 43, 59, 60, 73, 99, 100,
  168

Impact research measurement, 225–227
Independent production company, *see* Packager
Instantaneous rating systems, 34–36
 Arbitron, 34–35
 Nielsen, 35
In-store demonstrations, 57
Interlock, 104
Interview programs, 128
Intimate products, 256
Iris effect, 112

Jackson, Ruth, 74, 192
Jackson, Sheila, 192
Jell-O, 175, 180–182
Jingles, 88, 103, 149, 160–172
 emotional appeal, 170–171
 future, 171–172
 melody, 165–168
 public acceptance, 161
 qualities of good, 163–164
 recording, 168–170
 singers, 170
 "tag," 168
 what they offer, 162
 when to use, 161–162
 where they originate, 162–163
Johnson, Ginger, 170
Joint Council on Educational Television, 241

Kaiser Aluminum & Chemical, 205
Katz, Joseph, 193
Katz Agency, 51
Kinescopes, 14
Kraft Foods, 111

Late-night viewing, 52
Lead-in audience, 10
Legal considerations, 26–27
Lestoil, 42
Lever Brothers Co., 42
"Lineup," 48
Linkletter, Art, 194, 195
Live-action film, 87, 88, 89, 98
Live commercials, 71, 106–119
 advantages of, 108
 as spots, 45
 basic approaches, 110–111
 copywriter's task, 109–110
 costs, 118
 mechanics, 106–108
 opticals, 115
 "risks," 118–119
 steps, 116–118

Live commercials *(cont.)*
 visual effects, 112–115
 which "tools" to use, 115–116
Local business concerns on TV, 259–260
Local programs, *see* Programs, local
Local stations, *see* Stations, local
Loesser, Frank, 163
Lucky Strike, 46, 90, 91, 155–157
Lyons, Ruth, 65

Magazines, effects of TV on, 240
Markets, 150 top, 275–278
Marlowe, Christopher, 187
Marquand, Nancy, 198
Married print, *see* Answer print
Marx, Groucho, 195
Master control, 109
Match dissolve, 94
Mattes, 95
Matting amplifier, 112
Maypo, 175
MCA-TV, 48
McCarthy, W. Barry, 28
Meade, Julia, 192
Medical products, 252
Mellowlarks, 170
Menjou, Adolph, 193
Merchandising services, 52, 57–58
MGM, 48
Miniature shooting, 95
Minimum dollar volume, 7
Miss America pageant, 18
Models, 186, 195
Monroe, Vaughn, 193
Moore, Garry, 194, 195
Multiple images, 95
Multiple-track recording, 169

NAB Television Code, 146, 249–256
National Association of Broadcasters (NAB), 72
National Broadcasting Co. (NBC), 13, 48, 49, 55, 113, 114, 242, 244
National Labor Relations Board, 198
National Telefilm Associates (NTA), 48, 55
Nelson, George, 170
Network programs, *see* Programs, network
Networks, 6–12
 affiliation agreement, 6
 billing, 42
 minimum dollar volume, 7
 time rates, 7–8
*New York Journal American,* 161
*New York Times,* 151
News programs, 16, 18

Newspapers, effect of TV on, 240
Nielsen Co., A. C., 16, 21, 29, 31–32, 33
    Audimeter, 31
    average audience, 30
    coverage service, 31
    instantaneous Audimeter, 35
    station index reports, 31
    television index, 31
    total audience, 30
    year-by-year TV statistics, 238
Normandia, Alphonse, 86
NTA Film Network, 49

O'Brian, Jack, 161
Odell, Clinton M., 174
Official Films, 49
Opinion Research Corp., 207
Opticals, 85, 104
Order letter, 11
Original tunes, 165–166
Osborn, Alex F., 82
"Our Miss Brooks," 48

Parr, Jack, 130
"Package plans," see Spot announcements
Packager, 12
Participation programs, 18, 72
Participation spots, 43, 47
Pearson, Ken, 158
Pencil test, 104
Pepsi-Cola, 161
Pepsodent tooth paste, 168
Perrin, Mac, 170
Petersmeyer, C. Wrede, 240
"Piggy-back" announcements, 255
Pilot films, 14–15, 25
"Pitch" programs, 255–256
Polaroid Land Camera, 130
Politics, television and, 4, 242, 243–245
Polk, George, 15
Popular songs, 165, 167–168
Porter, Cole, 167
Premiums and offers, 252–253
Pre-testing of TV commercials, 230–232
Printers' Ink, 62, 158, 184
Prism camera lens, 95, 113
"Private Secretary," 48
Procter & Gamble Co., 42
Producer, 76
Product image, see Campaign
Production, film commercials, see Film
    commercials
Products, acceptability of, for television,
    250–251

Profile measurement, 22, 23, 24
Program ratings, see Ratings, program
Program research, see Programs
Programs, local, 44, 47
Programs, network, 12–28
    "climate," 12, 15, 25–26, 40
    costs, 17, 18, 19
    daytime, 8, 18, 19–20
    formulation, 12
    ideas, 14
    legal considerations, 26–27
    openings, 20–21
    publicity, 27–28
    ratings, 16, 29–40
    research, 21–26
    scripts, outlines, 14, 15
    sponsor identification, 20
    trends, 15
    types, 16
Prudential, 205
Public domain tunes, 165, 166–167
Publicizing the program, 27–28
Pulse, 34, 52

Qualitative Research, 222
Quiz programs, 16, 17, 19

Radio, effect of TV on, 239
Radio and Television Directors Guild
    (RTDG), 198
Radio Corporation of America (RCA), 123,
    124
Rates, network, 7–8
    contiguity, 8
    discounts, 8
Rates, spot, 43–44
    average number per week, 60
    local vs. national rate, 60
Rating services, see Ratings, program
Ratings, program, 16, 29–40
    ARB, 9, 29, 33
    criticisms, 36–37
    definition, 29
    factor in time-buying, 10
    improvements, 37
    local, 53
    new proposals, 39
    Nielsen, 29, 31–32, 33
    "rating trap," 39–40
    recommended standards, 37–39
    Trendex, 29, 33–34
Reagan, Ronald, 194, 195
Rear-screen projection, 95, 113
Regional advertiser, 47
"Rep," see Station "rep"

Reruns, 14, 48
Research, commercial, 109, 219–236
  appraisal, 235–236
  believability factor, 228
  climate testing, 233–235
  copy testing, 232–233
  corporate, 209–211
  costs, 235
  development, 220–221
  likability factor, 227–228
  methods, 221–224
  new areas, 233
  pre-testing, 230–232
  psychological factor, 228–229
  status, 219–220
  wearability factor, 229–230
Research, program, 21–26
  effect of program, on commercials, 25–26
    233–235
  entertainment value, 21, 25
  lie detector measurement, 23
  profile measurement, 22, 23, 24
  word-association study, 23, 25
Re-use payments, 84
Reverse scanning, 113
Robinson, William, 184
Rogers, Will, 173
Rooney, Mickey, 194
Rose Bowl, 4
Roster recall measurement, 34, 36
Rotoscope, 90, 100
Rough cut, *see* Work print
Rushes, 104

Saber, Bernie, 170
Sale, Chic, 174
"San Francisco Beat," 48
Sande, Bob, 170
Sarra, Inc., 91
Satisfiers, 170
Schaefer beer, 168
Schwerin Research Corp., 22, 191, 223, 224,
  226
Scott, Raymond, 163
Screen Actors' Guild (SAG), 87, 198, 199–
  201
Screen Directors' Guild of America
  (SDGA), 198
Screen Directors' International Guild, 198
Screen Extras Guild (SEG), 198
Screen Gems, 49
Scripts, commercial, *see* Commercials
"Sea Hunt," 48
Segment sponsorship, 17
Sell—"soft" or "hard," 180

Sheen, Bishop Fulton, 4
Shore, Dinah, 195
Short cuts in film production costs, 102–103
Silvers, Phil, 194
Singers, 170, 186, 195
Situation comedy, 16
Skip-frame printing, 96
Skylarks, 170
Slides, 45, 113
Socony, 174
Song Spinners, 170
Sound track, 81, 103, 104, 169
Special effects, 94–96, 112–115
Special events, 18
Specials, 4, 18, 19, 205
Spectaculars, *see* Specials
Spier, Carleton, 68
*Sponsor,* 47, 77
Sponsor identification, 20, 255
Sponsorship, methods of, 17–18
Sports programs, 16
Spot announcements, 42–47, 70, 72
  average schedule, 60
  copy, 44
  discounts, 44, 51
  forms, 42–43
  "package plans," 44
  production, 45–47
  rates, 43–44
Spot markets, coverage of, 278
Spot television, 41–52
  announcement, 42–47
  buys available, 42
  highest spenders, 42
  status of, 41–42
Standard Oil, 174
Star of the show, 109, 110, 195
Station clearances, 11
Station Managers Survey, 54–65, 257–261
Station "rep," 50
Stations, local, 53–65
  agreement with network, 6–7
  facilities, 56
  hours of network carried, 55
  hours of operation, 55
  live personalities, 64–65
  merchandising help, 57–58
  reasons for not using TV, 63
  revenue, 63–64
  spots sold by, 59
  Station Managers Survey, 54–65, 257–261
  studio size, 257
  types of concerns using, 61, 259, 380
Still photographs, artwork, 45, 92, 100
Stock footage, 102

Stone, Sid, 175
Stop-motion, 85, 100
Storyboards, 78–80
   testing, 230–232
"Strip," 48
Subliminal perception, 256
Sullivan, Ed, 195
Sullivan, Jean, 192
Superimposures, *see* Supers
Supers, 79, 90, 94, 104, 112
"Susie," 48
Swanson, Bob, 170
Syndicated films, 47–49, 127
   advantages of, 47–48
   examples of, 48
   "film network," 49
   growth of, 48–49
   time clearances for, 49

"Tag" jingle, 168
Talent in TV commercials, 186–203
   actors, actresses, 192–193
   AFTRA videotape code, 201–203
   announcer qualities, 188–189
   auditions, 197
   celebrities, 193–195
   children, 196–197
   female announcers, 191–192
   helping announcer give best, 190–191
   models, 196
   picking right announcer, 189–191
   SAG contract, 199–201
   singers, 195–196
   star of the show, 195
   talent unions, 198–203
Telephone surveys, 36
*Television Age,* 62, 65
Television Bureau of Advertising, 41
Television, picture of, 1–5, 237–245
   and politics, 243–245
   approaches, 5
   as a social force, 240–241
   color, 239
   coverage, 1, 238
   effect on family, 1–2
   effect on other media, 239–240
   growth, effect of, 237–245
   how local advertisers regard, 4–5
   how national advertisers regard, 3–4
   importance to advertisers, 2–3
   in education, 241–243
   top 150 markets, 275–278
   rise of, 237–239
   viewing patterns, 2, 9
Television Programs of America, 49

Telops, 45, 112
Ten-plan, 44
Texaco, 175
3-in-1 Oil, 174
*Time,* 161, 193
Time buying, 10, 11, 50
Time clearances, 49
Time periods, 10
Time standards for copy, 253–254
Title cards, 45
Total audience, 32
Transparent slides, 45
Tranum, Charles B., 189
Traveling mattes, 95
Trendex, 29, 33–34
   Television Advertisers Report, 34
   TV Program Ratings, 33
"Tune-in" advertisements, 27
Tune-in, tune-out, 21

UHF stations, 238–239, 241
Union Carbide, 205
Unions, talent, 198–203
United Artists, 49
United States Steel, 205, 263–268
Upjohn, W. John, 83

Variety programs, 16, 17, 19
Venus pencil, 174
VHF stations, 238–239
Videotape, 71, 120–128
   advantages, 120–122
   development, 123–125
   effect on film, 125–126
   effect on live, 126–127
   local station uses, 127–128
   program uses, 127
   splicing, 125
Vocal groups, *see* Singers

Warner-Lambert, 42
Westclox, 123
Westerns, 16
Westinghouse, 205
Wines of California, 90
Wipe, 94
Wipe amplifier, 112
Wisk, 136–138, 146
Wooley, Monte, 193
Word-association study, 23, 25
Words, 148–159
   grammar, 159
   guides to better copy, 149–157
   our complex language, 157–158
   to complete the picture, 159

Work print, 104
World Series, 4

Zerex anti-freeze, 164, 165
Zilboorg, Dr. Gregory, 83
Ziv Television Programs, 49

*Set in Intertype Fotosetter Times Roman*
*Format by Seamus Byrne*
*Published by* HARPER & BROTHERS, *New York*